TRACING YOUR
LANCASHIRE
ANCESTORS

FAMILY HISTORY FROM PEN & SWORD

TRACING YOUR LANCASHIRE ANCESTORS

A Guide for Family Historians

Sue Wilkes

Pen & Sword
FAMILY HISTORY

For all my family

First published in Great Britain in 2012 by
PEN & SWORD FAMILY HISTORY
An imprint of
Pen & Sword Books Ltd
47 Church Street
Barnsley
South Yorkshire
S70 2AS

ISBN 978-1-84884-744-6

Typeset by Concept, Huddersfield, West Yorkshire.
Printed and bound in England by CPI Group (UK) Ltd, Croydon, CR0 4YY.

Pen & Sword Books Ltd incorporates the imprints of
Pen & Sword Aviation, Pen & Sword Family History, Pen & Sword Maritime,
Pen & Sword Military, Pen & Sword Discovery, Wharncliffe Local History,
Wharncliffe True Crime, Wharncliffe Transport, Pen & Sword Select,
Pen & Sword Military Classics, Leo Cooper, The Praetorian Press,
Remember When, Seaforth Publishing and Frontline Publishing.

For a complete list of Pen & Sword titles please contact
PEN & SWORD BOOKS LIMITED
47 Church Street, Barnsley, South Yorkshire, S70 2AS, England
E-mail: enquiries@pen-and-sword.co.uk
Website: www.pen-and-sword.co.uk

CONTENTS

ACKNOWLEDGEMENTS

As ever, I must express my gratitude to the many archivists and librarians who have patiently assisted with my enquiries, in particular David Tilsley (Lancashire Record Office), Perry Bonewell and Caroline Furey (Bolton Archives and Local Studies), Nathan Williams (Borthwick Institute), Glenn Lang (Cumbria Archive and Local Studies Centre, Barrow), Kevin Bolton (Greater Manchester County Record Office), Paul Webster (Liverpool Record Office), Emma Marigliano (Portico Library), Christine Watts (Wigan Heritage Service), Teresa Nixon (West Yorkshire Archive Service), Kirsty McHugh (Yorkshire Archaeological Society). Marion Hewitt and Geoff Senior of the North West Film Archive were also extremely helpful.

I would also like to thank Andrew Leighton (Ancestry), Amy Sell (Find My Past) and Beth Snow (theGenealogist.co.uk) for their help. Contact details for FamilySearch Centres quoted from the FamilySearch website are by kind permission of Paul Nauta.

Information about the Society of Genealogists' resources is quoted from its website by kind permission of Else Churchill. Dr Craig Thornber also very kindly gave his assistance. Apologies to anyone I have inadvertently omitted. Any mistakes in the text are my own.

Records held by Lancashire Record Office, to which copyright is reserved, are reproduced by permission. Parish register transcripts quoted from Lancashire Online Parish Clerks (to which copyright is reserved) by permission of Paul Dixon. Parish registers held at Manchester Libraries, Information and Archives quoted by kind permission of Collections Manager David Govier.

Every effort has been made to trace copyright holders for images used in this work. The publishers welcome information on any attributions which have been omitted.

I would also like to express my gratitude to Simon Fowler and Rupert Harding of Pen & Sword Books for their help and encouragement.

Last but not least, I must once again thank my husband Nigel, and my children Elizabeth and Gareth. I could not have written this book without their help and support.

Map of Lancashire, c. 1730, by John Owen and Emanuel Bowen. (Nigel Wilkes Collection)

LIST OF ABBREVIATIONS

BMDs	Birth, marriage and death certificates
BTs	Bishop's transcripts
CARN	County Archives Research Network
CCALS	Cheshire and Chester Archives and Local Studies
CWGC	Commonwealth War Graves Commission
FHS	Family history society
GMCRO	Greater Manchester County Record Office
GRO	General Register Office (St Catherine's Index)
IGI	International Genealogical Index
LCRS	Lancashire and Cheshire Record Society
LPRS	Lancashire Parish Register Society
LRO	Lancashire Record Office
MIs	Monumental inscriptions
MLFHS	Manchester & Lancashire Family History Society
NCB	National Coal Board
NRA	National Register of Archives
PCC	Prerogative Court of Canterbury
PCY	Prerogative Court of York
TNA	The National Archives
UDC	Urban District Council

LIST OF ILLUSTRATIONS

All photographs, engravings and images are from the author's collection except where otherwise credited.

Part 1

THE STORY OF LANCASHIRE AND ITS PEOPLE

Chapter 1

ORIGINS

Lancashire was the cradle of the Industrial Revolution. It was famous for its textile and coal industries and helped to forge Britain's great empire. The county has had more than its fair share of notable inventors, authors, politicians and scientists.

Sir Richard Arkwright (1732–1792), a Preston barber, rose from humble beginnings to great wealth with his improvements to the 'water-frame', a cotton-spinning machine. Bolton's Samuel Crompton (1753–1827) invented the 'spinning-mule' which revolutionized the cotton-spinning industry.

Hall i' th' Wood, Bolton. Samuel Crompton is said to have invented the spinning-mule here. Engraved by Thomas Higham from a drawing by William Linton. (Revd G. N. Wright, *People's Gallery of Engravings Vol. 2* (Fisher, Son & Co., 1845))

Astronomer Jeremiah Horrocks (1618–1641) was born in Toxteth Park and physicist James Prescott Joule (1818–1889) was from Salford. John Mercer (1791–1866), a calico printer and chemist from Great Harwood, discovered the 'mercerization' of textile thread, which increased its strength.

Famous Lancashire authors include William Harrison Ainsworth (1805–1882), 'opium-eater' Thomas de Quincey (1785–1859) and Rochdale-born Edwin Waugh (1817–1890). Elizabeth Cleghorn Gaskell (1810–1865), who lived in Manchester from 1832 until her untimely death at the age of 55, wrote *Mary Barton: A Tale of Manchester Life*. *Mary Barton*'s vivid portrayal of the social gulf between mill-owners and their workers caused a furore in the city when it was published in 1848.

Lancashire's story is not just a collection of events and dates; it is also the story of its people. Our ancestors each played their part in county life, no matter how small. Perhaps they fought for Britain, spun cotton, hewed coal, tended a steam engine, tilled the fields or waved a Chartist or suffragette banner while campaigning for electoral reform.

Researching your family history is an addictive and increasingly popular pastime, but sometimes it is difficult to know where to begin. A bewildering variety of records and archives are available.

This book aims to provide a practical guide to researching ancestors who were born or lived within the historic county of Lancashire. Chapter 7 discusses the administrative boundary changes of 1974 and their consequences regarding the location of archive sources. However, readers researching Lancashire relatives born after 1974 should also find that many of the archives and other resources mentioned are extremely useful.

Tracing Your Lancashire Ancestors is divided into two parts. The first section is a brief sketch of Lancashire's social history. Some examples are given of the different records available for each topic under discussion.

Basic family history sources such as parish registers, wills and probate records, censuses, etc., are reviewed for family history novices. Particular issues relating to Lancashire records and their location are highlighted for seasoned genealogy campaigners.

The second part of the book is a directory of the most important archives, repositories and local studies libraries with collections relevant to Lancashire genealogists. Contact details are included for archives and repositories mentioned in the text. There are sections on family history resources, useful websites and places to visit.

Visiting a museum or heritage site can be a wonderful way to explore how your ancestor lived and worked. It is very important to set your ancestors' lives in context whenever possible. If you have an understanding of the times in which your ancestors lived, this can shed light on major changes in their lives such as moving house. During hard times such as the cotton famine of the early 1860s, for example, families often shared accommodation to save on rent and fuel. If work was scarce, the family breadwinner may have gone looking for work in other areas of the country.

By and large, the earlier back in time one looks for an ancestor, the more difficult it becomes, especially before the advent of civil registration in 1837. However, many different records can be utilized for family history, such as those of the medieval courts, government, church, trade and industries. If the documentary evidence exists, then with care and persistence you can break the 1837 'barrier' and trace your family tree back much farther than you imagine.

The Birth of the County

For our purposes, the story of the county 'proper' does not really begin until the late twelfth century. From ancient times England was divided into 'hundreds', also known as 'wapentakes'. Each hundred was further sub-divided into manors and townships, or vills.

When the Normans invaded England in 1066, 'Lancashire' did not yet exist. The lands between the Ribble and the Mersey contained the hundreds of Blackburn, Leyland, Newton, Salford, Warrington and West Derby. Before the end of Henry I's reign, Newton and Warrington became part of West Derby hundred, thus increasing its size.

North of the Ribble were the hundreds of Amounderness, Kendal and Lonsdale. Lonsdale was composed of two districts: Lonsdale North of the Sands (of the River Kent) and Lonsdale South of the Sands (Cartmel and Furness). Sometimes north and south Lonsdale were administered as if they were separate hundreds.

The Domesday Book (1086) was compiled for William the Conqueror. This inventory or survey of England detailed all the lands and any revenues derived from them. The hundreds north of the River Ribble, including Furness, were inventoried as part of Yorkshire. In the early 1060s, Earl Tostig and his thanes (thegns) held manors in Amounderness, Furness, Kendal and Lonsdale.

The lands 'between the Ribble and the Mersey' were inventoried under the description of Cheshire in the Domesday Book. At that time few people lived there and these lands produced little wealth, but they were richer than those north of the Ribble. The countryside was dominated by great forests, wastelands and dark peat mosses which could swallow up unwary travellers. Only a small proportion of land was available for the cultivation of the main crops of oats and barley.

Estates in south 'Lancashire' had many different owners. According to the Domesday Book, quoted by Edward Baines, in West Derby hundred: 'Four thanes [nobles] held Boltelai [Bootle] as four manors; there are two carucates of land. It was worth sixty-four pence', and in Salford hundred: 'King

Edward held Salford. There were three hides and twelve carucates of waste land; forest three miles long and the same broad; and there are many hays and an aerie of hawks' (*History, Directory and Gazetteer of the County Palatinate of Lancaster Vol. 1* (Longman, Hurst & Co., 1824)).

A 'carucate' was roughly 100 hundred acres of ploughing land. In the lands between the Ribble and the Mersey, there were six carucates to one 'hide'.

For many years, kings played 'pass-the-parcel' with north-west England, using its lands to reward noblemen for good behaviour, or confiscating their estates if they proved troublesome. Shortly after the Normans invaded, the victorious William the Conqueror presented his follower Roger of Poitou (third son of Roger de Montgomery) with the lands between the Ribble and the Mersey.

Roger, for his part, gave manors to his followers for their loyalty: the fortunes of the Molyneux (de Moliness), de Vilers and other Norman families date from this time. Apparently few Normans settled permanently in this area, however. Many decades after the Conquest, most landowners were still of Anglo-Saxon or Viking origin. Tradition has it that the de Trafford family were settled in Trafford at the time of King Canute, decades before the Normans arrived.

Roger temporarily lost the lands of south 'Lancashire' after rebelling against the king, but William's son Rufus later restored the estates to him and added Furness, Cartmel, Lonsdale and Amounderness for good measure.

A large feudal estate was known as an 'honour'. Roger's estates, which were not confined to the land between the Ribble and the Mersey (and included lands as far away as Suffolk), were called the 'honour of Roger of Poitou (Poitevin)'. His holdings were also known as the 'honour of Lancaster', because Roger had a stronghold there. He strengthened his strategic position by building a castle at Lancaster and occupying one at West Derby.

Around this time, Roger created the barony of Manchester, and gave it to his knight Nigel as his fiefdom. Roger kept Salford as a 'demesne' manor (for his own use) and it remained part of the 'honour of Lancaster'. When the duchy was later owned by the Crown, the monarch became lord of the manor of Salford.

In 1102, Henry I stripped Roger of Poitou of the honour of Lancaster after he rebelled against the Crown again. Roger was banished from the realm. But Roger's 'honour of Lancaster' kept this name long after the estate was forfeited (escheated) to the Crown. This great estate was the precursor of the Duchy of Lancaster. Because Manchester was no longer a 'demesne' manor, it was ruled by 'a lowlier line of lords', as historian James Tait noted.

Count Stephen of Blois now took possession of the honour of Lancaster. Stephen became king, but his reign was distinguished by a vicious power struggle with his cousin the Empress Matilda. These were the turbulent, violent times 'when Christ and his saints slept', and at one point Stephen gave the lands north of the Ribble to David I of Scotland after the Scots invaded. Following several changes of ownership, the honour of Lancaster was under the control of the English throne again by 1164.

The reign of Henry II heralded the first mention of the 'county' (*comitatus*) of Lancaster in the 'pipe rolls' of 1168 (see below). The 'honour of Lancaster', however, did not follow the 'county' borders because, as noted earlier, it was a large collection of estates.

After Henry II's death in 1189 Richard I gave the honour of Lancaster to greedy John, Count of Mortain. While Richard was away crusading in the Holy Lands, Prince John rebelled against his rule, aided by Lancashire barons such as Roger de Montbegon, owner of Hornby Castle. The barons backed down when Richard returned: Montbegon was fined 500 marks and his lands temporarily confiscated. When John succeeded to the throne after Richard died in 1199, Lancashire folk were taxed to the hilt.

King John spent large sums on strengthening Lancaster Castle. He improved the royal lodgings there, repaired the jail in Lancaster, and the castle in West Derby.

The barons, unhappy with John's grasping ways, were led by Simon de Montfort in open rebellion. They forced King John to accept Magna Carta, limiting his power. Roger de Montbegon, Robert Greslet (Grelley) of Manchester and John de Lacy of Clitheroe were present when this historic charter was signed at Runnymede.

When Henry III gave his son Edmund 'Crouchback' the Lancashire estates in 1265, he created the earldom of Lancaster. The first earl, Edmund, was succeeded in 1296 by his son Thomas, who came to a nasty end on the scaffold at Pontefract Castle after rebelling against Edward II and his infamous 'favourites', Piers Gaveston and Hugh le Despenser.

These were hard times for humble folk. During the ruinous wars against the Scots, the county provided men, weapons and taxes for the Crown. In 1297 Lancashire sent 3,000 men to war, and another 2,000 men 2 years later. The Scots won a great victory at Bannockburn in 1314 and celebrated their defeat of the English with several invasions of northern Lancashire. Robert the Bruce's 1322 expedition laid waste much of the county north of the Ribble, and Preston was attacked.

Worse than the marauding Scots was the visitation of the Black Death in 1349 and subsequent years. The archdeacon of Richmond estimated that over 3,000 people died in Preston alone and some 13,000 people perished in the hundred of Amounderness. At Didsbury, a new cemetery was opened in the chapel to cope with the ravages of the plague.

In 1351, a new chapter opened in the county's history when Henry, fourth Earl of Lancaster, was granted palatine powers by Edward III. Henry was also given the title of first Duke of Lancaster.

Palatine authority was extremely wide-ranging. In effect, Lancashire was Henry's own personal kingdom, although taxes were still paid to the Crown, and the county sent knights of the shire (MPs) to Parliament. Palatine status meant that 'the king's writ' was no longer current. Henry chose his own sheriff, judges and magistrates for the civil and criminal courts in the county palatine. Trials did not have to be held at Westminster, but offenders could still appeal to the king for pardon.

The palatine lapsed with the death of Duke Henry. John of Gaunt, second Duke of Lancaster, was granted palatine powers in 1377. When Henry IV became king in 1399, he inherited the dukedom and its vast wealth. From this time onwards the Duchy of Lancaster, and the palatinate powers, belonged to the king, but were kept as a separate inheritance through the male line, distinct from the Crown possessions. They were owned by the king himself, not the Crown. The palatine, a very important arm of the duchy, continued to hold separate courts from the king's courts. Our present Queen is Duke of Lancaster.

Although the duchy and the palatine were separate bodies, in practice, the two became highly interdependent. After 1471 the positions of chancellor of the duchy and chancellor of the palatine were always held by the same person, and the palatine was administered from the duchy office in London. The Duke of Lancaster appointed the sheriff and the chancellor for the county. The chancellor appointed the justices of the peace and other officers.

In the 1840s the chancery of the palatine court sat four times per year at Lancaster and Preston. The court of duchy chamber at Westminster was the court of appeal for the palatine chancery. The duchy chamber's business was largely concerned with hearing equity pleadings.

Serious criminals, such as those indicted for capital offences, were tried at the assize courts. Because the palatine had its own courts, Lancashire was not on the general assize circuit until 1876. Assizes and common pleas were held at Lancaster twice yearly. However, when the palatine lapsed between 1361 and 1377, common pleas and assizes were heard at Westminster and by the assize justices.

After 1835 the assize courts were held at Lancaster and Liverpool (for Salford and West Derby hundreds). In addition, 'three special sessions' were held regularly, with 'a fourth intermediately at Salford for the hundred of Salford ... at Lancaster for Lonsdale hundred; at Preston for the hundreds of Amounderness, Blackburn and Leyland; and at Liverpool for West Derby hundred' (Cyrus Redding, J. R. Beard and W. C. Taylor, *Pictorial History of the County of Lancaster* (George Routledge, 1844)). The palatine also held courts of common pleas at Lancaster and Liverpool during the assizes.

The records of coroners' inquests were given to the assize judges, who passed them on to the court of king's bench. After the early 1750s coroners' inquests were filed at quarter sessions instead. The quarter sessions courts were held by justices of the peace, who tried and punished petty criminals (see Chapter 5).

Until the end of the nineteenth century, during assize week, the justices of the peace and sheriff held administrative meetings in a special session (the Sheriff's Board or Table) but seemingly few of this court's records have survived.

The relationship between the duchy and the county palatine is explored in more detail in Robert Somerville's *History of the Duchy of Lancaster* (Chancellor and Council of the Duchy of Lancaster, 1953) and Helen Castor's *The King, the Crown and the Duchy of Lancaster* (Oxford University Press, 2000).

Medieval Records

Lancashire's inhabitants were subject to an elaborate system of rights and duties under the feudal system, and their lives are revealed in a variety of records. Your ancestor may have owned lands, paid rent or taxes or had dealings with the Crown, civil or ecclesiastical courts. The National Archives (TNA), Kew has hundreds of early legal documents that mention Lancashire people and estates.

Lancashire Pipe Rolls

The Exchequer pipe rolls were, in effect, the king's account books and are some of the earliest records available. The sheriff represented the king in the 'honour of Lancaster'. The pipe rolls record details of the money and property that he collected on the king's behalf: payments such as fines or levies, lands confiscated by the Crown or payments made on behalf of the Crown such as judges' expenses. Records were kept for each county and copies were sent to the Chancellor. For example, a pipe roll dated 1200–1202 for the reign of King John gives the names of Lancashire people and places paying tallage (tax) to the king, including Alexander de (of) Pilkington, Robert de Prestwich, Elias de Pendlebury and the towns of Middleton, West Derby and others.

Pipe rolls for Lancashire for some early reigns are catalogued in W. Farrer's *The Lancashire Pipe Rolls of 31 Henry I., A.D. 1130, and of the reigns of Henry II., A.D. 1155–1189; Richard I., A.D. 1189–1199; and King John, A.D. 1199–1216* (Liverpool, 1902). The pipe rolls are reproduced in their original Latin, but accompanied by copious explanatory notes.

Some medieval records were written in French (the language of the court), some in Latin, or an abbreviated form of Latin, and some in English. The later a record, the more likely it is to be written in English. TNA has online tutorials on Latin for beginners and palaeography (how to read old handwriting) at: www.nationalarchives.gov.uk/latin/beginners and www.nationalarchives.gov.uk/palaeography.

Assize Rolls

Large areas of land, even if they had villages on them, were subject to 'forest' laws which protected the king's game and the trees and plants that gave animals food and cover. People were savagely punished if they broke the forest laws. Visiting 'justices in eyre' dealt with these cases and others concerning forest land such as trespass, enclosures, felling timber and so on. The justices also held courts of 'common pleas'. They visited the northern counties every few years, dependent on how dangerous travel was in these parts.

The infrequent visits of the eyre justices caused great inconvenience to people because it might take many years to sort out their affairs, and litigants requested special assizes so that their cases could be heard more quickly.

Assize rolls record court cases heard by the 'justices in eyre', those heard by the justices in the duchy of Lancaster assize courts (when Duke Henry held the palatinate in Edward III's reign) and the 'pleas of the Crown'.

The assize rolls for Lancashire have been transcribed and summarized. For example, the roll for the thirtieth year of the reign of Henry III records the assizes and pleas held before the 'justices in eyre' at Lancaster for three weeks in October 1246.

One of many cases of 'novel disseisin' (recent dispossession) was brought by Robert de Birun against Robert de Biry and Roger de Shytlesworth, who had taken over 30 acres of common pasture in Shitlesworth (probably Shuttleworth). The judges found for the plaintiff Robert de Birun, and awarded damages of 2s.

The assize records have several missing years because the original court rolls were damaged beyond repair or lost. For example, when the Scots invaded in the late 1240s, coroner of Lancaster Matthew de Redman's house was ransacked and burnt down, and the coroner's rolls stolen.

Unfortunately, many early eyre rolls for Lancashire have vanished. The surviving records are calendared in Farrer's *Lancashire Pipe Rolls*, and in the introduction to the first volume of Colonel John Parker's *A Calendar of the Lancashire Assize Rolls Preserved in the Public Record Office Part 1* (Lancashire and Cheshire Record Society, 1904). The second volume of Parker's *Lancashire Assize Rolls* includes abstracts of fines and amercements (financial penalties) in the pipe rolls.

The British History Online website has a searchable digital version of Colonel John Parker (ed.), *A Calendar of Lancashire Assize Rolls* (2 vols, Lancashire and Cheshire Record Society, 1904 and 1905) at: www.british-history.ac.uk/source.aspx?pubid=504.

The vast majority of the county palatine's records, which includes Lancashire assizes and chancery court records, are kept at TNA: PL. The palatinate court of common pleas dealt with cases of trespass, land disputes and the recovery of debts, and this court's records are included in this series.

Calendars and abstracts (some indexed) of duchy and palatinate court rolls were published by the Deputy Keeper of the former Public Record Office (now TNA). Lancashire Record Office (LRO) has a collection of palatine records which includes papers relating to the appointment of the high sheriff.

The Duchy of Lancaster's records are also at TNA: DL. The Duchy of Lancaster office has its own archive but this is principally for working documents, and the first port of call for duchy records should be TNA. Section A of this book's Research Guide has more detailed information on duchy and palatine records and their location.

Land Records

There was no compulsory land registry until the mid-nineteenth century. In medieval times land could be registered in the court rolls by paying a fee, or by using special legal procedures, and deeds may be found in chancery close rolls, palatinate close rolls and plea rolls, and eyre rolls. After 1536 conveyances by 'bargain and sale' had to be enrolled in chancery or registered with the clerk of the peace. The clerk of the peace assisted local magistrates at quarter sessions and had many other local legal and administrative duties.

An early method of transferring the ownership of property and lands was by a 'final concord', in which a dispute over land ownership was settled and recorded in the rolls of the high court. Fictitious lawsuits using this method became a popular way to pass on an inheritance from a father to his children, say. People wanted the transfer of their lands to be properly recorded. This was because property deeds could be forged, or it might be difficult to prove that a deed was genuine if all the witnesses to it had died. Final concords were also known as 'feet of fines'.

After 1195 the 'fines' were recorded onto a large piece of parchment which was divided into three pieces. The Treasury kept one portion, and the plaintiff and defendant each had a portion, so there were three copies of the 'fine' or 'concord'. Each copy was called a 'chirograph'. The 'feet of fines', too, are held at TNA. They have been transcribed and published by the Record Society.

Royal grants, also known as the king's 'letters patent' or 'patent rolls', survive from the early thirteenth century. They include treaties, charters, grants of land, offices, titles and pensions, judicial commissions, pardons, licences, leases of Crown lands, the king's correspondence and much more. The patent rolls have been calendared (summarized). The palatinate issued its own patent rolls.

Case Study

For example, the roll for the thirtieth year of Edward I's reign mentions a pardon for Adam de Aveyse dated 23 February 1302. Adam had murdered his wife Emma de Preston, but was pardoned by the king because he had performed military service against the Scots.

Another patent roll dated 29 March 1305 records that the king granted a pardon to William of Eccleston, who was languishing in Lancaster Gaol after he had killed Richard de Fevre of Great Eccleston. The sheriff of Lancaster questioned the prisoner William, who was the son of Roger, son of Margery de Eccleston, and decided that he had killed Richard in self-defence.

The king's Exchequer raised money by personal taxation in addition to the dues payable on land under the feudal system, and these taxes were recorded in 'lay subsidy rolls' (taxes on the laity). A poll tax was introduced three times in the late fourteenth century, and was just as unpopular as in recent times because it impacted on the poor as well as the wealthier members of society. (Only the very poorest people were excused payment). A later tax (1662–1689), based on the number of hearths in a household, was paid by everyone except paupers, those with a low-value property or on a very low income (there were some other exceptions).

Clerical taxes, lay subsidy rolls, poll tax and hearth tax records are held by TNA (LRO has some copies of lay subsidy rolls).

Poll tax returns have been published: Carolyn Fenwick, *The Poll Taxes of 1377, 1379 and 1381* (3 vols, British Academy Records of Social and Economic History, new series, 1998–2004). The 1377 records for Lancashire do not appear to have survived.

More information on taxation before 1689 can be found in TNA's Domestic Records Guide No. 10 at: www.nationalarchives.gov.uk/records/research-guides/taxation-before-1689.htm.

Manorial Records

These records are very important sources of information for ordinary people. The manor was the basic unit of administration. It dealt with the day-to-day running of the land and the people living on it.

The boundaries of a manor did not necessarily coincide with those of a parish or village. A manor might hold land in more than one township, or land in a township might be divided up between different manors.

A tenant might have to do military service for the lord of the manor, or serve as a 'doomsman' or juror at his court. The lowest tenants had to plough the lord's lands for a specified number of days each year, or cart his fuel or manure, or help with the harvest. They had to grind their grain at the lord of the manor's mill: the miller took a portion of their flour as payment.

The lord of the manor, or his steward, held a court every two or three weeks. The 'court baron' or 'halmote court' dealt with civil matters such as changes in tenancies (perhaps if a tenant had died), settling neighbourly disputes such as trespassing or bad debts, or hearing complaints about misdemeanours such as slander.

Tenants were fined (had to pay an 'amercement') if they disobeyed or evaded their duties. Perhaps they had misbehaved by digging up another person's hedge, or maybe their animals had wandered off and damaged someone else's property. Pigs and horses seem to have been especially prone to escaping.

Tenants included 'freeholders', who had no time limit to their tenure, and 'copyholders'. Their tenancies were recorded on the manorial court rolls. Copyholders paid an 'entry fine' to the manor when they took over a tenancy, in addition to paying rent, and this fine was recorded as an 'admittance' on the roll. Copyhold could be inherited, and the names of family members are often mentioned in the records.

When a copyholder died, the land was surrendered to the lord, and the copyholder's heir (or the new tenant, if there was no heir) paid the manor a fee so that they could take over the tenancy. 'Customary tenant-right' was another form of copyhold. A 'heriot', perhaps the tenant's cow or horse, was often paid to the lord when a tenant died.

Lancashire had only one 'superior manor' with many different dependent manors subject to it: the 'honour of Clitheroe'. This manor had several courts associated with it.

In some manors, such as the non-incorporated towns, a court 'leet' was held in addition to the court baron. The court leet met more rarely, perhaps twice a year. It ensured that law and order was maintained (the 'view of frankpledge') and dealt with more serious criminal matters such as public order offences. It supervised the election of important manorial officers such as the borough-reeve and constable. Chapter 5 has more information on local government.

Other important manorial records which you may come across are 'rentals', 'custumals', 'compoti', surveys, 'terriers' and maps. 'Rentals', as their name suggests, were lists of the manor's tenants and the rents owing. 'Custumals' detailed the 'customs' of the manor: how much tenants should pay and what duties were expected of them. A 'terrier' was an extremely detailed survey of the land, right down to the smallest strip of farmland in the open fields. 'Compoti' were bailiff's accounts.

When a person died, if they were a 'tenant in chief', that is, a tenant of the Crown, an 'inquisition post-mortem' or 'escheat' was held before a jury to decide which lands the person held, and who was the new owner. If there was no heir, the lands reverted to the king. If the heir was under age, they were made a ward of court. The inquisitions included the tenant's name and date of death, the manors he or she held (sometimes with the names of tenants under them) and the name and age of the tenant's heir. These records, too, are at TNA and there are detailed guides to these record series on its website. Inquisitions post-mortem can also be found in the palatine records and duchy of Lancaster series.

Exploring Manorial Records

Records for manors may be found in local record offices, specialist re-positories or in private collections. LRO has a large collection of manorial court rolls and records.

Records for manors owned by the Crown and some other manors are kept at TNA: see series SC 2 and DL 30. The TNA guide to manorial records has details of the record series available and can be accessed at: www.national archives.gov.uk/records/research-guides/manorial-records.htm.

The Manorial Documents Register at TNA is a finding aid to manorial documents for England and Wales arranged alphabetically by county. There's a parish index to help locate the parish that a manor belonged to. Part of the register has been digitized and put online, including Lancashire North of the Sands (Furness) and can be accessed at: www.nationalarchives.gov.uk/mdr. The rest of the register can be viewed on microfilm at TNA in the Maps and Large Document Reading Room.

The Cumbrian Manorial Records website (University of Lancaster) is a comprehensive guide to manorial records and how to use them, with tips on searching the Manorial Documents Register. The website includes images of some records, has a useful glossary of terms used in the records and a directory of the manors and baronies in Lancashire North of the Sands: www.lancs.ac.uk/fass/projects/manorialrecords/index.htm.

Case Study

A search on the Manorial Documents Register online for 'Dalton' elicits several results, including one for Dalton-in-Furness, Lancashire. 'Clicking' on this result elicits over fifty types of manorial records with catalogue references for Dalton-in-Furness held at six different repositories: TNA, Cumbria Archives (Barrow), the John Rylands Library (Manchester University), London University Senate House Library, Northamptonshire Record Office and LRO.

The Access to Archives (A2) search engine can be used as a finding aid for Lancashire manorial records. The A2A index is now out of date, but is useful because not all archives have put their catalogues online yet: www.national archives.gov.uk/a2a/default.aspx.

The National Register of Archives (NRA) Accessions to Repositories index can be explored by the subject 'manorial' and by year, so you can see which repositories have recently acquired manorial records but which are not shown on A2A: www.nationalarchives.gov.uk/accessions/default.htm.

The Church also owned manors, and therefore these manorial records may be archived with ecclesiastical records (see the Chapter 2). For example, a search on the A2A index for the court records of the manor of Newton, Kirkmanshulme and Deansgate, which belonged to Manchester Cathedral, reveals that these records are kept in the Cathedral Archives: Mancath/2/A1.

Nottingham University has published an excellent online introduction to manorial records with images of the different types of records: www.nottingham.ac.uk/manuscriptsandspecialcollections/researchguidance/manorial/introduction.aspx.

Case Study

The Halmote Court

The Halmote Court at Ightenhill (Burnley) was held on the feast of St Clement the Pope in the seventeenth year of Edward II's reign (23 November 1323).

The 'perquisites' (payments) made to the court included:

John de Ourum, for breach of the peace	6d
...	
Ellot, wife of *William Hare*, for entry to 1 messuage 2 oxgangs and 9 acres of land	½ mark
The same, for administration of the goods of the said *William*, deceased	13s 4d
...	
Adam, son of *Adam*, son of *Watte*, for entry to 5 acres of land	2s.

(W. Farrer (ed.), *Some Court Rolls of the Lordships, Wapentakes, and Demesne Manors of Thomas, Earl of Lancaster, for the 17th and 18th years of the Reign of Edward II, AD 1323–4*, Vol. XLI (Lancashire and Cheshire Record Society, 1901))

Guides to manorial records for genealogists have been published, including P. B. Park, *My Ancestors were Manorial Tenants* (Society of Genealogists, 2002) and Mary Ellis, *Using Manorial Records* (PRO, 1997). The *Victoria History of the County of Lancaster* (8 vols, 1906–1914) has indexes of the manors, parishes and townships in each hundred.

Case Study

The Court Leet

At Manchester in 1619, the lord of the manor was Edward Mosley. He was only a young child; his father had died recently. A succession of different stewards supervised court hearings on his behalf. The steward for the 'court with view of frankpledge' held on 7 October 1619 was William Sparke, a Manchester gentleman.

Several tenants had deceased, including Francis Nuttall of Blakeley. The jury found that 'John Nuttall is his sonne and heire [*sic*] ... and his sonne James Nuttall hath some pte [part] of his land by conveyance'. John and James were ordered by the court to do their 'suite and service' to the lord (attend the court).

Other matters before the court included ordering Samuel Dickonson and Richard Hunt to clean out the gutter between their houses, and John Sorocould was told to remove his 'doungehill' [*sic*], which was causing problems with Francis Pendleton's brick wall, before Christmas, on penalty of paying a fine. (J. P. Earwaker (ed.), *The Court Leet Records of Manchester Vol. III* (Manchester, 1886)).

Case Study

Compoti

'Compoti' were detailed financial accounts for the manor and included rents paid by the lord's tenants. Henry de Lacey, Earl of Lincoln (1250–1311), was lord of the honour of Clitheroe and baron of Halton. He owned the rights to hold fairs at towns in his Lancashire estates including Burnley, Clitheroe and Rochdale. De Lacey held a manor court at Clitheroe.

His 'compoti' for his Lancashire manors for September 1304 to September 1305 includes accounts for Clivachre (Cliviger). The tenants mentioned include 'Oliver de Stanesfend', who paid a rent of 6*d*, 'Adam son of Matthew de Ormerode' and 'Matthew de Berecrofts'. (Revd P. A. Lyon, *Two 'Compoti' of the Lancashire and Cheshire Manors of Henry de Lacey, Earl of Lincoln, XXIV and XXXIII Edward I* (Chetham Society, 1884)).

Before 1733 most legal records, including manorial records, were written in Latin. Some early records have been translated and published.

Clearly, the most detailed entries on the rolls, with surnames as well as forenames, will be most useful. But even if a person's surname is not given, the rolls can be a good way to check if a property existed in an area at a certain date.

From the sixteenth century onwards, the manor's functions in local government began to be eclipsed by the work of the justices of the peace and the parish vestry. The system of land holdings by manor lasted until 1922, when copyhold was abolished.

Heralds' Visitations

The 'visitations of the heralds' are particularly interesting sources for genteel county families. The royal heralds were responsible for checking which families had the right to bear arms. They wrote down pedigrees for each family, sometimes including the female line. The heralds occasionally mention supporting evidence in other records, but they often relied on verbal evidence from the family. Lancashire was visited by the heralds in 1533, 1567, 1613 and 1664–1665.

For example, the visitation of 1533 has details of the Ashawe family: 'Roger Ashawe of the Hall of the Hill maried [sic] Jane daughter to Christopher Hulton of Farnworthe [sic] and they have issue Thomas, Leonard, Anthony, Margeret and Alice'. However, genealogy was in its infancy at that date, and some impressive pedigrees noted down by the heralds should be viewed with extreme caution unless they can be verified by checking them against other records. The heralds' visitations were published by the Chetham Society, and can also be found on the Ancestry website.

Finally, there's an extremely detailed guide to medieval records in England for genealogists on Chris Phillips' website. It lists sources in print and includes web links to books of records available free online and can be accessed at: www.medievalgenealogy.org.uk/about.shtml.

The Church played a very important role in the lives of Lancashire people. Before discussing its records in detail, it is necessary to explore the role played by religion in society. The question of which religion one followed was, quite literally, a matter of life and death.

Chapter 2

A MATTER OF RELIGION

O ur ancestors followed the Roman Catholic faith for centuries. Some time after Christianity was introduced into Britain, the embryonic 'Lancashire' and other counties were divided into parishes.

The Domesday Book mentions a church dedicated to St Mary in Manchester, perhaps the forerunner of the church that later became Manchester Cathedral: 'The church of St Mary's and the church of St Michael's held in Maincestre [Manchester] one carucate of land, free from all duties or rents except danegeld'. The Church of St Michael's may have been in Ashton-under-Lyne, where there is still a church with the same dedication.

There do not seem to have been any monasteries in the county prior to Roger of Poitou's ownership of the honour of Lancaster. Roger established and richly endowed a Benedictine priory at Lancaster in 1094. This priory was controlled by an abbey in Normandy.

Count Stephen of Blois founded the abbey of Furness in 1127, which was home to the Cistercian order. Whalley, another Cistercian abbey, was established by Henry, Earl of Lincoln in 1296 (Whalley's monks formerly had a house at Stanlaw).

At Cockersand by the River Lune there was first a hermitage, then a hospital for infirm monks, before the Premonstratensians founded an abbey on the site in about 1190. Augustinian priories were built at Burscough, Cartmel, Cockerham and Conishead towards the end of the twelfth and into the early thirteenth centuries.

Each diocese, or area controlled by a bishop, was subdivided into arch-deaconries, which in turn were divided into deaneries, then parishes. To complicate matters, some Lancashire deaneries were spread across more than one archdeaconry.

Lancashire south of the River Ribble belonged to the diocese of Lichfield and Coventry but was directly controlled by the archdeacon of Chester. Lancashire north of the Ribble belonged to the diocese of York.

The Church was a major landowner. Abbeys, priories and other religious houses derived most of their income from rent and tithes. The tithes system dates back to about the tenth century. The church received one-tenth of every crop or part of a flock or herd or its produce, such as wool from sheep. Sometimes tithes were paid in money instead of 'in kind'. The purpose of tithing was to pay for the clergy's maintenance, keep churches in repair, provide charity for the poor and funds for hospitality towards strangers.

Lancashire was still a poor county with few people, which meant slim pickings for the Church. Until about the mid-seventeenth century, the county's produce was chiefly derived from farming.

For example, Furness Abbey had many sources of revenue, including that from the rectory of Dalton. A survey in Henry VIII's reign found that each year Dalton received tithes of barley and oats (worth £13 18s 8d), lambs (£3 0s 8d) and wool (£2 13s 4d), plus another £13 6s 8d from lent oblations (offerings) and fines (West, Thomas and Close, William (ed.), *The Antiquities of Furness* (Ulverston, 1805)). Furness was the wealthiest abbey in Lancashire but it was 'small fry' compared with the great abbeys elsewhere in Britain, such as Glastonbury.

The Church defended its rights vigorously. People who refused to pay tithes were prosecuted in the ecclesiastical courts, and could be ex-communicated: a very serious penalty. Roughly one-quarter to one-third of cases brought before the consistory court of Chester in the late sixteenth century were related to tithe disputes.

In addition to collecting tithes on its own behalf, the Church leased out the right to collect tithes to lay people (impropriators). For example, the bishop of Chester leased the tithe for Cartmel parish to Thomas Preston of Holker. Because tithing rights were leased out, in some parishes vicars received only a tiny proportion of the income from their living and they endured great poverty.

Charters, rental rolls, 'Act books' (minute books), manorial, tithe and other records often include details of properties and tenants, or dealings with other landowners. People gave land or granted other privileges to religious houses. A gift to the abbey was seen as a pious duty, and in return the monks would pray for the soul of their benefactor and his family. The chartulary of Cockersand Abbey lists many grants to the abbey including one from Henry de Melling of a portion of his land in Melling 'with the consent of Thomas his heir, and Roger his son'.

During the sixteenth century, the Church's riches and the hedonistic life-style of some of its priests and monks brought the old religion and its ways increasingly into disrepute. The birth of Protestantism led to new ways of thinking.

Henry VIII was keen to swell his coffers with the Church's gold. In 1534 Henry VIII broke free from the Roman Catholic Church's rule and declared himself head of the Church of England. The following year, he ordered a Church survey, the *Valor Ecclesiasticus* (Liber Regis at TNA). It was a kind of ecclesiastical 'Domesday Book': a valuation of everything owned by the Church and religious houses.

Transcripts of the Lancashire returns, with an index, are at TNA: E 344/22. The Record Commission printed an abstract of the returns, with maps, in the early nineteenth century, and this is also available at TNA.

The foundation of the Anglican Church had an immense impact on our Lancashire ancestors' lives. Two years after the Act of Supremacy, Henry ordered the suppression of England's smaller monasteries. The monasteries had a great deal of support in the northern counties, especially among the poorer people. The monks looked after their tenants: they gave them beer and bread and educated their children. Travellers relied on charity from the monasteries.

The suppression sparked a great uprising in northern England with the aim of restoring the Catholic religion and re-establishing the monasteries. Thousands of Lancashire men answered the call to arms and beacon fires blazed on the hills.

The rising was crushed by the Earl of Shrewsbury and the Earl of Derby. John Paslew, the abbot of Whalley, was tried for treason after aiding some

Chapter House, Furness Abbey. Engraved by R. Sands from a drawing by T. Allom. (Revd G. N. Wright, *People's Gallery of Engravings Vol. 2* (Fisher, Son & Co., 1845))

of the rebels. He was executed in March 1537; one account says that he was hanged in a field called Holehouses, in front of the house where he was born. Four canons from Cartmel were executed, too. The last abbot of Furness, Roger Pyle, was forced to give up his high office or face execution like his brother clergy, and the abbey was taken over by the Crown.

After the Reformation

In 1541 Lancashire south of the Ribble became part of the archdeaconry of Chester, which belonged to the vast new diocese of Chester. This area of Lancashire included the deaneries of Manchester, Blackburn, Leyland and Warrington.

Lancashire north of the Ribble became part of the archdeaconry of Richmond, also in the diocese of Chester. It included the 'western deaneries' of Amounderness, Copeland, Furness, Kendal and Lonsdale.

The diocese of Chester was enormous. Each parish covered a very large area, so the parishes were further subdivided into chapelries. The biggest parish was Whalley, with over 100,000 acres, and Rochdale parish comprised over 40,000 acres.

The number of parishes has been disputed by historians, but in his *History, Directory, and Gazetteer of the County Palatine of Lancaster Vol. 1* (Longman, Hurst & Co., 1824) Edward Baines lists sixty-six parishes.

The diocese of Chester was later reduced in size. In 1847 the diocese of Manchester was created and the collegiate church (dedicated to St Mary, St Denys and St George) became a cathedral. The new diocese of Manchester was composed of the archdeaconries of Manchester and Lancaster. At the same time, the deaneries of Furness and Kendal were hived off from the diocese of Chester and became part of the diocese of Carlisle. The diocese of Manchester, in its turn, decreased in size when the diocese of Blackburn was created in 1927.

Liverpool was in the parish of Walton until 1658, when it became a parish in its own right. A new parish church, St Peter's on Church Street, was built in about 1704. Liverpool remained in the diocese of Chester until 1880 when the diocese of Liverpool, which included Warrington, was formed.

A Divided County

Lancashire remained a stubbornly Roman Catholic county after the Reformation. The Stanleys of Derby, the Molyneux family of Sefton and the Blundells of Crosby were among many important landowners in the county who clung steadfastly to the faith of their forefathers, even though they risked horrific penalties for doing so.

Some coats of arms and crests of the house of Stanley. (William Willis (ed.), *History of the House of Stanley* (Manchester, 1840))

These were perilous times, not least because the pendulum of religion swung first one way, then another. During the reign of Mary I, who was a Roman Catholic, Protestants were persecuted. George Marsh, a farmer who grew up in Bolton, preached the Protestant faith and was curate at Deane. He was arrested and questioned at Smithills Hall before being jailed at Lancaster Castle. In 1559, after refusing to recant, Marsh was sentenced to death at the ecclesiastical court at Chester. On 24 April, he was burned at the stake for heresy at Boughton, near Chester. Visitors to Smithills can still see the 'footprint' where Smith is said to have stamped his foot to assert his faith.

The Act of Uniformity (1559) in Elizabeth I's reign tried to steer a middle course between Calvinist doctrines and die-hard Catholicism. The new Prayer Book was designed in the hope that its form of words did not offend Catholics ('papists') or Puritans. However, like many compromises, it pleased no one with extreme views.

At first Queen Elizabeth, who did not wish to see the return of the fires of martyrdom that blackened her sister Mary's reign, trod softly on religious sensibilities. If people refused to go to their parish church ('recusants'), they were fined 1s (5p in decimal currency). There were many recusants in the Lancashire gentry (a recusant was not necessarily Roman Catholic). Attendance at church was enforced by the churchwardens, who collected the fines.

But a large number of Lancashire magistrates were Catholics and they were reluctant to prosecute backsliders, especially if they were neighbours. The great landowners had their own chapels where they worshipped in private, perhaps paying lip service to the Established Church by occasional attendance.

However, after Elizabeth I was excommunicated by the Pope, Catholics plotted against her. They wanted to remove her from the throne and restore the old religion. Sir John Southworth of Samlesbury, who was involved with the 'Rising of the North' in 1569, was lucky to escape with his life.

These plots led to much harsher recusancy laws. Fines were increased and were now collected by the sheriff (Exchequer records). Persistent offenders risked losing two-thirds of their estates. Priests who said Holy Mass were charged with high treason. After 1585, it was a treasonable offence for a Roman Catholic priest to be on English soil.

Cardinal William Allen of Rossall Hall on the Fylde fled England when Elizabeth was crowned. His determination to restore Catholicism caused many headaches for the government. He founded a priests' college (1568) at Douai in Flanders, and over twenty Lancashire families from the Fylde secretly sent their sons there and other colleges on the Continent to be trained as priests. Stonyhurst College at Clitheroe dates its inception to the Jesuit college founded at St Omer in 1593. It moved to its present site, the former home of the Catholic Sherburne family, in 1794. Priests risked the horrors of a traitor's death – being hanged, drawn and quartered – if caught when they returned to England.

Despite this deadly danger, Lancashire folk continued to shelter 'seminary priests'. Old houses like Speke Hall, home of the Norris family, and Towneley Hall at Burnley had 'priest's holes' where a priest could hide for days while the sheriff's men ransacked the house looking for him. The famous Jesuit priest Edmund Campion preached at Hoghton Tower, home of the Hoghton family. Campion also stayed with John Southworth at Samlesbury and visited the Hesketh family of Aughton.

In 1590 Richard Blundell of Crosby and his son William were convicted at Lancaster assizes of hiding Robert Woodroff, a Jesuit priest. Father and son were imprisoned in Lancaster Castle; Richard died there a few months later. Over half the Blundell estates were forfeited to the Crown until the reign of Catholic James I, who pardoned William and restored his lands.

When William Blundell discovered that Catholics were being refused burial at the nearby parish church at Sefton he set up a burial ground, the

Lancaster Castle. Engraved by T. Higham from a drawing by T. Allom. (Revd G. N. Wright, *People's Gallery of Engravings Vol. 2* (Fisher, Son & Co., 1845))

'Harkirke', on his own land. Catholics and priests were interred there for about ten years until the authorities got wind of it. Blundell was given a massive fine and the burial ground was flattened.

The persecution of Roman Catholics continued for many decades. The heads of James Bell and John Finch were displayed on the tower of the collegiate church in 1584 after they were executed at Lancaster for refusing to acknowledge the queen as head of the Church. In 1628 Father Edmund Arrowsmith (also known as Bradshaw or Rigby) from Haydock was executed at Lancaster for being a priest.

Meanwhile, Puritanism had gained ground in south-east Lancashire, particularly Bolton and Manchester. The busy traders and small manu-facturers there had plenty of money to spend on books and had links with the Continent. Historian Robert Halley felt that they became 'zealous adherents of the Reformation' because they were 'better educated than their rustic neighbours' and had 'a sturdy independence of thought'. Bolton was known as 'the Geneva of the North' (*Lancashire: Its Puritanism and Non-conformity* (2nd edn, Manchester, 1872)).

Alexander Nowell of Read (later dean of St Paul's), Edwin Sandys of Furness, Thomas Lever and James Pilkington of Bolton were noted Puritan preachers from Lancashire who were exiled during Mary I's reign. In

Manchester in the late 1580s, an illicit printing press for scurrilous Puritan tracts was set up by Martin Marprelate on Newton Lane.

This was a religious but superstitious age. Even highly educated people believed in the existence of witches, boggarts and fairies. Their belief in witchcraft had 'royal approval'. King James I wrote a book about witches which devoted many pages to their evil powers, and tried and tested methods of discovering 'real' witches.

In August 1612, nineteen women and men from the Pendle and Samlesbury areas were tried as witches at Lancaster Castle. Several confessed their guilt. The respectable Alice Nutter of Rough Lee, who stoutly maintained her innocence, was one of the ten people hanged. One of the prosecution witnesses, Jennet Device, was only 9 years old. Two decades later, Jennet was charged with witchcraft and imprisoned in the castle.

The loyalties of families were divided by religion during the bloody turmoil of the Civil Wars in England from 1642–1651. As always in wartime, the poorest people of Lancashire endured much suffering.

The Civil Wars began following bitter disputes between Charles I and Parliament. The king believed in the 'divine right' of kings to rule as they saw fit, without the consent of Parliament. To the dismay of many Protestants, Charles was suspected of Roman Catholic sympathies: his wife Henrietta Maria was Catholic. In the north and west of Lancashire, the Lune valley and the wilds of Furness, where Catholicism still had a stranglehold, most people supported the king and his Royalist 'Cavalier' forces. Preston and Lancaster were strongly Royalist.

The towns of south-east Lancashire, with some exceptions such as Salford, were on the side of the Puritan Parliamentary forces: the 'Roundheads'. They wanted to curtail King Charles I's power and steer the Established Church towards a stricter, more Puritan course. The people of Bolton and Manchester, where the Puritan ethics of hard work and thrift had found a ready audience, were fierce supporters of the Parliamentarians. Ralph Assheton of Middleton and Alexander Rigby of Wigan, both MPs, were important Roundhead leaders in Lancashire. The Roundheads were vastly outnumbered by Royalists in the Lancashire gentry, however.

The king's commander in the county was James Stanley, Lord Strange (1606–1651), who became seventh Earl of Derby in the autumn of 1642. The Stanleys were the most powerful family in the county, and they had houses at Knowsley and Lathom, near Wigan. When Lathom House was besieged by the Roundheads in 1644, Stanley's wife Charlotte de la Tremoille heroically defended their home.

William Willis (ed.), *History of the House of Stanley* (Manchester, 1840) tells the story of Charlotte's cool courage under fire while the Roundheads attacked the house with fire-bombs and mortars even when her children were inside. After weeks of stalemate, Colonel Rigby sent a messenger to

Knowsley Hall, Liverpool, seat of the Earls of Derby. Engraved by W. Taylor from a drawing by G. Pickering. (Revd G. N. Wright, *People's Gallery of Engravings Vol. 2* (Fisher, Son & Co., 1845))

demand Lady Derby's surrender. She declared: 'tell that insolent rebel Rigby, that if he presumes to send any other summons to this place, I will hang up the messenger at the gates'. Eventually the siege was lifted, but the Roundheads had the last laugh: they razed the old manor to the ground in 1645 following Charles I's defeat at Naseby.

James Stanley paid the ultimate price for his support of the king. The Roundheads believed that the earl was responsible for a dreadful massacre in the town of Bolton in 1644, and after he was captured they exacted a terrible revenge. The earl was tried at Chester and executed at Bolton on 15 October 1651.

Some family members fought on opposite sides. Thomas Standish of Duxbury was a Parliamentarian who died for the cause, to the sorrow of his Royalist father and younger brothers. Thomas was shot by a sniper during the Royalist siege of Manchester in 1642.

Royalist Composition Papers (TNA) list the fines paid by Royalists for their part in the war. The composition papers for Lancashire have been published by the LCRS and these volumes are also available on CD-ROM from genealogy suppliers.

The Civil War has wreaked havoc for family historians because those desperate times have left many gaps in parish registers. We need to retrace

Execution of James Stanley, 7th Earl of Derby, at Bolton on 15 October 1651. (Cyrus Redding, J. R. Beard and W. C. Taylor, *Pictorial History of the County of Lancaster* (George Routledge, 1844))

our steps a little to discover when this prime resource for genealogists first began.

Parish Registers

During the Reformation, one of the reforms of the Church instituted by Thomas Cromwell was proper record-keeping. In September 1538 the clergy was ordered to record every baptism, wedding and burial in each parish. (There was no compulsory civil registration of births, marriages and deaths in England and Wales until 1837.) Each parish register was kept securely in a coffer or chest.

The earliest surviving parish register in the county is probably that for the parish church of Whalley. The first entry is for the baptism of Emma Fielden, daughter of John Fielden, on 27 November 1538, followed the next day by that of Edward, son of Hugh Woode. The first wedding recorded at Whalley is that of Robert Talbott (*sic*) and Joan Cooke on 20 January 1539, and the first burial noted was of John Leghe on 6 December 1539.

Some early parish registers were written on paper, but after 1597 registers were required to be kept on parchment, and copies of the earlier registers were made on parchment. How much information was recorded was entirely at the parish incumbent's discretion.

Early parish registers were written in Latin. Denis Stuart's *Latin for Local and Family Historians* (Phillimore & Co. Ltd, 2006) discusses the Latin vocabulary used in parish registers, wills and other genealogical sources. (Chapter 1 mentions more resources to help you understand Latin documents.)

In 1754 Hardwicke's Marriage Act required parishes to keep records of banns and marriages in special books of printed forms, with four forms per page. All weddings – except those of Quakers and Jews – had to be solemnized in an Anglican church.

In 1812 George Rose's Act tightened up the recording of baptisms and burials. For baptisms, the date, occupations and dwelling place of the parents had to be noted in addition to their names and that of their child. Burial entries now had to include the date, the deceased's age and place where they lived. Churchwarden's accounts may include payments made for burials, so these can be used as a substitute for the parish register burials record if it is missing.

In spite of the penalties for recusancy, Roman Catholics preferred to be baptized and married according to the rites of their own church. If you have a Catholic ancestor, you may find that he or she was baptized twice: once in an Anglican church, and again secretly as a Roman Catholic.

Case Study

'Mary, the daughter of George Osborne and Sarah his wife, both of Backbarrow' was 'conditionally baptised' at St Mary's of Furness, Ulverston on 25 July 1815 'having previously been baptized in the rites of the established church' (*Lancashire Registers III: Northern Part* (Catholic Record Society, 1916)).

Some Catholics married 'twice', too. To give another example, on 15 May 1765, Robert Worden, son of John and Margaret, married Ellen Talbot, daughter of James and Mary, at St Joseph's Roman Catholic church at Brindle. The wedding was witnessed by Peter Heatley and Mary Stell. Bride and groom both lived at Walton (J. P. Smith (ed.), *Lancashire Registers IV: Brindle and Samlesbury* (Catholic Record Society, 1922)).

The next day, Robert Worden 'linnen weaver' married Ellen Talbot at St Leonard's, the parish church of Walton-le-Dale; the witnesses were Richard Cooper and John Tomlison (Gerald Clayton (ed.), *Registers of the Parish Church of Walton-le-Dale in the County of Lancaster* (LPRS Vol. 37, 1910)).

Original parish registers and bishop's transcripts (BTs) are deposited with the current diocesan record office. Generally only parish registers still in use are kept at their 'home' church. However, there are some exceptions, e.g., all original Manchester Cathedral registers are held at the Cathedral archive. See Chapter 7 for more tips on how to find parish registers.

Until the mid-nineteenth century, most marriages and baptisms in the Manchester area took place at the collegiate church (later the Cathedral) because, for historical reasons, it had a virtual monopoly on the fees payable. If people wished to be married or have a child christened at another church in the area, they paid two sets of fees: one to the parish priest and one to the collegiate church. But if the ceremony took place at the collegiate church, only one fee was payable.

In addition, at that time there were insufficient churches to serve Manchester's growing population. In practice this meant that marriages and baptisms were celebrated in large 'batches' at the collegiate church. The *General Weekly Register* (21 April 1822) reported that on 16 April (Easter Day), 17 marriages and 217 christenings were solemnized, followed by another 34 marriages the next day, and a similar number on the Tuesday. These crowded celebrations attracted scores of onlookers.

In his *Home Tour through the Manufacturing Districts of England during the Summer of 1835* (1836) Sir George Head described one of these mass

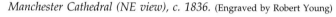

Manchester Cathedral (NE view), c. 1836. (Engraved by Robert Young)

weddings: 'About twelve couples were then to be married, the rest were friends and attendants ... The clerk ... performed the duties of his office in a mode admirably calculated to set the people at their ease'. The clergyman took great pains to ensure that everyone was standing in the correct place and gave the right responses. The happy couples removed their hats and gloves during the ceremony.

Bishop's Transcripts

In 1598 Anglican parishes were ordered to send copies or transcripts of their registers to the bishop of the diocese. These transcripts, which were made annually, may be the only record available if the original register is missing. Sometimes the clergy used a draft register when writing out the parish register or transcript, so the bishop's transcript and register do not always match exactly: names or dates may have been copied incorrectly. Occasionally the transcript may contain information not mentioned in the register, and vice versa. The original BTs are usually, but not always, kept at the diocesan record office.

Marriage Bonds and Allegations

If you have difficulty finding a record of a marriage, check if the couple was married by licence. Usually couples were married after the banns had been read, but sometimes people married by special licence. Perhaps they needed to be married quickly, or perhaps the bride or groom was a minor or maybe they wanted to marry away from their home parish. Roman Catholic couples who did not want to attend an Anglican church to hear the banns being read may have applied for a licence.

If the couple applied to the church court for a licence, the supporting documentation may have survived. In the 'allegation', the couple (or bride or groom) alleged that there was no reason, such as a previous marriage or a too-near blood relationship, why they should not be able to marry legally. The 'bond' set a high financial penalty which the groom (or a close relative who stood as his surety) agreed to pay if the allegation was later found to be untrue.

LRO holds marriage bonds and allegations for the western deaneries of the archdeaconry of Richmond from the early seventeenth century to the mid-nineteenth century. It also has a guide to 'Marrying by Licence'. Cheshire and Chester Archives and Local Studies (CCALS) holds marriage bonds and allegations for the diocese of Chester (which included south Lancashire) from the seventeenth century onwards. The Lancashire and Cheshire Record Society (LCRS) has published indexes to the bonds and allegations held by CCALS and LRO.

The Borthwick Institute holds bonds and allegations for licences issued by the Dean and Chapter of York, and some peculiar jurisdictions (see below). LRO reference library has copies of the indexes to these records: LG119.

Other Church Records

Wills and administration bonds ('admons') are some of the best sources for family history.

'Admons' were letters of administration granted to the person's next of kin if they died without leaving a will, or if the will could not be proved for some reason. For example, an 'admon' proved at Chester and dated 1633 for the estate of John Birchall of Culcheth gave his occupation as 'linen webster' (J. P. (ed.), *An Index to the Wills and Inventories now preserved at the Court of Probate at Chester 1621–1650* (Lancashire and Cheshire Record Society, Vol. IV, 1881)).

Wills often provide information about the members of the family still living at that date. 'Act books' are records of probates and 'admons' granted, and may have personal details of the person granted administration of the will. Probate records before the mid-eighteenth century sometimes include inventories of the deceased's personal effects and property, and these often make fascinating reading. Wills were proved in ecclesiastical (consistory) courts until 1858: see Chapter 7 for a discussion on how to find them.

Consistory courts dealt with a variety of matters such as matrimonial rights, divorce, adultery, defamation (slander), sexual offences (such as incest), clerical misdemeanours and tithe disputes in addition to wills and probate cases. Consistory court proceedings will be found in diocesan records. The consistory court records for the diocese of Chester held at Chester Archives and Local Studies mostly cover the archdeaconry of Chester (i.e., south Lancashire and Cheshire). Early consistory court records are written in Latin but the diocese of Chester records are summarized on the Chester Archives and Local Studies catalogue.

Consistory court cases for the archdeaconry of Richmond were heard by the commissary (bishop's) court. LRO has church court records for the western deaneries: ARR. However, disputed cases were referred to the archbishop's court at York (Borthwick Institute).

The tithe system caused many disputes in the ecclesiastical, exchequer and assize courts. Non-Anglican religious groups such as the Nonconformists and Quakers deeply resented paying tithes. In Cartmel in the mid-seventh century, Thomas Preston, who leased the parish's tithe from the bishop of Chester, kept up a running battle with local Quakers who refused to pay tithes and pursued them through the courts. LRO holds the Lancaster Society of Friends' records of their 'sufferings' for refusing to pay tithes: FRL.

The Ecclesiastical Survey of 1649 (sometimes known as the Common-wealth Survey) lists the clergymen of the county, names of lay impropriators and the names of tenants on Church lands. Edmond Wood, Richard Heyhurst and George Reads are among those listed paying rent for cottages on glebe land in the parish of Ribchester.

The survey found that although many of the clergy were 'godly' and took pains with their office, some were not as dutiful as they should have been. Mr Nicholas Marshall was vicar and master of the free school at Urswick, but he was 'scandelous [sic] in life and negligent in both his callings'.

Several important county families were lay impropriators, even though they were Roman Catholics. For example, the tithes of the parish of Dalton in Furness were collected by the heirs of the 'papist delinquent' Sir John Preston. The 1649 survey has been published: *Lancashire and Cheshire Church Surveys 1649–1655* (Lancashire and Cheshire Record Society, Vol. 1, 1879).

Clergy taxation records are held at TNA. From 1550 until the 1790s, when a clergyman took over a living, he paid a fee to the archbishop ('first fruits') and these records include the incumbent's name, the location of the benefice and the names of his sureties.

After the Restoration, religious tensions simmered beneath the surface and came to the boil again in the celebrated Manchester treason trial of 1694. Eight notable Lancashire gentlemen, including Viscount Molyneux of Sefton and William Blundell of Little Crosby, were tried for suspected complicity in a plot to murder William III and put James II's son James Edward Stuart on the throne. The men were all acquitted.

Lancashire folk in Manchester and Warrington gave a warm welcome to James Edward's abortive invasion in 1715. His son Charles Edward Stuart was similarly greeted with joy in the Jacobite rebellion of 1745. Colonel Francis Towneley of Burnley and two hundred soldiers – the 'Manchester Regiment' – raced to Bonnie Prince Charlie's standard at Manchester. But the Prince's fatal irresolution cost him the throne and many of his supporters like Towneley lost their lives on the scaffold.

However, many Lancashire people stayed loyal to their sovereign and steered clear of trouble during both rebellions. Roman Catholics remained under suspicion from the government and faced discrimination in public life until the Catholic Emancipation Act of 1829.

Chapter 3

RAGS TO RICHES

I n medieval times, the county's chief source of wealth was agriculture. Bowland and Lonsdale, Rossendale and part of the Fylde were important for their pastures. The lowland plains in the centre and some parts of the Fylde and Ribble valleys were devoted to arable farming. In south-west Lancashire, the richest area of the county, there was some arable and meadow land, but pasture for cattle and sheep was most important. Barley, oats, rye and other cereals were grown, and the cultivation of flax and hemp marked an incipient textile industry.

Most people lived off the crops they grew, the animals they bred or the rent collected from their tenant farmers. Crops were grown in a 'common field' subdivided into strips. Each adjoining strip was planted with the same crop. A tenant farmer's strips of land might be distributed over a large area, but in the county's central plain it was rare for people to own more than 15 acres. The fields were worked under the three-field rotation system in which land was alternately sown with a winter crop, or a summer crop, or left fallow to rest. Sometimes farmers let their livestock graze on the common fields.

The common-field system was very inefficient and it seems that in Lancashire, some common land and waste was being 'enclosed' as early as the thirteenth century. This process was still going on during the mid-sixteenth century, particularly in the Forests of Bowland and Rossendale, and in the Lune valley.

These enclosures, unlike elsewhere in Britain, were not necessarily to change arable land into grazing land for cows and sheep. They were simply the fencing off or hedging round of waste and common land to form more compact units. Or when forest land was converted into arable land, it could be fenced after the trees were cleared. Small farms became more prevalent as enclosures increased, but common-field farming continued in some manors for centuries longer. From the mid-eighteenth century, strenuous efforts were made to drain and improve the moss-lands such as Chat Moss and Trafford Moss to bring them under cultivation, too.

As previously noted, tenants and manorial lords had particular duties towards each other according to the customs of the manor, but from the seventeenth century onwards (possibly earlier) leases became more popular with landowners. Leases were usually held for a number of 'lives', for example, for the life of the tenant and his wife and son, or for a specified number of years. A tenant family might stay on the same piece of land for generations. Landlords charged a fee when a new lease was taken, or when one was renewed.

Some landowners, such as Ralph Assheton of Whalley, followed a firm but benevolent attitude towards their tenants, but others like Sir George Middleton of Leighton and John Brockholes of Lancaster were grasping and tyrannical.

By 1841 less than 10 per cent of the county's workers were employed in farming; over half were working in manufacturing industries. The growing population in the industrial towns provided a ready market for farmers. Cereals, milk, cheese, meat and vegetables were all needed, and Lancashire farm labourers earned good wages: £1 per week in some areas in the 1890s. Potatoes were an important crop. Even so, the demand for foodstuffs was so great that produce had to be imported from other counties such as Cheshire.

Records for Agricultural Areas

Sources mentioned in previous chapters such as manorial records, inquisitions post-mortem, rent rolls, surveys, tithe maps and records of tithe payments are all good starting points for research into ancestors living in agricultural areas. Family estate papers, too, should include rent records. Local record offices have collections of family estate papers, but some may still be privately held.

Case Study

The Shuttleworths of Gawthorpe Hall were major landowners in Padiham and Habergham Eaves in east Lancashire. The Chetham Society published many early deeds relating to the Shuttleworth estates, and also the house and farm accounts for the Shuttleworth family during the late sixteenth and early seventeenth centuries. For example, the steward's account for 1600 for Smithills (where the family lived prior to the building of Gawthorpe Hall) mentions tithe payments to James Anderton of Lostock for his demesne of Heaton and glebe lands in Bolton (John Harland (ed.), *The House and Farm Accounts of the Shuttleworths of Gawthorpe Hall Part 1* (Chetham Society Old Series XXXV, Manchester, 1856)).

The Shuttleworths were united with the Kay family in 1842 when Sir James Kay, a doctor from Rochdale well known for his social reform work, married Janet Shuttleworth, the last of her family's line. The Kay-Shuttleworth estate papers are held at LRO.

Enclosure awards, which may have been agreed privately or through an Act of Parliament, should include detailed maps or surveys of the land to be enclosed. Enclosure records at LRO are listed in *A Handlist of Lancashire Enclosure Acts and Awards* (Lancashire County Council, 1946).

Title deeds, leases, registers of leases, mortgages, land-tax records and solicitors' records are also potential sources. Land-tax records from the eighteenth and nineteenth centuries include owner name, tenants' names and tax paid by the owner; an address is not usually given. These taxes were paid annually, and these records may be found at local archives. A Return of the Owners of Land was made in 1873. It was published by HMSO two years later, and you may find a copy of the Lancashire returns in reference libraries or on CD-ROM available from genealogy suppliers.

Following the 1910 Finance Act, a nationwide land valuation survey was carried out, and the field books and plans from this survey may yield information on a property, its owner or use. This survey was nicknamed the '1910 Domesday' and the finalized valuation plans are kept at TNA, but some working valuation books and maps are kept at local record offices, e.g., LRO and Greater Manchester County Record Office (GMCRO). (The working valuation office records for Liverpool were destroyed during the Second World War.)

After 1862 the ownership of land was registered at district land registries, which also recorded changes in ownership after first registration. Copies of land registers can be obtained (a fee is payable) from the district land registry at Preston or HM Land Registry: www.landregistry.gov.uk.

Equity Suits

If a dispute arose between business partners, family members or trading partners which could not be settled using the common law, then equity suits or 'pleadings' were brought in the chancery or exchequer courts.

An equity suit could relate to matters as diverse as apprenticeships, cargoes, land ownership, marriage settlements, manors, mortgages, shipping, slavers or wills. Several members of a family may be mentioned in a suit over the content of a will, say.

The plaintiffs and defendants set out their respective cases in a statement or 'pleading'. 'Depositions' were statements of evidence written for the court. As mentioned earlier, the county palatine had its own chancery and exchequer. Appeals against judgements made in the palatine's chancery court were heard in the Duchy Court of Lancaster at Westminster; further appeals were heard in the king's court.

Pleadings and depositions for the Duchy Court for some reigns were calendared by the LCRS (volumes 32, 35 and 40). See also C. Fishwick (ed.),

A Calendar of Lancashire and Cheshire Exchequer Depositions by Commission from 1558 to 1702 (Lancashire and Cheshire Record Society, 11 (1885)).

Records of chancery suits date back to the late fourteenth century and are kept at TNA. They are mostly written in English. The earlier records (before 1558) are listed in series C1, which can be searched online.

Formerly, equity pleadings after 1558 have been particularly difficult to research owing to a lack of finding aids, but recently more indexes have become available.

A broader discussion of equity suits, with details of available indexes, can be read at: www.medievalgenealogy.org.uk/guide/cha.shtml.

The Bernau Index

This index of surnames relates to people mentioned in chancery and exchequer court depositions and proceedings from 1714–1758. It is available on microfilm at the Society of Genealogists' Library and from FamilySearch (the Church of Jesus Christ of Latter-day Saints). A guide has been published: Hilary Sharp, *How to Use the Bernau Index* (Society of Genealogists, 2000).

There's more information on chancery records at TNA, with a discussion of the Bernau Index, in Henry Horwitz, *Chancery Equity Records and Proceedings 1600–1800* (2nd edn, PRO, 1998).

Some series of chancery and exchequer records at TNA can be explored online. The Court of Chancery Six Clerks' Office (C 6) series is currently being indexed. It can be explored online by piece number, person, place or subject using the Equity Pleadings Database at: www.nationalarchives.gov.uk/equity/default.asp. TNA Guide to Equity Suits before 1558 is at: www.nationalarchives.gov.uk/records/research-guides/chancery-equity-before-1558.htm. TNA Guide to Equity Suits after 1558 is at: www.nationalarchives.gov.uk/records/research-guides/chancery-equity-from-1558.htm.

The Birth of the Textile Industries

Long before the birth of Lancashire's famous cotton industry, it was home to the spinning and weaving of linen, fustians and woollens. The county was blessed with certain natural advantages for textile production. It had plenty of flowing streams, essential for fulling-mills and dye-works, and the moorlands were more suited to raising sheep than growing crops. Later, when mechanized spinning was introduced, Lancashire's damp climate was highly suited to processing yarn.

Textile manufacture began as a sideline for small farmers: for example, the people of Rossendale wove flax and wool into cloth to help supplement their income.

Flax was grown locally around Wigan and other areas, and linen yarn was imported from Ireland via the ports of Chester and Liverpool.

For some people, however, spinning or weaving was their main occupation, although they kept a small plot of land for their own cow, pig or growing potatoes. They helped out local farmers at busy times like the harvest.

Lancashire historians have speculated that the textile industry was given its first major boost when skilled Flemish weavers settled in the Manchester, Bolton, Rossendale and Pendle areas at the invitation of Edward II. It is said that the sabots (wooden shoes) worn by these weavers were the ancestors of the clogs worn by the factory hands in the textile towns.

By the early 1640s the textile industries were firmly established, and the county was noted for its 'cottons'. These early 'cottons' were still made from wool, however. Yarn from the cotton plant was first used in Lancashire early in the seventeenth century, when it was woven with linen yarn to make sturdy 'fustian' cloth.

Families such as the Chethams of Manchester became very wealthy buying and selling woollen cloths, linens, cotton yarn and fustians. The wholesalers and master-manufacturers of Manchester (who bought the yarn and put it out to weavers to be woven into cloth) became famous. As the 'Manchester men' became richer they built smart brick homes and warehouses for their goods. Bolton had a regular market for fustians, and the Oldham district had many small-scale dealers or 'chapmen'.

Towns like Bolton, Blackburn, Manchester and Rochdale, which were not yet incorporated and had few restrictions on their trade, had an advantage over boroughs like those of Preston, Lancaster and Wigan which were strictly regulated by their guilds or corporations.

Strange to relate, all-cotton goods and the calico-printing industry, which later brought immense wealth to Britain, faced severe restrictions from government at first.

In the early eighteenth century, the woollen trade was threatened by calicoes imported from India and the East. It became very fashionable to wear beautiful, light, practical clothes made of printed calico instead of heavy, difficult to clean woollens. These calicoes were woven wholly from cotton. Imports of printed or dyed calicoes were banned in 1700 to protect the livelihoods of silk and woollen workers.

However, this Act boosted the manufacture, printing and dyeing of calicos in Britain at the expense of woollen weavers. To ease the depression in the woollen industry, an Act of 1721 banned the weaving or selling of any printed cotton 'stuffs', whether imported or made in Britain, and it became illegal even to wear them.

Luckily for Lancashire workers, 'fustians' made from cotton mixed with linen were exempted from the 1721 Act (fustian was still taxed, however).

Norwich worsted manufacturers and London woollen weavers, 'feeling the pinch' of competition, put pressure on Parliament to include fustians in the 1721 Act. Lancashire manufacturers in their turn petitioned Parliament: thousands of people depended on the fustian industry for a living. The 'Manchester Act' of 1736 upheld the exemption of fustians from prohibition but all-cotton printed goods were still banned.

Prior to the introduction of the factory system, the processing, spinning and weaving of cotton, wool, fustian and linen was primarily done in a domestic setting. Weaving was performed by men and women. Some weavers rented their looms; others owned several looms which they housed in work-shops, and employed others to help with the weaving. Spinning was done by women and girls at home. The smallest children helped to clean and prepare raw materials like cotton wool so that it could be spun into yarn.

Spinning and weaving by hand were slow processes and merchants struggled to satisfy their customers' demand for cloth. Bury inventor John Kay's 'flying shuttle' (1733) made weaving faster and easier, although it was a couple of decades before it was widely used. Faster spinning was made possible by Bolton weaver James Hargreaves' 'spinning jenny', patented in 1770. The flying shuttle and spinning jenny were used for cotton and wool yarns.

Preston barber Richard Arkwright's 'water-frame', which built on the ideas of Thomas Highs and Lewis Paul, was powered by a waterwheel. Arkwright's machine produced cotton thread strong enough to replace the linen warp thread used in fustian weaving, so a lighter, all-cotton cloth could be woven. In 1774 Arkwright succeeded in overturning the ban on all-cotton goods and the cotton industry was unfettered by legislation at last. Arkwright's patents and factories brought him riches and a knighthood.

The 'spinning-mule' was invented by Samuel Crompton (1779), who lived at Bolton. The 'mule' produced a particularly fine, strong cotton thread suitable for weaving delicate muslins. News of his invention soon leaked out and Bolton became known for its fine-spun cotton.

As the technology for cotton carding (a preparatory process) and spinning became more advanced, textile machinery grew too large to be housed in the home. The factory system was born. Water, and later steam, was needed to power machinery. Formerly workers could please themselves what hours they worked (and many families worked very long hours in order to earn a living). Now the spinners had to start and finish work when their master wanted. Their lives were ruled by the factory whistle.

Some districts specialized in particular products but others made a range of textiles. Manchester made 'velveteens' (a type of corduroy) as well as fustians, cottons and 'small-wares' such as tapes. Blackburn was famous for its 'greys' (fustians). Sturdy linen sail-cloths were woven in Warrington and the cotton town of Preston had silk factories.

Velveteen cutting, Platt's works, Warrington. Illustration by H. E. Tidmarsh. (William Arthur Shaw, *Manchester Old and New Vol. II* (Cassell & Co., c. 1894))

Fortunes could be made in the bleaching, finishing and textile printing industries, too, which were also major employers of men, women and children. The Peel cotton dynasty began with farmer Robert Peele (later Peel) (1723–1795) who lived in Blackburn. Like other Lancashire farmers, Peel eked out his income by spinning and weaving cloth.

Fish Lane, Blackburn, traditional birthplace of Sir Robert Peel, first baronet (1750–1830). Engraved by Evans from a drawing by Cardwell. (Cyrus Redding, J. R. Beard and W. C. Taylor, *Pictorial History of the County of Lancaster* (George Routledge, 1844))

In 1744 Robert married Emma Howarth of Lower Darwen. The newly-weds lived at Holehouse Farm before moving to Fish Lane, Blackburn in about 1750. Peel ventured into the calico-printing trade with Emma's brother Jonathan. Howarth had learned the art of calico-printing in London, then the centre of the trade.

Peel and Howarth began printing cloth by hand: applying dye using a traditional wooden pattern or block. Hand-printing was very slow and time-consuming.

Peel conducted several experiments, and successfully mechanized calico printing by applying coloured patterns onto cloth using rollers. His first pattern was a parsley-leaf, and he acquired the nickname 'Parsley Peel'. Sometime around 1760, he set up a calico print-works at Brookside near Blackburn in partnership with his brother-in-law Mr Howarth and Mr William Yates.

Robert Peel junior was the third son of 'Parsley Peel'. Authorities disagree about his birthplace, but local tradition says he was born in his father's house at Fish Lane. Robert was baptized on 23 April 1750 at Blackburn church, and educated at Blackburn Grammar School.

Parsley Peel wanted his children to be prosperous and started them in the industry early. His sons Robert and Jonathan served apprenticeships in calico-dyeing so that they learnt the trade from the ground up.

Chamber Hall, home of Sir Robert Peel (first baronet), Bury, after he moved from Fish Lane.
(Alfred Rimmer, *Summer Rambles Around Manchester* (John Heywood, c. 1890))

When Parsley Peel's partnership with Howarth and Yates ended, he continued manufacturing at Brookside, but his partners moved to Bury. Robert junior entered into business with his father's former partners when he was about 20 years old. Parsley Peel is said to have given him £500 (a tidy sum) to kick-start his business.

The new Peel, Yates & Howarth firm set up calico print-works and later cotton-spinning mills. The Bury firm became very successful and founded more mills at Ramsbottom, Summerseat and elsewhere.

At first money was tight and young Robert lodged with Mr Yates's family. He became great friends with their daughter Ellen ('Nelly'), then only 5 years old. According to biographer Samuel Smiles, Robert often teased Nelly. He asked if she would marry him when she was grown up, and Nelly answered 'Yes'. Robert said, 'Then I'll wait for thee, Nelly, and wed no-one else' (Samuel Smiles, *Self-Help* (John Murray, 1860)).

Mills at Summerseat. Sir Robert Peel (first baronet) and his partners owned mills in this valley. (Alfred Rimmer, *Summer Rambles Around Manchester* (John Heywood, c. 1890))

Nelly grew into a beautiful young lady. When she was 17, Robert kept his word, and they were married on 8 July 1783. Their third child, Robert (1788–1850), was destined for a dazzling future. His father had his heart set on a political career for Robert, so he and his brother William were educated at Harrow.

Robert Peel's mills at Bury prospered and in 1790 he became MP for Tamworth. Peel was a strong supporter of the Pitt administration and was made a baronet.

When he died on 3 May 1830 his estate was worth over £2 million. His children were allied by marriage to several noble families. Sadly, Peel did not live to see his son become Prime Minister four years later, but Robert was clearly destined for greatness. The Lancashire family that began life in a farmhouse was now a great dynasty.

Innovation did not guarantee financial success. John Kay and James Hargreaves's inventions were greeted by mob violence because workers feared for their livelihoods. The inventors were forced to flee their native towns. Kay and mule-spinning inventor Samuel Crompton died in poverty.

Cotton factories like those owned by the Peel family relied on cheap labour. Apart from the highly professional art of mule spinning (which was done by men), many jobs in the factory did not require great skill and were done by women and children.

Sir Robert Peel (1788–1850) second baronet, Prime Minister from 1834–1835 and 1841–1846. He was born at Bury. (The Story of Lancashire (London, c. 1898))

42

The earliest factories were water-powered and sited alongside rivers. Workers were scarce in rural areas so conscript labour was used in the form of pauper apprentices (see Chapter 5). Mill-owners didn't have to pay them a wage (just bed and board) as they were 'learning a trade'. Waggon-loads of children were transported from parishes in London to mills in Lancashire such as Backbarrow. Some child apprentices at Backbarrow were from Liverpool workhouse. Parish apprentices were usually bound to the mill-owner until the age of 21. The children slept in custom-built 'apprentice houses'. All too often, mill children shared beds and were given insufficient food.

Joseph Dutton, who gave evidence to a parliamentary select committee on children's work in factories in 1816, said that children working at Ainsworth & Catterall's cotton-spinning mill at Preston worked up to fifteen hours per day, including one hour for meals.

Ironically, one of the first pioneers of factory reform was mill-owner Robert Peel (first baronet). Around 1,000 of Peel's 15,000 workers were pauper apprentices. Peel's factories were managed by overseers, because he was too busy to look into his mills' day-to-day running. In 1784 the welfare of his child employees was forcibly brought to his attention when several parish apprentices at his Radcliffe factory died of 'putrid fever'. Local doctors condemned the children's living conditions.

Peel was shocked, and enquired further. He told the 1816 select committee on factory children that he was 'struck with the uniform appearance of bad health and ... stinted [stunted] growth of the children' in his own and other factories. He successfully pushed the first legislation to regulate factory labour through Parliament.

Peel's Health and Morals of Apprentices Act of 1802 limited apprentice children's hours in cotton mills to twelve hours a day. But just a few years later, apprentice labour in mills was far less common. The introduction of steam-power meant that factories did not need water-power and could be built anywhere. Now concern grew over the 'free labour' children sent to work by their parents.

In 1815 Peel proposed a bill to protect all factory children, He wanted children's hours limited to ten (not including mealtimes). Peel's bill was lost after opposition from other mill-owners, but he continued his campaign. He told the House of Commons it was 'notorious that children of very tender years were dragged from their beds some hours before daylight, and confined in the factories not less than fifteen hours'. (*Edinburgh Annual Register* (1818)).

Over the following decades, Parliament ordered several investigations into factory children's working conditions. Children were employed as 'piecers': they joined together broken threads on the spinning-mule. Scavengers cleaned waste cotton dust from under the machinery. If the

Weaving shed, Haworth's Mills, Ordsall, Lancashire. Illustration by H. E. Tidmarsh. (William Arthur Shaw, *Manchester Old and New Vol. II* (Cassell & Co., c. 1894))

machinery began to move while they were still underneath, they were badly injured or killed. Children also worked as bobbin winders and 'doffers'.

Thomas Wilkinson, a 34-year-old mule spinner from Bolton who worked in Crook's mill, told a select committee in 1819 that children as young as 6 years old were employed as piecers.

Crook's mill ran from 6 in the morning until 7 at night in the summer (7 a.m. until 8 p.m. in winter), but the piecers 'very often' were at the factory to clean and oil the machinery half an hour before work started. On Saturdays the mill closed at 4 p.m. (4.30 p.m. in winter).

The children had just one hour for lunch, with 'no other' mealtimes, but for two or three days each week their lunchtimes were spent oiling the machinery. They ate their meals as they worked; their food often got covered with cotton dust. Thomas said this was the usual practice 'in all' the Bolton factories he had worked in.

Piecers were not employed directly by the mill-owners. They worked for the mule spinners. Child workers were often beaten 'to keep them awake, and drive them on'. The spinners were paid by piecework, and they paid the piecers from their own wages. Sometimes the spinners employed their own children, in which case the wages were kept in the family.

The heat in the factories was 'overpowering'. Cotton was easier to spin in a warm, moist atmosphere, so the mill hands worked barefoot and only lightly clad. Mule spinners were extremely well paid: Thomas earned about 20s per week after he had paid his piecers.

Wilkinson did not say exactly how much he paid his piecers but William Royle, a spinner at Thomas Ainsworth's factory at Warrington, told the same select committee that he paid his piecers from 2s to 6s per week. The older, more experienced piecers earned more than the youngest children.

Factory work was exhausting, and it was rare for people to be employed in the mills after the age of 40: the mill-owner would 'turn them away' if they could not do the work.

In 1819 a Factory Act was passed that banned children under 9 from working in cotton mills. Children under 16 were limited to a twelve-hour day. The law was ignored and factory reformers spent many years campaigning for better protection for children in textile mills. The 1833 Act limited hours for children in all textile factories (not just cotton) and banned night work. This Act established the factory inspectorate, which was responsible for enforcing factory regulations and ensuring that children had a minimum amount of education.

Factory inspector Leonard Horner reported that in 1840 in Lancashire, over 8,200 children (5,103 boys and 3,099 girls) under the age of 13 were employed in cotton, wool and flax mills (*Reports of the Inspectors of Factories for the Half-year Ending 31 December 1840* (1841)).

The 1847 Factory Act limited the working day for females and young persons to ten hours per day. More legislation on hours, working education and conditions was passed throughout the nineteenth century. Factory children had to attend school for a set number of hours per week ('half-timers') and they were not permitted to work without a school attendance certificate signed by a teacher.

The factory Acts required employers to keep registers of children and young persons, and local archives may have copies. Local government records may have registers of children exempted from school under the factory and workshop Acts in the school attendance record series. Proof of age certificates include the youngster's name, parents' names, place of residence and date when the child was examined.

There is always a possibility that your ancestor was cited in the factory inspectors' reports, which were published half-yearly from 1834, and annually from 1878. The reports included records of prosecutions against employers and parents for infringements under the factory Acts, e.g., for underage working, illegal hours, failure to attend school, unsafe machinery, etc.

Case Study

The 'returns of prosecutions' in the *Reports of the Inspectors of Factories for the Half-year Ending 30 April 1876* (1876) [C.1572] include a summons brought by sub-Inspector Mr Cramp against James Nuttall. Nuttall, an overlooker at Lower Clowes Mill, Tottington Higher End, Rawtenstall, was summonsed for 'allowing his child, a girl under eight years of age, to be employed in a cotton mill'. He was also summonsed for obstructing the inspector 'by attempting to conceal a child' (i.e., Nuttall tried to hide his daughter from the inspector). The case was heard at Bury Petty Sessions on 16 March 1876. Nuttall was fined £3 for obstructing the inspector and 13s 6d for making his underage daughter work in the mill.

Weaving by hand was not displaced by machinery for many years. The long, painfully slow decline of the Lancashire handloom weavers is a desperately tragic story. At first the abundance of yarn owing to mechanized spinning led to a golden age for cotton weavers: wages were good and food plentiful. Fustian weavers were not as well paid, however, and the county's linen industry unravelled as demand for cotton grew.

The cotton weavers' good fortune was short-lived. The wheel turned full circle with the invention of the power-loom ('steam' loom). Edmund Cartwright's patents in 1785 and 1787 were not an immediate success because power-woven cloth was of poor quality. But the handloom weavers sensed that the writing was on the wall, and power-loom factories were attacked in 1790, 1812 and 1826.

A trade slump after the end of the Napoleonic Wars led to handloom weavers' wages being slashed. All the weavers in the cotton towns went on strike for higher wages in 1818 and locked up their shuttles. They won a short reprieve, but the overall trend for wages was downwards. Large numbers of people were affected: Geoffrey Timmins has estimated that there were roughly 200,000 handloom weavers in Lancashire in the 1820s.

A parliamentary select committee on handloom weaving in 1835 heard that Bolton textile weavers lived 'under the most incredible privation'. At Bolton, an average weekly wage was 4s 1½d net, and at Manchester 5s to 7s 6d net.

John Scott was a Manchester silk weaver with three children too young to work. He and his wife earned 8s–10s per week after deductions, but it was not enough to feed and clothe his family even though he worked from fifteen to seventeen hours a day, and he was in debt. (John's rent was 3s 6d per week; bread was 1½d per lb).

Weavers' low wages were not just owing to mechanization; the trade was overstocked with workers. Some left the trade, but all too many continued to try and scrape a living. A high proportion of handloom weavers in Manchester and Salford were Irish immigrants. Weavers taught their children how to weave, hoping to increase the family's income, and piece-work rates fell sharply.

The cotton masters worked hard to improve the quality of machine-woven cloth, and by the mid-1830s there were 110,000 power-looms nationally. In the Lancashire textile towns the number of power-loom workers began to overtake handloom weavers (except in Bolton and Wigan) by the mid-nineteenth century. Power-looms did not need physical strength to work them and the machines were tended by women and children. It must have been a bitter moment for a skilled weaver if he could no longer earn a living and his wife and children went into the factory to make ends meet.

Ancoats mills at dinnertime, Manchester. Illustration by H. E. Tidmarsh. (William Arthur Shaw, *Manchester Old and New Vol. II* (Cassell & Co., c. 1894))

The cotton business boomed: demand for raw cotton rose from 8,000 tons p.a. in 1760 to 300,000 tons p.a. in 1850. Cotton machinery was one of the main attractions at the Great Exhibition in the Crystal Palace. In 1853 Britain exported £30 million of cotton goods and yarns yearly.

When in full employment, some operatives owned their own homes and thrifty families had money in the bank. But the industry's total reliance on imported raw cotton was its Achilles heel. In 1861 the Civil War in America led to the blockade of its ports. Lancashire's lifeline was snipped in two. No cotton from the slave plantations could reach the mills, and four years of terrible suffering followed: the 'cotton famine'.

The *Illustrated London News* (22 November 1862) reported on the scale of the disaster, which particularly affected cotton workers in Lancashire and Cheshire. The newspaper estimated that in normal trading conditions, around 355,000 people were employed spinning and weaving cotton. In February that year, only 92,000 operatives had full-time work. By November, just 40,000 operatives were in full-time work. In the Blackburn district, which had 155 mills, 48 had closed their factory gates, and 17,120 of 39,435 workers were unemployed. The Rochdale area was very badly hit, with 19,093 of the 24,361 mill-hands out of work.

Donations of clothes for starving Lancashire operatives arriving at the Bridewell Hospital, London, during the cotton famine. (Illustrated London News, 22 November 1862)

Desperate to save money, families huddled together to save rent, perhaps six to eight people living in one small room. Savings in the friendly societies and co-operative banks were raided. Every stick of furniture and household goods were sold off, and families slept on straw. Many were ashamed of their poverty. They tried to keep up a respectable appearance, and washed their clothes regularly even if they were in rags.

The Poor Law Boards of Guardians struggled to cope with the sheer numbers of people out of work. Soup kitchens were set up but thousands of people 'clemmed' (starved). Cotton famine relief funds and committees were set up in the north-west and in London to provide food and clothing for the unemployed, and some minute books and payment books are kept by local record offices.

Before the famine, wages ranged from 13s per week for a piecer to nearly 30s weekly for a mule spinner. Now men were set to public works such as breaking rocks for road-making so that they could earn a shilling a day.

The cotton famine was also disastrous for the collieries and mill engineering firms whose businesses depended on the mills. Grocers and other shopkeepers suffered, too, because no one had any money to buy their wares.

Helpers making up clothing parcels at the Industrial Institution, Manchester, for unemployed Lancashire workers. (Illustrated London News, 22 November 1862)

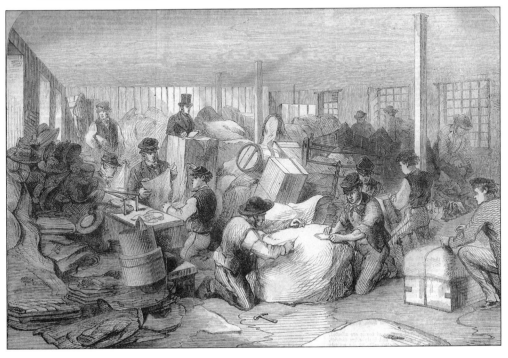

Ironically, raw cotton was available, but it never reached the stricken mills. Liverpool brokers who had stockpiled raw cotton during a period of over-production made a fortune when they shipped it out to North America, where cotton was also in demand and high prices paid.

The Cotton Spinners' Association (a masters' association) was formed at this time to protect themselves against speculators and suppliers of sub-standard raw cotton, which became increasingly prevalent as the cost of cotton rocketed.

One way of escaping the famine was emigration. Tens of thousands of Lancashire people left for a new life abroad. Trade revived again in the mid-1860s and cotton exports kept on growing until the century's end.

Textile-related Records

The censuses (Chapter 6) and parish registers may give the first clue that an ancestor was a textile worker. Although it was not compulsory for baptismal records in parish registers to include the father's occupation until 1812, textile workers are recorded in earlier registers. A parent's occupation may be mentioned when a child was buried.

The 1851 census recorded over 1,250 different types of job related to cotton manufacture alone in Lancashire. Common job titles in the censuses include: cotton weaver, power loom weaver, cotton spinner, doffer, throstle doffer, cotton overlooker, piecer, tackler and so on. Be aware of possible problems with the census data, for example, if an ancestor was working a night shift, they might be recorded at the factory rather than at home.

The county palatine's chancery court records may record financial disputes between merchants, businesses and out-workers. Accident books, apprentice-ship records, business records, cash books, company wage books and wage slips, debt records, minute books, financial accounts, friendly society records, letters, pension records, stocks and shares registers, title deeds, trade-union records, wills and probate inventories are all useful sources. (See Chapter 4 for more information on apprenticeship and trade-union records.)

Fire insurance records date back to the late seventeenth century and many different types of business were covered. Cotton mills and warehouses contained lots of highly flammable materials and often burnt down. Records for insurance policies include policy holders, property addresses and names of tenants living in the building insured. One of the earliest fire insurance companies for which records survive is the Sun Fire Office (1710) and its records are kept at the Guildhall Library in London.

For more information on how to use fire insurance records, and their location, see David T. Hawkings, *Fire Insurance Records for Family and Local Historians* (Francis Boutle, 2003).

National Register of Archives Index

Business records may be scattered across several archives. If you know the name of the firm or family business that your ancestor worked for, you can use the NRA index as a finding aid. Search by corporate name, family name, personal papers or alphabetical listings at: www.nationalarchives.gov.uk/nra.

Access to Archives (A2A)

Use the Access to Archives search engine to find records such as wage books, staff records or trade-union records. Limit your search by time period so you don't get overwhelmed with results. For example, a general search for 'cotton industry wage' + 'Lancashire' elicits nearly 150 results. Narrow down your search by including as much information as possible, e.g., the name of your ancestor's employer: www.nationalarchives.gov.uk/a2a.

Parliamentary Papers (Blue Books)

Parliamentary select committee reports and royal commissions on the cotton industry like those mentioned in this chapter are often overlooked by family historians. The government ordered investigations into mining and many other trades and manufactures as well as cotton, such as the Children's Employment Commission reports of the 1840s and 1860s. These 'Blue Books', which comprise 'sessional papers' and 'Command' papers, were ordered to

Case Study

Henry Ashworth & Co. was a firm of Bolton cotton spinners. A search on the NRA's corporate index for 'Henry Ashworth' generates the names of two businesses, but only one is a cotton-spinning firm. 'Clicking' on this firm's name elicits the names and contact details of six repositories with records relating to the company.

The John Rylands University Library at Manchester has the firm's accounts and stock book for 1831–1879. Bolton Archives and Local Studies hold family papers, valuations and correspondence, and registers of children employed for 1823–1887: ZWL 50-69, ZZ/31. LRO has records of the Ashworth family, H. & E. Ashworth and Henry Ashworth & Son for 1800–1894: DDAS. Blackburn Museum and Art Gallery has business and other letters to Henry Ashworth c. 1841–1865, and cotton samples. Henry Ashworth's notebooks are held privately. Finally, Staffordshire and Stoke-on-Trent Archive Service (Staffordshire Record Office) holds the firm's business and personal diaries and papers from 1841–1975: D3016.

be printed by the Houses of Parliament. They include interviews with workers and overviews of the industry under discussion. Factory inspectors' reports are 'Command' papers.

Each 'Blue Book' or parliamentary paper is numbered. Large reference libraries may have copies of 'Blue Books' and catalogues and indexes are available. You can access digital images of parliamentary papers in the reading rooms of TNA. The Parliamentary Archives have copies, which can be viewed in the search room at: www.parliament.uk/archives and www.parliament.uk/business/publications/parliamentary-archives/archives-electronic/parliamentary-papers.

A limited number of Command papers and factory reports are available free on Google Books: http://books.google.com.

A huge number of books have been published on the cotton industry. Terry Wyke and Nigel Rudyard, *Cotton: A Select Bibliography on Cotton in North-West England* (Manchester, 1997) not only has a comprehensive list of reference works but also an excellent overview of archival sources (with locations) including business, employment and trade-union records.

The 'Spinning the Web' website is a wonderful resource for the history of the cotton industry with images of workers, detailed information on working conditions and oral histories. 'Spinning the Web' also has a free downloadable copy of Wyke and Rudyard's *Cotton: A Select Bibliography* at: www.spinningtheweb.org.uk/bibilog.php.

The cotton industry's success in Lancashire owed a great deal to the creation of speedy communications: the transport revolution.

Chapter 4

SPEED KINGS: TRANSPORT AND INDUSTRY

Turnpike Roads

Today we expect travel to be quick and easy, and grumble if we are delayed for a short time. But until the eighteenth century, England's roads were little better than mud-filled, deeply rutted tracks, virtually impassable during the winter. If you needed to travel somewhere, you walked (if you were poor) or rode, if you could afford it. Goods were transported on the backs of pack-ponies or in slow, lumbering waggons. The first coaches appeared towards the end of the sixteenth century, but they were really glorified carts, with no springs.

In 1555 the Highways Act made parishes responsible for the roads in their area. A surveyor of highways (unpaid) was appointed by local magistrates, and each householder had to spend six days each year helping to maintain the roads, or provide labour and materials. Road-mending duty was not popular, and quarter sessions and assize records may reveal indictments against people (including the surveyors) for non-repair of roads.

Despite the shocking state of the roads, the first stage-coaches began running in the 1650s. Edward Parker travelled from Preston to London in 1683. He wrote to his father: 'My journey was noe [sic] ways pleasant ... I am resolved never to ride up again[e] in ye coach' (Samuel Smiles, *Brindley and the Early Engineers* (John Murray, 1874)).

As traffic increased, parishes found it even more difficult to keep their roads in good repair. But a parish did not have the power to build new roads, nor could it levy a toll to pay for repairs without Parliament's consent. Local communities felt it was unfair for them to keep funding major repairs when so many outsiders used their roads without paying for the privilege.

The answer was 'turnpike trusts'. A local statutory body was set up (sanctioned by an Act of Parliament) which controlled a particular section of road, with a toll-bar at each end. Travellers paid a toll to use the turnpike, with some exceptions, e.g., pedestrians, flour-millers, the mail-coaches and people attending church.

Turnpike trusts found the money to repair or build their roads by mortgaging the tolls to be collected. Usually, a trust was set up for twenty-one years, but it could apply for a fresh Act of Parliament to renew its authority. Unfortunately, many trusts could not keep up their mortgage payments, so they did not spend enough on keeping their roads in good repair.

The first road to be turnpiked in Lancashire was from Liverpool to Prescot in 1725, and another seven roads followed during the next quarter century. The period from 1750 to 1754 was exceptionally busy: another thirteen trusts were formed. The General Turnpike Act of 1773 made it easier for turnpikes to be established.

Because these were local initiatives, Britain's road 'system' became a patch-work of turnpikes and un-adopted roads. But journey times did improve. In the 1730s intrepid stage-coach travellers took six days to reach London from Chester. Three decades later, a stage-coach from Liverpool to London took two days during the summer, and three days in winter.

Great strides were made in road construction techniques, too. John Metcalfe (Blind Jack of Knaresborough) built several new Lancashire roads including one from Bury to Blackburn, with a branch to Accrington, and one from Bury to Haslingden. His road from Manchester to Huddersfield, built over extremely marshy ground, was no mean feat.

Turnpike trust records include minute books, maps, details of toll charges and sometimes toll-house keepers' daybooks. Plans for turnpikes were deposited with the clerk of the peace (quarter sessions records). Roads were convenient markers for property boundaries.

Trust records may also be found in solicitors' accounts at local archives. Turnpike records may have detailed information on toll-houses on the road's route. If your ancestor invested money in a turnpike road, their name could be listed in the trust's accounts; reports on trusts were sometimes printed in local newspapers.

However, the formation of a turnpike trust did not exempt parishioners from their obligation to maintain the road, or from their compulsory days of labour or provision of materials to that end.

The Highways Act of 1835 freed parishes from the burden of providing labour and materials and enabled them to levy a rate to pay for road repairs and for a salaried road official. The coming of the railways greatly reduced turnpike trusts' profits, but some trusts survived into the early 1880s. The Local Government Act (1888) transferred responsibility for main roads to county councils, rural and urban district councils.

Coal Mining

Coal was mined in Lancashire from medieval times. Early pits were small-scale, shallow workings. Families such as the Bradshaws of Haigh Hall and the Egertons (Bridgewater estates) had mining interests since the sixteenth century. Mines were sunk deeper and deeper as the topmost seams were exhausted.

Men dug out or 'hewed' the coal. Miners earned good money (£1 4s per week at Ringley Bridge, Bolton in the 1840s) but paid for their own tools, candles and gunpowder. Investigators for the Children's Employment Commission in 1842 interviewed mine managers, miners and child workers. Women, boys and girls worked as 'drawers' and 'thrutchers'. They were harnessed like animals by a belt and chain to incredibly heavy coal waggons which they dragged, pushed and pulled from the coal face to the main shaft.

Betty Wardle of Outwood, near Lever, 'had a child born in the pits ... I brought it up the pit-shaft in my skirt'. Henry Jones, who was just under 6 years old, worked at Messrs' Cleggs at Pauldin Wood, Oldham: 'I am the youngest in the pit, excepting Jack Jones ... we are working two shifts of eight hours'. Henry worked as a 'thrutcher' for his 13-year-old brother James. Child labour was used because seams in Lancashire mines could be as narrow as 20in high. The 1842 Mines Report shocked society: all females and boys under 10 were banned from the mines that year, but the law was widely flouted.

Many colliery workers were employed at the pit brow. There were firemen, winding-engine men, wheelwrights, blacksmiths, carpenters and men to tend the colliery engine. Women and girls cleaned and sorted the coal.

Work-girls at Wigan collieries. (*Cassell's Illustrated History of England Vol. IX* (Cassell, Petter and Galpin, c. 1874))

In the early 1860s Lancashire had over 370 collieries which produced over 12 million tons of coal annually. The county had one of the highest accident rates in Britain. Deaths and accidents from roof falls and explosions from gases were common. Over 300 men were killed in Lancashire's worst mining disaster at the Pretoria Pit near Atherton in 1910.

Parliamentary papers such as mining inspectorate reports list fatalities, with names of casualties where known, in mining accidents (see also POWE 7 at TNA).

For a general overview of coal-mining sources for family history, see David Tonks' *My Ancestor Was A Coalminer* (Society of Genealogists, 2010), which also has a glossary of mining terms. The section on industry records later in this chapter lists fruitful sources of information. Chapter 6 discusses coal-mining records in detail; Section F lists some online sources.

Coal was needed for fuel to smelt iron and generate steam in engines. Industry's ever-growing appetite for coal ignited the next stage of the transport revolution. The continuing poor state of turnpike roads led to the construction of canals and railways. Once again, Lancashire people set the pace for the rest of Britain and built some of the wonders of the age.

Canals, Docks and Shipping

Merchants and traders who wanted to move heavy, bulky cargoes like coal and salt faced great difficulties. There was a limit to how much pack-ponies could carry, and it was slow and extremely costly to send goods by waggon.

It was easier to move large cargoes by water. Merchants sent their goods by sea or river. River navigation could be difficult and dangerous, impeded by weirs or waterwheels used to power mills. Rivers were made straighter, deeper and wider to make voyages quicker and easier.

At the beginning of the eighteenth century, ships travelling up the Mersey estuary could not advance beyond Warrington, to the frustration of local businessmen. The earliest canal pioneer in Lancashire was southerner Thomas Steers (1672–1750). He was responsible for the Mersey & Irwell Navigation (1721) which made the Irwell navigable from Bank Quay at Warrington to Manchester. He also promoted the Douglas Navigation, which was fully open in 1742.

Pressure from salt and coal merchants such as John Blackburne of Liverpool led to the construction of Britain's first 'true' canal, the Sankey Brook Navigation, built by Henry Berry. (Berry may have been born in Lancashire.) The canal, which opened in 1757, enabled coal from St Helens collieries to be conveyed cheaply to Liverpool, and also to Cheshire salt-fields via the Weaver Navigation.

Francis Egerton, 3rd Duke of Bridgewater, kept a watchful eye on these successful waterways. The Duke (1736–1803) had considerable mining interests at Worsley. The towns of Manchester and Salford were the largest customers for his coal, but it cost the hefty sum of 10s per ton to convey it by road.

The Duke spent a fortune constructing a canal from Worsley to Manchester. Engineers James Brindley and John Gilbert overcame immense challenges such as the construction of the Barton Aqueduct over the Irwell. When the Bridgewater Canal opened in 1761 it caused a sensation.

The canal halved the cost of coal carriage to Manchester and generated much-needed income for the 'Canal Duke'. Later he extended his canal to Preston Brook, where it joined the Trent & Mersey Canal. The canal then continued to Runcorn, thus giving the Duke's boats a link to the Mersey. The Duke's huge financial risk now finally paid off, and money poured into his coffers.

The Duke's successes launched the great age of canal-building. The chief canals in Lancashire constructed after the Duke's were the Leeds & Liverpool Canal, Lancaster Canal, the Manchester, Bolton & Bury Canal and the Rochdale Canal. These canals were primarily funded by coal and cotton business owners and eventually most Lancashire textile towns had a canal link.

The canal companies made their profits by charging tolls, like the turnpike trusts. The carrying of passengers on packet boats was a profitable sideline. Canal boats also carried produce like potatoes, milk and butter to hungry townsfolk.

Sustained investment in new docks and harbour facilities for shipping was another major factor in the growth of Lancashire's industrial centres. The biggest success story was the port of Liverpool, which began life as a small fishing village.

During the sixteenth century imports of linen yarn from Ireland landed at Liverpool. Later, tobacco was imported from Virginia. However, nearby Chester had the lion's share of overseas trade until the River Dee silted up, to Liverpool's advantage. Trade gradually increased during the eighteenth century and Liverpool's imports included Irish wool and linen, cotton from the West Indies and dyestuffs for textiles such as indigo and logwood.

The construction of Liverpool's famous docks began with Thomas Steers' wet dock (the Old Dock) which opened in 1715 and by the end of the century, the city had nearly 2 miles of docks.

The wealth of some Liverpool and Lancaster merchants in the eighteenth and early nineteenth centuries was founded on the misery of men, women and children. Lancashire cloth was used to buy slaves in West Africa. Thousands of Africans were transported across the Atlantic to be sold as slaves in the West Indies, to work on sugar plantations (or they were taken to the southern states of North America to labour in cotton fields).

New Custom House, Liverpool (first stone laid 12 August 1828). Engraved by R. Finden from a drawing by T. Allom. (Revd G. N. Wright, People's Gallery of Engravings Vol. 2 (Fisher, Son & Co., 1845))

Conditions on the slave ships were disgracefully inhumane and untold numbers never survived the voyage. Typical slave-ship cargoes included sugar, tobacco, cotton, gunpowder (there was a factory near Backbarrow), dyestuffs, iron goods from Furness and timber.

The first slave ships left Liverpool in 1700 and by the 1750s the city had the dubious distinction of being Britain's busiest slaving port. The American War of Independence caused a setback for Liverpool slavers. The number of slave ships dropped from ninety-six in 1770 to just eleven vessels in 1779, but trade had recovered by the early 1790s. (John Britton, *The Beauties of England and Wales* (London, 1807)).

Merchants involved in the slave trade included Samuel Touchet and his family, the Hibbert family (both Manchester firms) and William Davenport of Liverpool.

In 1799 there were fifty-seven ships involved in the euphemistically named 'West India trade' at Lancaster. The treacherous navigation of the Lune caused difficulties with shipping, however. In the 1820s only small ships reached Lancaster via the river; larger vessels unloaded at Glasson Point, where there was a 'spacious dock'. (Edward Baines, *History, Directory and Gazetteer of the County Palatine of Lancaster Vol. 1* (Longman, Hurst & Co., 1824)). The slavers invested their money in factories in the town.

The grave of 'Sambo' at Sunderland Point. Alone but not forgotten: this poignant memorial to a nameless slave or servant is cared for by local schoolchildren.

Many thousands of Lancashire people helped to campaign against slavery. Liverpool's great rival port, Bristol, gave up the slave trade first. Slavery's abolition in Britain (1807) caused violent acrimony in Liverpool. However, historian Henry Smithers felt that the loss of the slave trade, which forced Liverpool to concentrate on other markets, led the port to have 'a more rapid state improvement and of progressive increase than at any other time in its history' (Henry Smithers, *Liverpool: Its Commerce, Statistics and Institutions* (Liverpool, 1825)).

After Lancaster's slave trade had declined it focussed on commerce with Russia and North America, and the coasting trade. But its significance as a port became overshadowed by Liverpool's spectacular success. In 1891 over £115 million of imports and over £108 million of exports flowed through Liverpool. There were also ports at Preston and Poulton.

LRO has a guide to 'Black and Asian Sources' which includes materials on the slave trade. Merseyside Maritime Museum and Archives has collections relating to many Liverpool merchants, both pro- and anti-slavery.

Railways

The next stage of the transport revolution was the birth of the railways. Canal carriage was not always ideal: like road transport, it could be slow and subject to delays. A prolonged spell of frosty weather could shut down a canal for weeks if the water froze.

The opening of the Stockton and Darlington Railway (1822) demonstrated the possibilities of steam-powered haulage. The first railway in Lancashire was the Bolton and Leigh line, financed by local colliery owners. It opened for goods traffic in 1828.

Paradoxically, the canal companies' success launched the building of the Liverpool and Manchester Railway. Cotton money was the engine driver of change in this instance. Liverpool merchants became fed up with paying the high charges demanded by canal carriers, in particular on the Duke of Bridgewater's canal.

The historic Rainhill trials were held on 6 October 1829 to decide which locomotive would perform best on the planned railway. The trials attracted a host of excited spectators. Stephenson's *Rocket* won the £500 prize when it reached a record-breaking 29mph.

The famous Rainhill trials, 1829. (*Monthly Chronicle of North Country Lore and Legend* (Walter Scott, 1889))

When the Liverpool and Manchester Railway opened on 15 September 1830, it was the first 'inter-city' railway for passengers. Investment in railway building, however, did not reach its peak in Lancashire until the 1840s. The textile towns all had rail links by the middle of the century.

The Liverpool and Manchester Railway reinforced Liverpool's importance for cotton imports. Railways stimulated the growth of the industrial towns even more and were a boon to areas like Rossendale which as yet had no canal link.

The railways made it much easier for the working classes to enjoy a trip to the seaside on the rare occasions when they were able to take a holiday. Southport and Blackpool both saw increases in visitor numbers when their railway links to the manufacturing towns were completed.

Railways enabled swift transport for perishable goods such as fish and shellfish from Morecambe Bay and the Mersey estuary to industrial districts. There were fishing trawlers based at Southport until the new port of Fleetwood (built 1836) began to entice them away. At the end of the nineteenth century, the introduction of steam trawlers greatly boosted Fleetwood's fishing industry.

The St Helens and Runcorn Gap Railway Co. built a large dock for sea-going ships at Garston in 1830. The new dock attracted a significant proportion of coal exports formerly exported from Liverpool and Widnes, and exports of copper smelted at St Helens.

Postcard of Blackpool from the beach, c. 1905.

Canal companies like the Leeds and Liverpool continued to prosper for some time after the coming of the railways, but later in the century, they were undercut by railway freight.

During the 1880s Britain suffered a deep, prolonged trade slump. Manchester merchants became increasingly angry about Liverpool's stranglehold on cotton imports. Dock duties and rail freight charges on cargoes passing through Liverpool were so high that it was sometimes actually more cost-effective for Manchester traders to import cargoes overland from Hull instead.

Manchester businessmen floated the idea of building a canal broad and deep enough so that ships could sail from the Mersey estuary all the way to Manchester. Cargoes could then be unloaded straight onto canal boats or onto railway waggons.

In 1882 a bill to construct the Ship Canal was proposed in Parliament, but rejected by the House of Lords the following year. The scheme was bitterly opposed by Liverpool businessmen who did not want to see potential profits sailing past their collective noses.

At last the Manchester Ship Canal bill was approved by Parliament in 1885. The Canal's construction gave employment to over 12,000 men and boys. Mechanical diggers – 'steam navvies' – were used to carve out the

'Manchester-sur-Mer'. A Punch *cartoonist has fun with the proposed Manchester Ship Canal, which opened to traffic in 1894.* (Punch, Vol. 83 (1882))

channel, but thousands of tons of earth were still shifted by sheer physical labour. Over 100 men were killed on site. When the Ship Canal opened in 1894 it rejuvenated trade and industry and the docks at Manchester bustled with cotton, grain and other imports.

Transport Records

An Act of Parliament was required before a canal, railway or dock could be built. Acts of Parliament also authorized the raising of funds so that construction could begin. New transport schemes often met with sustained opposition from competing interests which feared they might lose trade as a result. Parliamentary records include select committee reports and minutes of evidence with detailed witness statements from engineers or landowners affected by the scheme. Parliamentary papers can be accessed at the Parliamentary Archives (see Chapter 3).

Plans for new roads, bridges, docks, harbours, canals and railways had to be deposited with the clerk of the peace (quarter sessions records).

Sanitary inspections of canal boats became a legal requirement in the late 1870s and local record offices may have inspectors' records ('health registers') relating to the Canal Boat Acts of 1877 and 1884 in their public health collections.

The Waterways Archive at Ellesmere Port has many records relating to canals and inland waterways including some copies of health registers. (Please note that the waterways archive at Gloucester Docks has now moved to Ellesmere Port.) Use the Virtual Waterways Archive Catalogue to explore records for British Waterways and its predecessors, including early canal companies and canal carriers at: www.virtualwaterways.co.uk/Home.html.

One of the best histories for the birth of Lancashire canal system is Charles Hadfield and Gordon Biddle, *Canals of North-West England* (2 vols, David & Charles, 1970). Edward Paget-Tomlinson's *Illustrated History of Canal & River Navigations* (Landmark Countryside Collection, 2006) has a helpful section on staff and histories for canal and river navigations. The author's *Tracing Your Canal Ancestors* (Pen & Sword, 2011) includes a social history of canals and canal workers, with a comprehensive guide to inland waterway sources.

Several books have been published on researching your railway ancestors, most notably David T. Hawkings, *Railway Ancestors* (History Press, 2008), Di Drummond, *Tracing Your Railway Ancestors* (Pen & Sword, 2010) and Frank Hardy, *My Ancestor Was A Railway Worker* (Society of Genealogists, 2009). There's a family history society (FHS) devoted to railway ancestors and it publishes CD-ROMs of staff lists, which are available at: www.railwayancestors.org.uk.

British registered vessels kept records of their crew members (crew lists and agreements). The Crew List Index Project (CLIP) is a finding aid for merchant seafarers on British registered ships for 1861–1913 and can be accessed at: www.crewlist.org.uk/index.html.

London Metropolitan Archives holds Lloyd's registers of captains and mates of merchant ships who held masters' certificates from 1869–1947 (see Section A).

TNA is home to hundreds of collections on railways, canals and shipping. Its British Transport Historical Records (BTHR) collection is one of the most important sources for railway and canal history. Use the BTHR card index in the document reading room as a finding aid. A booklet with notes on how to use the finding aids is available. There are more finding aids in the research enquiries room. The BTHR archive has almost 150 records series: the RAIL series of railway records includes private canal companies which were later nationalized and those taken over by railways.

LRO has records relating to canals and shipping, including registers of vessels for the ports of Fleetwood, Lancaster and Preston. The Merseyside Maritime Museum Archive and Library has many collections for the area's shipping history.

A Hive of Industry

The construction of canals, docks and railways, coupled with better roads, made it easier for factories to access the raw materials they required, which boosted industrial growth even further. Lancashire became 'the workshop of the world'.

In 1794 John Holt commented on the county's immense variety of factories: 'hats, … cast iron; copper works; paper … pins and needles … plated glass, vitriol works, glass works, stockings, glue, lamp-black works, white-lead works, salt works, nailors [sic], tobacco-pipe makers, tobacco and snuff manufactories, black and brown earthenware, English porcelain, clock and watch makers, tool makers for both these branches' and so on (John Holt, *General View of the Agriculture of Lancashire* (London, 1794)).

Metal manufacturers were the second largest employer next to cotton in Lancashire in the 1860s. Of the 51,748 males employed in metals, around 12,000 were under the age of 18. Only a tiny proportion of the workforce was female.

Lancashire mines, textile factories and other mechanized industries required engines, machinery and spare parts. Iron foundries and forges were needed to cast machine parts and forge tools.

One of the most important innovations in iron manufacture was by Lancaster man Henry Cort (1740–1800), who in 1784 perfected a more efficient method of refining molten iron. Unfortunately, he lost his patent after the business capital he borrowed from a friend turned out to have been originally stolen from public funds. Although Cort was innocent of wrong-doing, he could not repay this money and was ruined financially.

When Scot William Fairbairn set up as a 24-year-old millwright in Manchester in 1814, every piece of machinery was built from scratch by hand. Fairbairn had no capital but brains, great practical experience and skill. Fairbairn had a partner, James Lillie, and their first 'big break' was to improve the gearing of the machinery in McConnell & Kennedy's spanking new spinning mill (1818). Soon Fairbairn had his own works at Ancoats, where he constructed an iron ship in 1831. He became the chief engineer and machine-maker for Manchester cotton mills.

Advances in tool-making technology led to Manchester becoming a centre of excellence for making machinery used in textiles, railways and heavy engineering industries. The first steam-hammer in Britain was built in 1842 at James Nasmyth's foundry at Patricroft. Joseph Whitworth's works at Chorlton Street, Manchester, turned out machine tools manufactured to a precision hitherto unknown.

At Oldham, thousands of people were employed by Platt Bros making textile machinery. The boys in the factory earned 3s 6d per week; labourers earned 14s per week. Mather & Platt (no relation to the Oldham firm) at Salford made textile machinery before branching out into dynamo manu-facture in the 1880s. The firm later moved to Newton Heath.

Pin and nail-makers, by contrast with metal-workers in the foundries, were extremely poorly paid. In Warrington, children as young as 5 put heads on pins using a special machine; they earned about 1s 6d per week. Young children and women in south Lancashire made nails by hand for pitifully low wages in filthy, squalid conditions. Nails were needed for heavy engineering such as ship-building.

Liverpool had a thriving ship-building industry in the early nineteenth century, but it was undermined by competition from across the Atlantic. The foundation of Laird Brothers Ltd (later Cammell Laird & Co.) by the banks of Mersey drew customers away and later in the century, Liverpool shipyards switched from building vessels to repairing them. Ships and boats were also built at Lancaster and Ulverston.

The development of iron and steel industries in Furness led to the birth of the new town of Barrow and its ship-building industry. The Furness district had plentiful supplies of iron ore; the lodes at Dalton-in-Furness had been mined since medieval times.

Furnaces to smelt iron were fuelled by charcoal made from Furness timber. The first blast furnace at Backbarrow was built in 1711 by William Rawlinson, John Machell, Stephen Crosfield and John Olivant. Another blast furnace was constructed at roughly the same time at Cunsey by Daniel Cotton and his partners. (J. D. Marshall (ed.), *The Autobiography of William Stout of Lancaster, 1665–1752* (Chetham Society 3rd series No. 14 (1967)).

The construction of the Ulverston Canal, which opened in 1795, meant that iron ore from Furness could be shipped out from Ulverston's newly built port. This canal was partly financed by slave-trade profits from investors such as Daniel Backhouse of Liverpool. The locks on the canal could accommodate ships of 200 tons. Ulverston also had a ship-building works. By the 1840s, iron exports from Furness were estimated at 75,000 tons per year.

The opening of the Furness Railway in 1846 opened up this previously remote area even further. Barrow, a small fishing village of about 300 souls, underwent a massive population boom. In 1857 it had 2,000 inhabitants; 10 years later its population had increased 6-fold. A new town was built by James Ramsden, one of Barrow's chief entrepreneurs.

Meanwhile, Henry Bessemer's invention of his 'converter' (1856) made it possible for iron to be converted into steel. Pig-iron made from Furness iron ore was particularly good for making steel, and in 1859 the firm of Schneider, Hannay & Co. founded a massive steel-works at Hindpool. Within five years the works produced 160,000 tons of iron annually. When the Barrow Haematite Steel Co. bought Schneider's in 1866 there were ten blast furnaces in continuous operation. The steel-works was the biggest in Britain and employed almost 2,000 men.

Barrow's famous docks were built by the Furness Railway in 1863 at a cost of £200,000. The new docks enabled cargoes to be loaded directly onto ships from railway waggons. Copper and slate were exported from Barrow as well as iron.

The *Annual Register* (September 1867) reported that when the docks officially opened, the town's streets were 'gay with flags' and 'thronged with people'. Barrow, which already had a small ship-building yard, was now a prime site for ship-building and the Barrow Shipbuilding Company was founded four years later. Steel-making suffered a decline later in the century but military contracts for warships gave the town a vital lifeline. In 1897 the ship-building company was taken over by Vickers, Sons & Maxim Ltd.

One could continue almost indefinitely listing all the different types of Lancashire engineering-works. Railway locomotives were built at Gorton by Beyer-Peacock; over 1,000 people worked there in the 1860s. Ferranti set up an electrical engineering-works at Hollinwood in the 1890s. Ford cars and Westinghouse electrical equipment were made at Trafford Park, and vans and lorries at Leyland.

The salt trade was one of Liverpool's most important exports and a key ingredient in its growth. Rock salt from Cheshire was refined in Liverpool as early as the 1690s. The salt was dissolved in sea water; then the brine was boiled over a coal furnace so that fine salt evaporated out. The smoke from the works caused so many complaints that the refinery's owner, John Blackburne, moved it to Garston. Salt was imported from Cheshire along

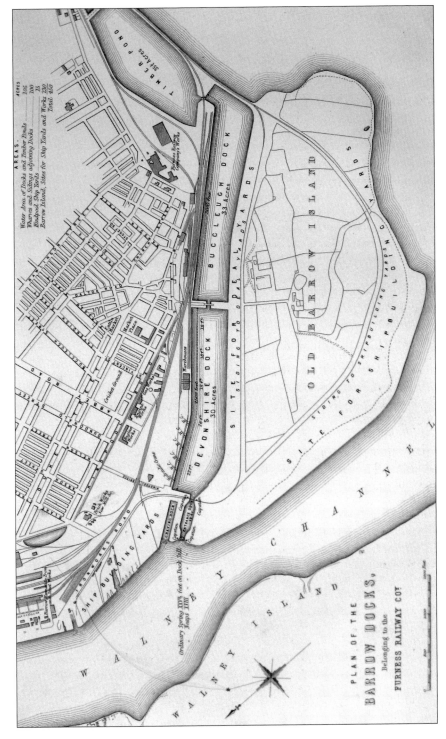

Plan of Barrow-in-Furness docks. (Thomas Baines, *Lancashire and Cheshire Past and Present Vol. II* (William Mackenzie, c. 1884))

the Sankey Canal (1757), Mersey and Irwell Navigation and the Weaver Navigation.

Investigators for the Children's Employment Commission (*5th Report,* XXIV (1866)) visited the Garston Salt Refinery. Investigators found that 'boys begin to help their fathers at the salt pans at nine or ten years old'. They worked for eight hours per day. Boys carried out ashes from the furnace, ladled wet salt into moulds and turned it out of the moulds when firm. Sometimes the boys carried the lumps of salt, which weighed from 12lb to 16lb, one at a time to a drying room.

Salt was used in soda ash manufacture, which was also needed for glass-making. Glass had been produced in Lancashire as early as Roman times. During the eighteenth century glass-makers could be found at Warrington, Liverpool, Prescot and Ormskirk. Glass-making was a highly skilled craft. Glass was made entirely by hand until the late eighteenth century.

St Helens was an ideal centre for glass-making because the resources needed for its manufacture were plentiful: good quality sand, Cheshire salt and coal for the furnaces. In the 1770s the British Cast Plate Glass Manufacturers at Ravenhead introduced the French invention of 'casting': pouring molten glass onto a table so that it formed an even layer.

In 1826 the St Helens Plate Glass Co. was founded. Among its founder members were Peter Greenall (of the brewing dynasty) and his brother-in-law William Pilkington, the son of a prosperous doctor. William (1800–1872) had a brother, Richard, who also became a partner in Greenall & Pilkington's firm. The business later became known as Pilkington Bros.

The Pilkingtons, a very old Lancashire family, had links with other wealthy business dynasties. William and Richard Pilkington's father was Dr Pilkington, whose sister married Joseph Rylands. Joseph's son John Rylands made a massive fortune in textiles. Richard Pilkington married Ann, the daughter of Richard Evans, who owned collieries at Haydock.

Plate, sheet glass, crown and flint glass was made in Lancashire. Men and young lads were employed in the furnaces or 'glass-houses'. Shift times depended on the type of glass being made. Flint glass workers worked six hours on, six hours off until all the molten glass or 'metal' in the furnace was used up. It was blisteringly hot, thirsty work. Glass workers were well paid: crown glass-makers could earn up to 37s 6d per week in the 1840s. Women and girls worked in the glass cutting and polishing rooms. Pilkingtons set up a school and recreation club for its workers.

Chemicals were manufactured in Lancashire on a small scale in the mid-eighteenth century. 'Heavy' chemical industry was first introduced by James Muspratt's alkali-works at Liverpool in 1822. But the smoke and chemical pollution it generated blighted the landscape for miles around. Muspratt moved his works to St Helens in 1828, and later founded more factories in Newton-le-Willows and Widnes.

> *Tip*
>
> Alkali factories came under government inspection following the Alkali Act of 1863, which aimed to limit their emissions of noxious gases. The *First Annual Report of the Inspector* C.11887 (1865) lists all the registered alkali manufacturers in Britain in 1863. There were alkali factories in Bolton, Gorton, Leigh, Liverpool, Manchester, St Helens and Widnes.

Alkali factories provided employment but their workforce and local inhabitants suffered from industrial pollution for many years despite efforts to clean up the manufacturing process. Soda from these factories was used in soap manufacture and there were soap factories in Widnes (Gossage's) and Warrington (Crosfield's, William Hesketh Lever).

In some areas of Lancashire traditional industries continued side-by-side with heavy industry. Oak, ash, birch and hazel wood was grown in the Leven valley and put to a variety of uses. Charcoal-burners or 'colliers' made charcoal from coppiced birch wood. The charcoal was sent to iron-works like the one at Backbarrow for fuel. Birch was used to make bobbins; there was a mill at Stott Park. 'Hoopers' made wooden hoops for barrels from oak. Sturdy, shallow oak baskets or 'swills' were made by hand; a good workman could make seven baskets per day. These baskets were used in agriculture and on coaling steamers.

Splitting wood for baskets, Finsthwaite. Engraved by Charles Brabant from a drawing by G. H. Thompson. (English Illustrated Magazine, 1883–1884 (Macmillan, 1884))

Industry Records

The historic societies have published studies of businesses, trades, shipping, slavers, industries and notable Lancashire families. These works are authoritative and include references to original documents.

Manchester University recently launched a searchable database of family and small businesses in north-west England (see Section D) from 1760–1820, which could be a useful tool for breaking the pre-1837 civil registration barrier.

Remember to use the NRA index to locate businesses, people, firms, trade unions, etc., and the A2A search engine to look for records or to explore record office collections not yet online. Check your local record office catalogue, too.

Look for firms' wage books, cash books, company minutes, pension (superannuation) records and so on. Businesses that provided tied accommodation for their workers (e.g., cotton, coal, canals, railways) may have left rent records. Tied accommodation was also common in rural districts.

Statutory compensation for injured workers was made compulsory in 1897. Injured employees who were not fit to work could be listed in accident registers, company pension books, insurance records or in Workmen's Compensation Act judgements in county court cases. Accident registers and compensation records may be closed to researchers for privacy reasons for a number of years.

For construction projects (canals, railways, etc.), engineers' day books or company cash books may include payments to workers. The archive at the Institution of Civil Engineers Library has collections on civil engineers such as James Brindley and William Fairbairn.

L. A. Ritchie, *The Shipbuilding Industry: A Guide to Historical Records* (Manchester University Press, 1992) has chapters on the history of the shipbuilding industry in the nineteenth and twentieth centuries. It discusses the different types of records available and lists archival sources for shipbuilders such as Vickers and trade organizations.

Trade Directories

Use street and trade directories to locate firms, businesses and people. For Lancashire, early trade directories are listed in G. H. Tupling, *Lancashire Directories 1684–1957* (Manchester Joint Committee on the Lancashire Bibliography, 1968).

The earliest surviving directory for Liverpool is Gore's *Liverpool Directory* (1766). Early directories like Gore's were often just alphabetical lists of surnames; later directories became more sophisticated in approach and listed inhabitants by area and business specialization. For example, Pigot & Co.'s *National Commercial Directory 1828–1829* lists over twenty ship-building firms for Liverpool, including Bland & Chaloner on Baffin Street and Grayson & Leadley at Salthouse Dock.

The reader should note that only the principal citizens and traders of a town are likely to be listed in early directories and small shopkeepers and ordinary workers were often omitted. The first telephone directories were published towards the end of the nineteenth century, but not many of these have survived.

Local record offices and reference libraries have copies of trade directories. Some directories have been reprinted, or are available on microfiche, or can be browsed online at: www.historicaldirectories.org/hd/index.asp.

Apprenticeship Records

In medieval times, trade and craft guilds strictly controlled the training and apprenticeship of new entrants to their profession. Later the Statute of Artificers (1563) regulated entry to the trades and professions: no one could enter a 'craft, trade or mystery' without first serving an apprenticeship. The Statute was repealed in 1814. New manufactures such as mechanized cotton spinning were not covered by the Statute because they did not exist when it was first enacted.

Parents who wanted their child to learn a trade paid an entry fee (premium) to the craftsman, tradesman or merchant. When a youngster was apprenticed, a legal document or 'indenture' was drawn up noting the child's name and age, date when apprenticed, name of new master and premium paid, and conditions and length of service. Local archives may hold apprenticeship indentures, although they are more likely to keep records of parish apprenticeships than privately arranged indentures. For more recent times, if you know which firm your ancestor worked for, search its records for apprenticeships.

Stamp duty was payable on indenture premiums from 1710 to 1804. The Commissioners of Stamps kept records of these payments. These registers (IR 1 at TNA) record when the tax was paid, the name of each apprentice (mostly boys, but some girls are included) and the name and address of their

Case Study

A good example of a private contract made by a child's parent is an indenture dated 22 September 1813. It records the apprenticeship of Jonathan Booth by his father Thomas Booth of Manchester for seven years to Samuel Crosfield of Manchester 'cloath manufacturer' to learn the 'art, trade or business of a finisher of woollen cloaths' (LRO DDX 31/1).

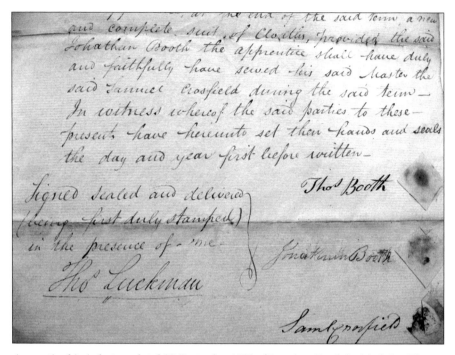

Apprenticeship indenture dated 22 September 1813 of Jonathan Booth by his father Thomas Booth for seven years to Samuel Crosfield of Manchester, 'cloath manufacturer'. (Lancashire Record Office DDX 31/1)

master. The tax was sometimes paid several years after a child or young person was apprenticed. Parish and charity apprenticeships were exempt from this tax, so they are not recorded in the registers.

The IR 1 apprenticeship registers are available free at Ancestry.co.uk (an indexed version) and as a free 'digital microfilm' (un-indexed) from TNA website.

Trade Unions and Friendly Societies

Friendly Society and trade-union records may have membership registers, or record payments made by or to workers relating to sick pay, funerals or other expenses. Records for the Register of Friendly Societies from 1784–1999 are at TNA (series FS), although trade unions were not necessarily formally registered.

The Labour History Archive at the People's History Museum (Manchester) has some union records. The Working Class Movement Library at Salford has trade-union archives and related materials for organizations such as the Amalgamated Society of Boilermakers, Shipwrights, Blacksmiths and

Structural Workers. The library also has collections on co-operative and friendly societies.

The Modern Records Centre at Warwick University library has records for employers' associations, trade associations and trade-union records for many different industries including dockers, miners, transport workers and foundry men.

London Metropolitan Archives hold the records of the Trades Union Congress, which includes many trade-union journals. Journals often printed biographical information about union members. There's a website devoted to the collections at: www.unionhistory.info.

Chapter 5

STRUGGLE FOR SURVIVAL

Whis commented that 'it was the fairest, best builded [*sic*], quikkest
[*sic*] and most populous tounne [*sic*]' of all Lancashire, with two 'fair'
market-places.

As the Industrial Revolution accelerated, the manufacturing towns witnessed massive population increases as people came looking for work,
stayed and had families. The county's population almost tripled between
1801 and 1841 and contemporaries ascribed this massive increase to the
'wonderful success of the cotton manufacture' (Cyrus Redding, J. R. Beard
and W. C. Taylor, *Pictorial History of the County of Lancaster* (George
Routledge, 1844)).

But there was virtually no 'town planning'. Workers' houses were built on
the cheap and crammed together, with primitive sanitation, no drainage and
limited access to clean water. Just a short walk away from the glittering shop
fronts of the town centres, families lived in streets awash with human and
animal waste. Pigs roamed around the 'closed courts' where little fresh air
penetrated. In Manchester, the rivers Medlock and Irk stank with pollution
from the factories that lined their banks.

By 1851 Lancashire was the most populous county in England outside
the London area, with 2,067,301 inhabitants. Bolton, Liverpool, Manchester
and Salford were the chief districts where more than one family occupied
the same house. In Liverpool, 258,263 people (47,271 families) lived in
35,293 houses. In the Manchester area, 228,433 people (44,621 families)
occupied 36,701 houses.

Diseases like cholera, typhus and smallpox exacted a fearful toll on
families, especially the most vulnerable members like babies. On average
over half of working class children died before they were 5 years old. In 1839,
the average age of death in Manchester for the operative classes was 17 years
old; in Bolton it was 18 years. High infant mortality was not confined to
Lancashire, however.

The industrial towns had large immigrant populations: Irish and Jewish
immigrants were among the most destitute members of society. Many Irish
people had fled from the potato famine of the late 1840s. Liverpool was
home to over 83,800 Irish-born inhabitants in 1851, and Manchester and

Emigration vessels Nimrod *and* Athlone *departing from Cork for Liverpool. Many Irish emigrants stayed in Lancashire instead of continuing their journey to America.* (*Illustrated London News*, 10 May 1851)

Salford had over 52,500 Irish folk. Over 14,000 people of Scottish origin lived in Liverpool, and over 6,500 in Manchester and Salford. Ten years later, over 10 per cent of Manchester and Salford's population were Irish.

Irish families were accustomed to a low standard of living in their native land and they lived in the dankest and most miserable 'homes', particularly the notorious cellar dwellings of Manchester and Liverpool.

Liverpool and Manchester had Jewish communities as early as the 1740s. It seems that eighteenth-century Liverpudlians had a fairly tolerant attitude towards the Jews, perhaps because this seafaring port had a cosmopolitan outlook. But in Manchester, Jewish traders were originally regarded with suspicion because people feared they would carry the secrets of cotton manufacturing to foreign competitors during their travels.

Some Jewish immigrants were well-heeled, like Nathan Meyer Rothschild, of the well-known banking family. Rothschild, who settled in Manchester at the turn of the nineteenth century, acted as an agent for his father in Frankfurt. He bought cottons for the Continental market.

During the 1860s and 1870s many poor immigrant Jews from Eastern Europe, desperate to escape famine and persecution, arrived in Manchester, especially in the Red Bank, Cheetham Hill and Strangeways areas. They had their own schools and places of worship. Some grew wealthy enough to become accepted members of the city's middle class. The ranks of the Jewish communities were swelled during the 1930s and 1940s by refugees from Nazism.

The Manchester Jewish Museum has a library, photographic and oral histories collections through which you can explore community life. The North West Sound Archive has some oral histories relating to Jewish families.

Boroughs and Corporations

Few members of the working classes were entitled to vote before the 1830s. Voting rights were dependent on property qualifications. The franchise differed in counties and boroughs. In counties votes were limited to freeholders of property worth 40s per annum. Voting rights in the boroughs depended on their charters, or local custom, but were usually based on a property qualification and/or residence.

A borough's charter gave it the right to a degree of self-government, with its own council, mayor, borough-reeve (so it was not under the sheriff of Lancaster's jurisdiction), coroner and other officials. The burgesses or freemen agreed to pay a fixed fee ('farm') to the Crown in lieu of many other taxes.

In 1179, Henry II granted Preston a charter of incorporation; some historians date the town's charter as early as 1100. Lancaster was next in 1193, possibly even earlier. King John granted Liverpool its charter in 1207. Salford became a borough in 1230 followed by Manchester in 1301, but Manchester was downgraded to a market town half a century later.

Borough charters are extremely detailed documents because it was necessary to spell out exactly which privileges had been granted by the Crown. Borough status conferred the right to hold courts, markets or fairs, and sometimes a 'guild merchant' to control its trades and crafts. Burgesses had voting rights, such as the right to send MPs to Parliament or to vote in local elections.

Preston Guild Merchant

In Preston virtually all adult male inhabitants, including craftsmen and traders, had voting rights, and the borough sent two MPs to Parliament.

Preston had a Guild Merchant (trade association) and the names of Guild members or burgesses were inscribed on a roll. A regular court was held at which a new roll of burgesses was compiled.

The custom of holding Preston's Guild Merchant every twenty years began in 1542. People who had died since the last court were removed from the Guild roll, along with the names of those who had left Preston, and those who had disobeyed the Guild statutes and lost their privileges.

The names of burgesses still living were confirmed, and the sons of burgesses who were previously too young to take the oath and pay the requisite fine (fee) were added. Apprentices who had served out their time (if apprenticed to burgesses) could be added to the roll. Newcomers to the town could become burgesses (after paying the fee) if their name was put forward by guild members. As the Guild Court was held so infrequently, a provisional category of membership could be obtained by court roll.

It was a mark of distinction to have the freedom of the borough. Local gentry like the Earls of Derby were invited by the corporation to be burgesses, or bought the privilege. Burgesses who lived out of the town ('foreign' burgesses) did not have the right to vote in elections.

The right to be a burgess was passed down from father to son, and the Preston Guild rolls are an exceptionally fine source for genealogists. Over 400 different surnames were recorded in the Guild rolls from the 1390s to the 1680s. The only time women's names appeared on the rolls was in 1397. Their names were written on the back of the parchment, and this list seems to have been of widows or female relatives of burgesses.

Trades in the Guild Merchant included blacksmiths, clock-makers, cutlers, glaziers, goldsmiths, grocers, gunsmiths, salters, vintners and weavers. Becoming a burgess gave tradesmen and craftsmen the right to follow their trade in the borough and many other privileges. They could trade without paying tolls, have a market stall free of charge and the right to pasture livestock on the town waste and other places in the borough. Burgesses' rights were strictly controlled by the corporation and disputes were dealt with in the court leet.

The carnival that marked each Guild Merchant was unique in the county and famed nationwide. Great feasts were held and a grand time had by all.

Case Study

The rolls were originally written in Latin. Those rolls that have been published have an index of names in English. Each family relationship mentioned relates to the previous entry. For example, the Guild Merchant for 1682 includes the names of the Bullock family.

George Bullock, Joyner [sic]
James filius ejus (his son)
George frater ejus (his brother)
William frater ejus (his brother)

So this entry is for George Bullock and his three sons James, George and William. George paid £3 for admission to the Guild (W. Alexander Abram, *The Rolls of Burgesses of the Guilds Merchant of the Borough of Preston 1397–1682* (Lancashire and Cheshire Record Society, Vol. IX (1884)).

The Beauties of England and Wales (1807) reported that the Guild Merchant on 30 August 1802 was attended by 'an immense concourse of people of all ranks'.

Processions took place through all the town's 'principal streets'. On the first day everyone took their allotted place in the parade: the mayor, corporation and 'the wardens of the different companies at the head of their respective incorporated bodies, each in their official dresses' to represent each branch of trade and commerce. A band of musicians marched with each group.

On the second day the mayoress did the honours. 'The girls of the cotton manufactory' headed a procession followed by nearly 400 ladies 'superbly dressed, and profusely decorated with jewels'. A 'miniature model of a complete steam-engine' was displayed which 'performed every operation of the cotton manufactory' (John Britton, *The Beauties of England and Wales Vol. IX* (London, 1807)).

When the Municipal Corporations Act of 1835 reformed the boroughs, burgesses lost their ancient privileges. But 'proud' Preston did not want to see its traditional festival disappear, and the Guild Merchant has continued to the present day, apart from wartime interruptions.

Friar Gate, Preston, c. 1920. (Deas Cromarty, *Picturesque Lancashire* (Valentine & Sons, c. 1920))

A Radical County

There was an immense social gulf between rich and poor. Some employers such as John Fielden of Todmorden adopted a paternalistic attitude towards their workforce and tried to keep on good terms with them. Others, like Pendleton mill-owner Elkanah Armitage, who grew up in Newton Heath, were notorious for their penny-pinching attitude to their workers.

Workers had few means open to them to improve their daily lives. Their class was virtually disenfranchised. Ordinary people had no voice when legislation was enacted that affected them directly, for example, the combination laws that made trade unions illegal. Destitute workers like handloom weavers tried to better their lot by striking or machine-breaking. Others, like Middleton weaver Samuel Bamford, pinned their hopes on electoral reform.

One of the great injustices affecting large, populous towns like Manchester was their lack of parliamentary representation. Lancashire had only fourteen MPs, whereas sparsely populated counties such as Cornwall had forty-two. Parliament was dominated by farmers and the owners of large estates. Even wealthy mill-owners and merchants found it difficult to influence government policy when they had no MPs to fight their corner.

There was consternation in the industrial towns when the Corn Laws were introduced in 1815. The Corn Laws protected farmers' profits but had the effect of raising the price of bread. The trade slump that followed the end of the Napoleonic Wars led to great distress, exacerbated by the high price of corn.

In March 1817 starving cotton spinners and weavers from Lancashire began a march from Manchester to London to present petitions to the Prince Regent asking for relief and parliamentary reform. They carried blankets so they could sleep on the road. But the 'Blanketeers' were swiftly dispersed by yeomanry cavalry; only one man reached London to hand in his petition.

The authorities relied on the Army and militia, night-watchmen, special constables and the yeomanry cavalry to keep the king's peace. The county had no professional police force until 1839, although some towns like Preston had their own police. The yeomanry could ride swiftly to any flash-points and deal with angry mobs, such as the food rioters in Manchester in April 1812. Several people were hanged at Lancaster the following month for their part in the riots, including Hannah Smith of Ardwick.

The infamous Peterloo massacre on 16 August 1819 caused great ill-feeling towards the yeomanry cavalry. There were 60,000 to 80,000 people – men, women and children – assembled at St Peter's Field, Manchester, to hear a speech by the Radical Henry Hunt in favour of electoral reform.

Local magistrates ordered Hunt's arrest. The yeomanry cavalry were sent into the tightly packed crowd to clear a way. The horses panicked; the

Henry Hunt addressing the people of Manchester in 1819. (Cassell's Illustrated History of England Vol. VI (Cassell, Petter and Galpin, c. 1864))

yeomanry lost their temper, and hacked people with their sabres. Shouts, prayers and threats rang out as people desperately tried to escape. Over 400 people were injured and several people died. The fatalities included Thomas Buckley from Chadderton and special constable Thomas Ashworth. The yeomanry cavalry were called out again to deal with anti-Corn Law rioters at Accrington in April 1826.

The prosperous middle classes in Lancashire wanted free trade. They believed it would make food cheaper for the masses and increase their profits. Mill-owners Richard Cobden (1804–1865) and John Bright (1811–1899) were the leading lights of the Anti-Corn Law League, formed in 1838. Quaker John Bright was born at Greenbank, near Rochdale. Cobden, who was born in Sussex, was a Manchester calico printer.

Peterloo plaque, Peter Street, Manchester.

Right: Richard Cobden (1804–1865), Manchester calico printer, writer, anti-Corn Law campaigner and MP for Rochdale. (Thomas Baines, Lancashire and Cheshire Past and Present Vol. I (William Mackenzie, London, c. 1867))

Below: John Bright, the cotton-mill-owner who fought for the repeal of the Corn Laws, but opposed factory reform. (The Story of Lancashire (London, c. 1900))

The Anti-Corn Law League campaigned vigorously for the law's repeal, despite opposition from Lord Edward Geoffrey Smith Stanley (1799–1869), later the 14th Earl of Derby. The horrors of the Irish potato famine persuaded Prime Minister Robert Peel (1788–1850) to repeal the Corn Laws in 1846.

John Bright also campaigned fiercely for electoral reform. The electoral system was corrupt to the core. Parliamentary seats were bought and sold, and there was no secret ballot. Elections were distinguished by riots and vast sums of money spent by the candidates on 'treating' voters. The Earls of Derby fought bitterly with Preston corporation for control of the borough's parliamentary seats. Unscrupulous landowners put pressure on their tenants to ensure that they voted for the 'right' candidate.

The 1832 Reform Act swept away the 'rotten' boroughs that had only a couple of voters. Lancashire's parliamentary seats were increased to twenty-six. Towns like Blackburn, Bolton, Oldham, Manchester and Salford now had MPs. In the boroughs, the vote was restricted to men with property worth £10 per annum. For county elections, some copyholders, leaseholders and tenants were enfranchised in addition to 40s freeholders. In Preston the Act had the effect of decreasing the franchise as the town's old burgesses gradually died out over the years.

Edward Geoffrey Smith Stanley, 14th Earl of Derby. (Thomas Baines, *Lancashire and Cheshire Past and Present Vol. I* (William Mackenzie, London, c. 1867))

Chartism

Working class agitators were bitterly disappointed by these limited reforms. The ill-fated Chartism movement, founded in 1837, was rooted in mass unemployment, resistance to the new Poor Law (see below) and dear food prices. The aims of the People's Charter included universal male suffrage, secret ballots and annual parliaments. The movement was particularly attractive to the distressed handloom weavers of Manchester and Bolton, and there were mass meetings on Kersal Moor. Little Bolton Town Hall suffered an arson attack and in August 1842 there was a massive 'turn-out' of Lancashire cotton workers: the 'Plug Plot' strikes. Striking workers stopped the factories by removing the plugs from the steam boilers.

The Chartist Land Company was a utopian but ill-judged attempt to give workers another means of subsistence by owning their own plot of land. Mark Crail's Chartist Ancestors website has lists of Chartist Land Company officials, and subscribers from eleven Lancashire towns and can be accessed at: www.chartists.net/Chartist-land-company.htm#index and www.chartists. net/Land-Company-officials-1849.htm.

The Chartist Land Company was later re-named the National Land Company. It was a registered company, and its official registration (with lists of shareholders) is in the Board of Trade records at TNA. The Chartist Ancestors website also has a guide to Chartist records at TNA at: www. chartists.net/Chartist-archives.htm.

The co-operative movement was one way in which workers could help themselves, for example, by founding a store where they could buy reason-ably priced food (employers often insisted their workers buy goods from a shop owned by them). The Rochdale Pioneers' shop at Rochdale (1844) was the first commercially successful co-operative store in Britain which offered a 'dividend' to its customers.

The National Co-operative Archive and some local record offices have collections on the co-operative movement and societies. The Working Class Movement Library (Salford) and People's History Museum (Manchester) have collections on labour history.

The 1867 Reform Act further broadened the franchise. In 1869 women ratepayers (unmarried) were allowed to vote in local elections and to serve as Poor Law guardians. After 1888 unmarried women could vote in county and council elections.

The fight for women's right to vote in national elections was long and bitter. Suffragette Emmeline Pankhurst (née Goulden) was born in Moss Side, Hulme in 1858. Emmeline and her daughters Christabel and Sylvia spent years campaigning and risked their health for the cause. Universal male suffrage (for men over 21) was finally achieved in 1918. Women were given the vote that year, but to the suffragettes' disgust they had to be over

30 years old. Another decade passed before women were accorded the same voting rights as men. The voting age was set at 18 in 1969.

Burgess Rolls, Electoral Registers, Poll Books

From the late seventeenth century onwards until 1872, when a secret ballot was introduced, 'poll books' recorded the names of people who had voted in elections. From 1780–1832, since voting depended on the amount of property held, land-tax assessments were made to verify voters' entitlement, and these assessments will be found in quarter sessions records.

After 1832 electoral registers were kept of everyone entitled to vote in a constituency. They were compiled by local authorities such as the parish overseers, county councils or boroughs.

As noted earlier, the right to be a burgess or freeman, and voting rights in elections, differed from borough to borough. Burgess rolls or registers of voters exist for boroughs such as Accrington, Bolton, Liverpool, Oldham and so on. Broadly speaking, more people had the right to vote in local elections than parliamentary ones.

The Preston Guild rolls can be found in the corporation records at LRO; some years are available on microfiche (CNP/2). LRO has a guide to Guild sources. For the historical background to the Guild, and a detailed explanation of the different types of burgesses, see Alan Crosby, *History of Preston Guild: England's Greatest Carnival* (Carnegie Publishing, 2012).

The records of Liverpool Corporation, or 'Town Books', were published by the LCRS in 1999. They include portmote (quarter sessions) records, the admissions of freemen to the borough and the appointment of town officers. Some years covered by the town books are available on CD-ROM.

Electoral registers are particularly valuable for family research purposes because they were updated annually. From 1832 onwards, voters' names in the registers were listed by alphabetical order within a township. If you find an ancestor's name and address, you can use this to check the census record for that address (see Chapter 6). The date when a young person first appears on the voting register will enable you to infer their date of birth.

After 1884 the registers become more difficult to use because they were arranged in street order within polling districts, so you will need an address before you try to locate a person. Surname indexes are sometimes available. Electoral registers can be found in local libraries and record offices; the British Library has collections.

For a comprehensive listing of poll books, see Jeremy Gibson and Colin Rogers, *Pollbooks 1696–1872: A Directory to Holdings in Great Britain* (3rd edn, Family History Partnership, 2008). Jeremy Gibson, *Electoral Registers 1832–1948 and Burgess Rolls* (3rd edn, Family History Partnership, 2008) has a detailed discussion of voting qualifications and archival holdings.

The Poor

There was no national state provision for the poor and sick until the mid-twentieth century. Families in need relied on relatives or neighbours for help, but when times were hard they turned to the parish or charity for aid.

Until the Poor Law Act of 1834, every parish was responsible for its 'paupers'. People who were destitute, unemployed, too young, too old or infirm to work were offered a place in a poorhouse or workhouse. Or families were given practical help – 'outdoor relief' – in their own homes, e.g., food, money, blankets or perhaps some means of earning a living such as a loom.

It was not easy for people to look for work outside their parish because of the 'settlement laws' dating back to Elizabethan times. Men, women or children could not stay in another parish without a 'settlement certificate' from their home parish to say it would pay for their upkeep if they became 'chargeable' to the parish, i.e., they needed support.

The parish did not want to pay for other parishes' poor people. If some-one living in the parish needed help, but was believed to have a settlement elsewhere, justices of the peace (JPs) conducted a 'settlement examination' to discover the true facts. These examinations often contain lots of family information. If the person's settlement was in another parish, JPs signed a 'removal order' and the person was forcibly taken to their home parish.

If an unmarried woman became pregnant, and had no means of support, the overseers tried to find the father and make him pay for the child's maintenance. Magistrates would write a 'bastardy order' compelling the father to pay up.

To relieve the parish of their upkeep, parish overseers apprenticed pauper children into trades such as textiles, coal mining, farm labour, domestic

---

Case Study

Having an illegitimate child could be an expensive affair. At Liverpool quarter sessions on 29 January 1817, the court ratified a bastardy order dated 3 January made by the justices of the peace. Weaver 'John Crook of Aspull is adjudged to be the reputed father of a male bastard child, born upon the body of Ann Whittle of Newton', a single woman. John was ordered to pay the churchwardens and over-seers of the poor £1 8s for the expenses of the child's birth, a further 8s shillings for its maintenance up to the time of the order, plus 14s 'for the costs of apprehending and securing the said John Crook'. John was further ordered to pay 1s 9d weekly for the child's maintenance. (LRO DDX153/3/17).

service, the Navy, etc. Sometimes people bequeathed money to the parish to be spent on charitable purposes, and money was used to pay apprenticeship premiums. As discussed in Chapter 3, apprenticeship indentures were drawn up when a child was 'bound' to a trade or master. However, it was expensive to have formal indentures drawn up, and some parishes did not bother.

Hanway's Act of 1767 required parishes to keep registers of their child apprentices. These registers contain similar details to indentures. Peel's 1802 Act also required registers of apprentices to be kept, and these sometimes include details of apprentices' parents.

Parish records may include parish overseers' accounts, vestry accounts, parish rate books, poorhouse or workhouse accounts, apprenticeship indentures, etc. Quarter sessions records will include bastardy maintenance orders, settlement papers and removal orders. Registers of Irish vagrants deported to Ireland from the county (usually via Liverpool) record their names, details of family and name of ship.

Following the 1834 Poor Law Amendment Act, Lancashire was divided into thirty Poor Law Unions. The Act abolished family allowances and curtailed 'outdoor relief'. More workhouses were built, and conditions inside made as strict and uninviting as possible as a deterrent. Families were split up when they entered the workhouse and segregated by sex. Old married couples might only see each other once a week. Ordinary people hated and feared the workhouse and only applied for help if in direst need. The new law had the effect of compelling families to send even very young children out to work. The 1834 Act was deeply resented in Lancashire, where trade slumps could throw thousands of people out of work at once, and local authorities initially dragged their feet over complying with the law.

Medical care was expensive. The only hospitals or asylums available to poor people were those provided by charities and workhouses. Thomas Henshaw of Oldham, who died in 1810, bequeathed '£20,000 for a Blind Asylum, £1,000 to the Infirmary, £1,000 to the Lunatic Hospital, and £500 to the Ladies' Jubilee School' at Manchester. (Charles Henry Timperley, *Manchester Historical Recorder* (Manchester, c. 1875)).

Some workhouses had infirmaries or hospitals but provision was patchy. As late as the 1860s, Prestwich and Oldham Poor Law Unions had no hospital or dispensary. People who were injured or seriously ill had to travel to Manchester Infirmary for treatment.

Mentally ill paupers were sent to an asylum or institution with a 'reception order' for their admission, and you may find these reception orders in quarter sessions records.

Workhouse, hospital and infirmary records may include admission and discharge registers, staff records, vaccination registers and creed registers (1876 onwards). Creed registers give each inmate's name, date of birth, date and place of admission, creed, date of discharge or death; some give occupation, last address or details of next of kin. Vaccination registers were returns made to the vaccination officer of children's births and deaths.

For more information on Poor Law Union records, see Simon Fowler, *Poor Law Records for Family Historians* (Family History Partnership, 2011). For details of Lancashire records, consult Jeremy Sumner and Colin Rogers, *Poor Law Union Records: Midlands and Northern England Pt. 2* (3rd edn, Family History Partnership, 2008). A useful gazetteer is also available: Jeremy Gibson and Frederic A. Youngs, *Poor Law Union Records: 4. Gazetteer of England and Wales* (2nd edn, FFHS, 1997).

The Poor Law Boards were dissolved in 1929 and their duties were taken over by the county and borough councils, which appointed public assistance committees to care for the poor. The introduction of the National Health Service Act (1946) and National Assistance Act (1948) finally banished the Poor Law. The fear of the workhouse was lifted at last.

Education

Education was one way out of the poverty trap, but in general, good schools were only available for the middle and upper classes until late Victorian times. There was no state system of education, but Lancashire was fortunate because it had some excellent free schools dating back to Tudor times.

These charity schools were founded by wealthy benefactors like Hugh Oldham, who founded the Manchester Free Grammar School in 1515. Its scholars staged a rebellion in 1690. They locked out their schoolmasters for two weeks before they were forced to surrender. Sympathetic locals gave the young rebels not only food and bedding, but also firearms and ammunition!

One of Manchester Grammar's most famous pupils was rich merchant Humphrey Chetham. Chetham (1580–1653) founded a charity school (Chetham Hospital) and library which still bears his name.

For many working class children and adults, Sunday schools were their only access to education. The first Sunday schools in Lancashire were founded by Andrew Chadwick of Longsight, grandfather of the famous sanitary reformer Sir Edwin Chadwick (1800–1890).

Apart from charity schools and Sunday schools, parents paid for their children's education. (Some Sunday schools charged a nominal sum.) During the nineteenth century, some free schools such as Manchester Grammar began charging fees to cover their costs, although they had bursaries for poor pupils.

Growing awareness from the early 1810s of the ocean of illiteracy among children and adults led to the formation of the National School Society and the British and Foreign School Society. These societies founded many schools. The factory Acts (see Chapter 3) were an educational measure to ensure children had a set number of hours' schooling each week.

Charities such as the Manchester and Salford Boys and Girls Refuges and Homes (now the Together Trust) provided help for destitute children so they did not have to go into the workhouse. A basic education might be provided, and perhaps a bed for the night. Orphans were given industrial training so that they could earn their own living and sometimes assistance to emigrate abroad to start a new life.

Workhouses had schools for their pauper children, either attached to the workhouse or sited separately. They were generally industrial schools, like those at Kirkdale, Swinton and Manchester, and gave children occupational training. School registers may be found in Poor Law Union records.

The 1870 Education Act enabled the founding of school boards in areas where there was no provision, but education was not compulsory for children aged 5 to 10 years old until 1880. Children aged 11 to 13 could leave school providing they attained a set educational standard. School authorities issued labour certificates to show that a young person was permitted to

Labour certificate, possibly for the author's great-uncle William Hollis Dickman, dated 22 October 1894. The certificate, which gives his family's address, shows that William had reached the sixth standard at school (William was about 12 years old).

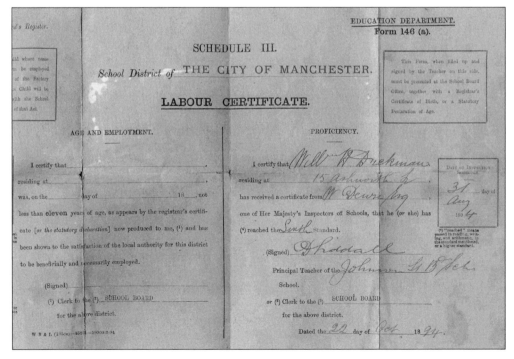

work full or part-time; sometimes these certificates have birth certificates attached to them as proof of age. Labour certificates may be found in school board or local education authority archives or family papers. In 1902 the county councils became responsible for primary and secondary schools.

School Records

Admission registers are the most likely records to include your ancestor's name and details such as address and date of birth. School log books (diaries) record day-to-day occurrences but it is unusual for a particular child to be named unless they were punished by the head teacher, or perhaps won a prize. Some early school admissions registers for the grammar schools at Manchester and Blackburn were published by the Chetham Society.

Schools did not have to keep permanent records so there is no guarantee that records for the school you are interested in have survived. Records for schools that are still open will normally be kept at the school; local record offices hold collections of records for schools that have closed. Some schools such as Manchester Grammar School and Manchester High School for Girls have their own archive.

Case Study

The admissions register for Manchester Grammar School includes the occupation of each scholar's father. To pick an example at random, three boys with the surname 'Ogden' attended the school in the late eighteenth century. Samuel, son of John Ogden, hatter of Manchester, joined on 20 January 1783. The name of Thomas, son of John Ogden, a Failsworth weaver, appears on 17 January 1791. Then a few months later, William, son of John Ogden, a farmer at Failsworth, joined the school on 19 September 1791. (Jeremiah Finch Smith (ed.), *The Admission Register of the Manchester School*, Vol. 2 (1776–1807) (Chetham Society Old Series 73, 1868)).

Samuel is unlikely to be a relative of the other two boys. Although Failsworth and Manchester were only a few miles apart, hatting was a specialized occupation. Thomas and William could be related, but they only joined the school eight months apart. However, their ages are not given. Both are from Failsworth and some farmers did weaving as a sideline. However, Ogden is a common name in Lancashire and further research (e.g., the parish registers) would be need to be carried out to establish if there was more than one John Ogden living in Failsworth at that date.

Law and Order

People, including children, who broke the law faced harsh penalties ranging from hanging, transportation, a flogging or a spell in the stocks. Routine criminal cases and law enforcement matters were dealt with at quarter sessions by justices of the peace. County quarter sessions were held at Lancaster, Preston, Wigan or Ormskirk (this court moved to Kirkdale after 1817).

Boroughs held their own quarter sessions, for example, Bolton from 1838, Manchester after 1839, Wigan from 1886 and Salford after 1890. There were prisons at Lancaster, Manchester (Strangeways), Preston, Salford (the New Bailey) and Kirkdale.

Magistrates also dealt with issues such as regulating trade, commerce and work, caring for the poor, maintaining roads and bridges, ensuring that people conformed to the state religion and licensing victuallers, ale, wine and beer houses.

As the county's population grew, there was too much judicial business to be left until quarter sessions, and in the nineteenth century 'petty' sessions were instituted. Petty sessions for minor offences were heard by two or more magistrates, without a jury. Collections of quarter and petty sessions records are held at local record offices.

The quarter sessions courts and assizes at Liverpool and Manchester were replaced by Crown courts in 1956: Manchester Crown Court took over Salford's assize work. Elsewhere in the historic county, Crown courts did not replace quarter and petty sessions and assizes until 1972.

Criminal registers list people indicted for offences, the assize or quarter sessions court where the case was heard and whether they were convicted or found innocent. You should check these registers first if you do not know which court heard a prisoner's case. Criminal registers and prisoners' registers are kept at TNA. Prison registers are held by some local record offices; they may contain physical descriptions of prisoners or photographs.

Reformatory schools tried to instil discipline into juvenile offenders and set their feet on the right path. Quarter sessions records may include committal orders to send youngsters to reform schools and parental orders for maintenance for their children while they were at the schools.

The Lancashire Constabulary records at LRO include photographs of people arrested and their criminal records (PLA/16/1). The archive also has a searchable database of police officers in Lancashire County Constabulary. The Greater Manchester Police Museum has some registers of aliens and a calendar of prisoners at Manchester Assizes.

Coroners looked into cases of sudden or suspicious death. Coroners' expenses may include names of persons for which an inquest was held. Local newspapers often reported on inquests and their reports may include biographical material on the deceased. Coroners' records may be found in quarter sessions archives (record offices) or at TNA in records of the court of the King's Bench, palatinate records or Duchy of Lancaster files (DL 46).

Life in the crowded cities saw slow, piecemeal improvement during the nineteenth century. Towns like Liverpool and Manchester introduced sanitary Acts and appointed Medical Officers of Health. More hospitals, sewers, and cemeteries were built. Reservoirs were constructed at Gorton, Hollingworth, Rivington Pike and in Wales to make fresh water available for townsfolk. Public baths were built at Liverpool, Bury and elsewhere.

Public parks were provided so that workers could enjoy some fresh air during their time off. In the 1840s and 1850s, several parks were opened in Manchester and one in Blackburn. Alexandra Park at Oldham was created during the cotton famine: it was a construction project to provide work for unemployed factory hands.

Tip

As with all sensitive data for individuals, coroners' files and records from schools, hospitals, institutions and workhouses may be subject to a closure period from the date when the record was first created. The length of closure varies according to archive policy.

Postcard of Alexandra Park, Oldham, postmarked 1908.

The 1888 Local Government Act reformed local administration. The historic counties, including Lancashire, were divided up into county councils and county boroughs. These new administrative bodies took over responsibility for quarter sessions, levying rates, industrial and reform schools, providing asylums for mentally ill people who were poor, the main roads, polling for parliamentary elections and several other duties.

Local authority records include cash books, financial reports, letter books, rate books, Medical Officer of Health reports, education records, hospital records, building plans, fire department records, police records, staff records, unemployment relief schemes, wage books, etc.

Council committee minutes may cover subjects such as provision for children, education, mothers, senior citizens, sanitation, the poor, housing, town planning, etc. Your ancestor's name may not be mentioned in council minutes, but these records can give a fascinating insight into living conditions. Local authority records are kept at record offices: see Chapter 7 for the effect of boundary changes.

Chapter 6

SACRIFICED

As Britain's population and industries multiplied, and as local and government machinery became more advanced, the need for accurate statistics of the population and its occupations became increasingly urgent.

How many men were of the right age for military service? How many workers were there in a particular industry? Were the numbers of poor people rising or falling? The nation's vital statistics were a measure of its economic health. The best way to answer these questions was to count the people living in every city, town and village.

Censuses of the population can help to 'fill in the gaps' for the years between ancestors' birth, marriage and death records.

Censuses

Local Censuses

Occasional local censuses were undertaken for various ecclesiastical, government or administrative purposes. These were often just 'head counts' to provide statistics, but they sometimes included names and brief addresses. For example, there was a partial census of Manchester – the 'Pole Book' – on 22 May 1690. This was not a voting register; it was compiled for a poll tax to raise money for the 'reduceing [sic] of Ireland and carryeing [sic] ye war on France'. The census is incomplete because there were exemptions from the tax, such as people receiving charity from the parish and their children under 16 years old. The tax was levied on a sliding scale according to a person's income. The 'Pole Book' lists the inhabitants street by street and mentions if they were Roman Catholic.

In Deansgate 'Humphrey Booth gent[leman]' was living with his 'wife, child and one maid'. Mrs Mary Goolden and her maid, both 'Roman Catholick', lived in the same street. One hopes that William Mather's house in 'Ould Mealgate' (Old Millgate) had plenty of room because it contained Mather, his wife, five children, an apprentice and four men. The 'Pole Book' was published by the Chetham Society: *Chetham Miscellanies*, Old Series 57, Vol. 3 (1862). The same volume also includes the names of 800 Manchester residents who took the oath of allegiance to Charles II in April 1679.

To give another example, at Preston in the early nineteenth century Friar Joseph Dunn wrote down the names and addresses of his Catholic congregation. Dunn noted the family relationships of some parishioners, and sometimes their ages. His 'census' has been published: Revd Joseph Dunn, *Census of the Catholic Congregation of Preston 1810 and 1820* (Ancestral Data Publications, 1993). The book is available for purchase from the Sanctuary Bookshop, St Wilfrid's Centre, Chapel Street, Preston (no mail order available).

National Decennial Censuses

From 1801 the government took censuses of the population of Britain every ten years. The 1801–1831 censuses were extremely basic: parish overseers and other local officials were just requested to count the people in each parish, without any additional information. Generally, census returns with more detailed information are only available from 1841 onwards. However, in a few cases for 1801–1831, luckily for family historians, local officials compiled lists of householders and some early censuses are still extant, e.g., for the Ashton-under-Lyne area. Some have been transcribed and put online (see Section D).

Censuses before 1841 are kept at local record offices and Table 1 below lists some available for Lancashire. Lists of householders may have only a brief address, or none. Census records that are only population statistics are included for completeness. Associated records such as officials' bills for services are not included.

Table 1. 1801–1831 Censuses

Bolton Archives and Local Studies
Great Bolton township census returns: 1811, 1821, 1831: PGB/8
(available on CD-ROM from Manchester and Lancashire FHS)

Bury Archives Service
Elton township census return 1801: ABP/4/8

Lancashire Record Office
Lancashire census returns 1821: QDV/17
Ashton copy of census return c. 1802: QSP 2466/10
Ashton-under-Lyne 1811 (incomplete): PR 2583
Bolton by Bowland parish census 1829: DDX 1459
Billinge Higher End, Up Holland, Winstanley: copies of summary census 1831:
　PR 2907/5/4
Broughton census returns 1811–1841: PR 1892/1, undated census book PR 1892/2
Clitheroe census returns 1801: MBC/650, MBC/839, 1831 (in two parts): DDX 28/262
Croston census returns 1801: PR 2644 and 1811: PR 2645
Great Crosby copy parish register: notes on census figures 1811–1861: PR 2944/1/2

Formby (St Peter) parish register includes census statistics 1811–1831: PR 3360/1/1
Haigh copy of census return c. 1802: QSP/2474/87
Hambleton draft census return undated: PR 3013/4/15
Longton, St Andrew parish summary census 1821: PR 3007/5/2
Middleton 1802: QSP/2463/13
Newton census return c. 1802: QSP/2462/15
Southworth with Croft census return 1802: QSP/2462/18
Standish, St Wilfrid's parish, assorted memoranda re 1801 census: PR 3134/2/4
Tarleton census returns of population 1821: PR 3168/7/78, and 1831: PR 3168/7/79
Tatham census forms 1821, 1831: PR 2920/6/5
Tatham St James the Lesser census forms 1821, 1831: PR 551
Thurnham census of Roman Catholic congregation 1830: RCTm 1/2

Liverpool Record Office
Liverpool partial census has some names, but no ages or places of birth 1801: MF 7/14.

Greater Manchester County Record Office with Manchester Archives
Lumb (St Michael's) notes from census returns 1811–1891: L104/1/15/1–2
Rochdale (St Chad) assorted census papers 1801–1821: L48/1/8
Walmsley (Christ Church) census figures 1831: L99/1/8/2

Preston Harris Library
Preston 1801 census transcript: LQ81/CEN

Wigan Archives Service
Wigan Census Book 1811: ABWi

There is more information on local and early censuses and their locations in Jeremy Gibson and Mervyn Medlycott, *Local Census Listings 1522–1930: Holdings in the British Isles* (Federation of Family History Societies, 3rd edn , 1997, repr. 2001) and Colin Chapman, *Pre-1841 Censuses and Population Listings* (Lochin Publishing, 1998).

Censuses After 1841

The 1841 census was the first compiled by the General Register Office (GRO). For this and successive censuses, enumerators listed the inhabitants of every household with details of ages and occupations. On a specified date, each householder filled in a schedule, which was collected by the enumerator. If the householder was illiterate, another family member or the enumerator completed the schedule. People in workhouses, hospitals and other institutions were included in the schedule for that institution. The enumerator used the schedules to fill in a summary book. The householders' schedules were destroyed, but the enumerators' books or 'returns' were preserved.

The enumerator worked his way methodically around the census district, listing the households one by one in a pre-printed form in a book. For most censuses, a 'double line' was drawn under the entry for each house to mark its end and the beginning of the next one. If more than one family lived in a house, a single line was used to denote the start of each family. A page of the summary book may cover more than one street and contain several households, and a household's entry may cover more than one page.

The 1841 census has several shortcomings. Enumerators were ordered to 'round down' the ages for people aged 15 and over to the nearest five years, so a 22-year-old's age was written down as '20'. (In a few cases the enumerator cheerfully ignored their instructions and wrote down the exact ages anyway.) So you must bear this in mind when trying to infer a person's date of birth from the 1841 census. Also, a person's birthplace was not noted in detail: people were asked if they were born in or out of the county, or were from Scotland, Ireland or abroad.

The information gathered became more sophisticated and comprehensive over time. The 1851 census was the first to list precise ages, marital status and family relationships, and detailed birthplaces.

Which County?

The boundaries of census districts can cause confusion when trying to locate the returns for a particular place. Prior to 1841 the returns were compiled using the ancient county boundaries, subdivided into parishes and townships.

When the GRO compiled the census in 1841 it used 'registration districts' and sub-districts based on the civil registration districts (for births, marriages and deaths), which in turn were based on the Poor Law Unions. These registration districts did not necessarily follow the ancient county boundaries. For this census only, the GRO re-ordered the completed census books into historic districts such as hundreds.

For the 1851 census the GRO divided England and Wales into eleven 'divisions' and introduced 'registration counties', an amalgam of the registra-tion districts in each historic county. Each registration county was sited in its historic county but did not necessarily follow the same boundaries. The registration county of Lancashire was in the North Western Division of England: it comprised twenty-six registration districts. For the 1851 and successive censuses, the returns were archived in registration district order, not rearranged into historic counties. The 1881 census is the easiest to search; it has been fully indexed and transcripts for England and Wales are available at LRO and reference libraries.

Before you search the censuses, find out the correct registration county for your place of interest. For example, the parish of Reddish was in the ancient county of Lancashire, but in 1834 it became part of the Stockport Poor Law Union. This meant that Reddish was in the Stockport Registration District, which was in the registration county of Cheshire. Therefore its census returns were filed under Cheshire.

The Association of British Counties website has a gazetteer of places in England and Wales that were in a registration county with a different name to their historic county in the 1851 and 1881 censuses. It includes the registration county, district and district number for each place listed. For 1851: www.gazetteer.co.uk/appendixc.html. For 1881: www.gazetteer.co.uk/appendixd.html.

Census Returns

The enumerators' summary books were bound into volumes ('pieces'). Because each summary book had numbered pages, each page number would recur, so to make it easier to identify each record, the front of each page was stamped with a 'folio number'. So for 1841–1901, each page of the book is defined by a unique reference number comprising four parts. The first part is the original Home Office or Registrar General series code, followed by a 'piece number', folio number and page number (each folio number relates to two pages).

For example, the 1851 census return for Bolton Registration District enumeration district number 1e, Bolton Western Sub-Registration District, has a TNA reference number: HO 107/2211, folio 162, p. 20. This refers to Home Office series 107, piece 2211, folio 162, p. 20.

For the 1911 census, the household schedules were preserved as well as the summary books, and colour images of schedules are available online. Each schedule was completed and signed by the householder. The 1911 census schedules were extremely detailed. For the first time, married women were asked how many children were born alive in their current marriage, how many had died and how many were still alive.

The 1911 census schedules and summary books are linked by a unique reference number comprising three parts: Registration District Number (RD), Registration Sub-District Number (RS) and Enumeration District Number (ED). Each summary book correlates to its own set of schedules.

A detailed discussion of the variations in the types of data gathered by each census is beyond the scope of this book: see Peter Christian and David Annal, *Census: The Expert Guide* (TNA, 2008), which includes case studies and the 1911 census, and Edward Higgs, *Making Sense of the Census Revisited: Census Records for England and Wales 1801–1901* (Institute of Historical Research/TNA, 2005).

The census returns for England and Wales are kept by TNA; they can be viewed on microfilm at Kew and at local archives and reference libraries. LRO holds copies of censuses for Lancashire for 1841–1901. Local record offices and reference libraries may only keep censuses for their particular area, but many offer free access to one of the subscription services.

Census returns for 1841–1911 have been digitized, transcribed and indexed and made available online (see Section E). Lancashire County Libraries offers free access to the Ancestry website via its library computers. Census returns are also available at FamilySearch (the Church of Jesus Christ of Latter-day Saints) centres (see Section C).

Some free census returns for Lancashire have been transcribed by volunteers and put online (see Section D). The Lancashire Family History and Heraldry Society has published some 1851 transcripts and indexes for the North Lancashire and the Fylde areas. Indexes and/or transcripts for several Lancashire towns have been printed in book form, fiche or CD-ROM by family history or record societies.

The Society of Genealogists' Library has some surname indexes, place-name indexes and returns for Lancashire censuses. It also has some copies of censuses prior to 1841 and census 'substitutes' such as lay subsidy rolls (see the Society's online library catalogue).

Problems Finding Ancestors in the Online Censuses

The advent of online censuses has reduced much of the legwork needed to search for ancestors. In theory it should be 'easy' to trace your family back to 1841 but sometimes you may hit the proverbial 'brick wall' almost straightaway. There could be several possible reasons for this.

Location, Location, Location

As noted previously, the type of information gathered differed for successive censuses. The 1841 census presents a real stumbling block because people were only asked if they were born in or out of the county. So a person born in Lancashire but living in Yorkshire, say, in 1841, will just have 'N' (not born in the county) as their birthplace.

Places of birth are potential sources of confusion. If a family moved several times, or had a large number of children, they may not have remembered exactly where a child was born. Adults may not have known precisely where they were born. Very often you will find that a person's place of birth varies slightly from census to census (although it should be roughly in the same locale).

Your ancestor may have moved away from Lancashire, or possibly travelled around because of their job. This is where the online censuses can potentially save a great deal of time, because you can search through the returns for the whole of England and Wales in one go. However, occupational data was not always gathered consistently in the censuses and this problem is particularly acute for shipping vessels, canal boats, Army and Navy personnel.

If your ancestors were immigrants, or emigrated overseas, you will need to check the censuses for their home country or destination, or passenger lists for vessels.

Spelling and Transcription Errors

Ancestors may not have been sure of their name's exact spelling, or it may have changed slightly over the generations. In addition, old handwriting can be notoriously difficult to read and transcription errors often creep into the online databases. Generally, forenames are easier to read than surnames (and easier for transcribers to guess the correct name), so transcription errors are far more common for surnames.

Some websites offer a way around this by offering 'wildcard' searches for your ancestors' surname, i.e., the first three for four letters of their surname plus a *. For example, you could use 'Tom*' to search for 'Tomlinson'. Alternatively, some websites offer a 'Soundex' search for similar-sounding names.

If you still can't find your ancestors using a 'wildcard' search, try another approach. Assuming that you know what their occupation was from a marriage or death certificate or a parish register, try searching by occupation plus first name. This will generate many results, but you can limit your search by location, age or the names of your ancestor's children if known.

How Old?

The ages of ancestors recorded in the censuses, and on documents such as marriage certificates in particular, should be viewed with caution. People may have been shy about putting down their real age, or made an honest mistake. The date when a birth was registered is the most reliable guide to an ancestor's birthdate. A baptismal record is only an approximate guide because a child may not have been christened until several weeks or months after the birth. However, a baptism may be the only record available of a birth for ancestors born before civil registration began.

Case Study: The Dickman Family

In the late 1870s, the author's great-great-grandmother Annie Mary Hollis, a Yorkshire lass, married William Kirkwood Dickman from Manchester. William's death certificate in 1931 gave his occupation as railway coach painter and his age as 73: hence he was born in about 1858.

Searching through the online censuses (such as those available on the Genealogist.co.uk and other subscription websites), in 1901 we find six results for a William Dickman, of which the most likely is a William (43) and Annie (40) who lived at 189 Wellington Street, Manchester with ten of their children. The age of their oldest child, Margaret (23?), is hard to read on the census return image but the youngest child, the author's grandfather Frank, is 3 years old.

William and Annie's birthplaces on the census return were Manchester and Sheffield respectively. The four oldest children's birthplaces were also Sheffield, so this is a clue that the couple lived in Sheffield for a time. William was employed as a railway waggon coach painter (RG 13/3763 folio 46, p. 27). Neither William nor Annie's middle names are given, but the birthplaces and names of the children matched the author's previous information on the family.

Working backwards through the censuses, in 1891 William and Annie lived at 59 Libby Street, Openshaw, Manchester with six children and a lodger (RG 12/3177, folio 48, p. 39). This time Annie's middle name Mary is noted. Margaret is not mentioned, so she must be staying elsewhere. A possible match is a Maggie Dickman (13) working as a domestic servant for the Sinclair family at 10 Alexander Grove, Chorlton-on-Medlock (RG 12/3185, folio 80, p. 19).

Searching the online 1881 Lancashire census for William Dickman poses some puzzles. Four results appear, but none of the ages or birthplaces match 'our' William, who was about 23 years old. (One of the results is for a painter named William Dickman (51), living at 12 Tipton Street and born in 'Whit[e]church, Shropshire' with his wife Elizabeth, born in Wigton, Cumberland, and a stepdaughter, Elizabeth Pearson. One can hazard a guess that wife Elizabeth's maiden name was Pearson. We will return to this family presently (RG 11/3908, folio 38, p. 36).)

Some subscription websites allow you to search by 'keyword' or by a wildcard search (for example, a keyword search is available on the Genealogist.co.uk). A search for William + 'D*' + 'painter' + 1858 yields a possible match: a 'William Kirwood Dickinson' a coach painter (23), married but living as a lodger at 3 Mitchell Street, Openshaw. His birthplace is given as Hulme, but age, marital status and occupation match. The name on the return is extremely difficult to read but looks very similar to the one we are looking for (RG 11/3907, folio 92, p. 32).

Turning now to the 1871 census and concentrating on William, as he was Lancashire born, neither a quick initial search nor a wildcard search as above gives us any promising results.

After trying several different combinations, and searching through many results, a 'William K Dickenan' was found living at 6 George Street, West Gorton with his father William (41), born in Whitchurch, William's wife Elizabeth, born in Wigton, and a brother 'John T', born in Shoreditch, Middlesex (RG 10/3981, folio 37, p. 20). Both John and young 'William K' (14) are coach painter's apprentices, so the occupation is correct. There is another son, Joseph, born in West Gorton, and Elizabeth Pearson is living there too.

At first glance, although the surname is once again hard to read on the image, occupations and ages match and it seems likely that we have discovered William Kirkwood Dickman's father, mother and other siblings.

However, if we go back further in time to the 1861 census, we find a family of Dickmans living at 39 Wovendens Buildings, Openshaw, Manchester. The head of the family is William Dickman, a labourer in an iron-works (RG 9/2872, folio 74, p. 12). This William, born in Whitchurch (36), was living with his wife Margaret Frances (26), born in Wigton, Cumberland, and sons John (born in Shoreditch) and William Kirkwood Dickman, aged 3, born in Manchester. Their mother-in-law Sarah Thompson, born in Wigton, was living with the family.

It is most unlikely that there is another William Dickman with such an unusual middle name of 'Kirkwood'. A search of the parish registers at Manchester Archives and Local Studies confirmed that a William Kirkwood Dickman was baptized at St Silas's Church, Ardwick on 5 September 1858, and his parents were William and Margaret Frances. Their address was given as 3 Elizabeth Street, Openshaw (MFPR 1214).

Therefore, the Elizabeth Dickman first mentioned in the 1871 census was William Kirkwood Dickman's stepmother, not his mother: his father had married a second time, to another Wigton girl. This example clearly shows how searching the online censuses can solve some problems, but also generate fresh lines of enquiry. (Of course, an alternative approach would have been to infer William's birth date from the censuses, search the GRO indexes and order William's birth certificate.)

Missing and Damaged Censuses

Some census records were lost over the years. Others could not be recorded on microfilm because they were damaged during storage and were too fragile to survive being filmed. For example, the 1851 census returns for several districts in the Manchester area were badly damaged by water, and some of the Preston returns from the 1871 census are missing.

The Find My Past website has a useful overview of known missing and incomplete census returns for 1841–1901 at: www.findmypast.co.uk/help-and-advice/knowledge-base/census/known-issues.

The damaged returns for Manchester in the 1851 census were a major blow for Lancashire family historians because the records for over 200,000 people were 'lost'. The affected districts included Ashton-under-Lyne, Chorlton, Manchester, Salford and Oldham.

Fortunately, in the early 1990s, the Manchester and Lancashire FHS launched a rescue mission to transcribe those records that were still readable but too fragile to film. This volunteer project took many years to complete but over 80 per cent of the census returns were recovered. There's a website dedicated to the 'unfilmed' 1851 Manchester census at: www.1851-unfilmed.org.uk. The website explains which districts were affected and how much data was recovered. There's a free surname index and street index which you can search online, and information on where to find copies of the transcripts.

The 1911 census is particularly poignant for family historians because it gives us a last glimpse of the generation that suffered in the First World War. Thousands of the men listed in this census did not survive the war years, or were left physically or mentally scarred by their experiences.

Tip

Get into the habit of making a note of the reference number, location and date for each record relating to your ancestor, whether it is a census return, parish register, newspaper report or any other type of record. When looking through online census images, for example, it is all too easy to lose track of the date of a census return unless you print out the reference, write it down or 'label' the downloaded document image clearly on your home computer. Noting a record reference is also vitally important for records held at the archives. It can be extremely annoying if you need to double-check a fact about your ancestor, but have no idea in which archive you found the original information or in which series of records.

The World Wars

The county has a proud history of military service dating back to at least the early eighteenth century. LRO has a guide to its records of militia and volunteer regiments from 1757 onwards, including the modern Territorial Army (from 1908).

Britain greeted the outbreak of the First World War with an outpouring of patriotic fervour and Lancashire men were quick to volunteer. Local recruiting centres opened in cities like Manchester and Liverpool. Lord Derby (later the 17th Earl) at Liverpool was one of the most enthusiastic recruiters. Men from the same families, and towns, joined the ranks together and the battalions raised became known as the 'Pals'. They trained together and went into battle together. 'Pals' battalions were formed at places like Accrington, Liverpool, Manchester, Oldham, Salford and Preston.

Unfortunately, because members of the famous 'Pals' battalions were mostly from a small geographical area, it had a devastating effect on local communities if most of a battalion perished.

Lists of casualties and gallantry awards were printed in the national and local newspapers, and the mind-numbingly large numbers of people lost make shocking reading. Local papers printed short obituaries and biographies for their local heroes, sometimes with a photograph of the deceased or decorated soldier.

You can order death certificates for soldiers who died in the world wars from the GRO (not local register offices). The GRO also issues birth and death certificates for people on ships registered in Britain (1837 onwards) and British-registered aircraft (1948 onwards).

Military Sources

This is a vast subject. A wealth of published material is available: books on the volunteer movements, militias and world wars, autobiographical accounts of the Lancashire regiments, regimental histories, war diaries, 'how to' guides for genealogists, etc. A good starting point is Terry Wyke and Nigel Rudyard, *Military History in the North West* (Manchester: Bibliography of North West England, 1994).

An enormous amount of information can be found online: see Simon Fowler, *Researching Your Military History on the Internet* (Pen & Sword, 2007). Some resources and regimental archives for Lancashire military family history are listed in Section G below.

TNA has Army service records from the 1730s to the late 1890s: muster rolls, pay lists and description books (which have information on each soldier). TNA's Our Online Records has digitized service records for the world wars including the Army, Navy, Air Force, nurses and merchant

---

Tip

The TNA images of First World War medal index cards only show the front of each card. Some cards had information on the back such as the name and address of next of kin. The cards can be viewed free (WO 372) at TNA. Alternatively, Ancestry.co.uk has images of both sides of the medal index cards.

---

seamen. A selection of these record series and 'rolls of honour' are available on genealogy subscription websites.

Some men could not cope with the horrors of war. They became ill, or went absent without leave or deserted. Deserters from the armed forces were listed in the *Police Gazette* (which also detailed wanted criminals and illegal aliens).

You can use TNA's Hospital Records Database to find the location of medical records, e.g., for the Grangethorpe military hospital at Rusholme, but these records may be closed for privacy reasons. The database can be accessed at: www.nationalarchives.gov.uk/hospitalrecords/default.asp.

Absent Voters' Lists (1918) recorded men who were eligible to vote but were away on active service. The list should include each man's address, rank and number. Surviving lists will be held at local record offices.

The Commonwealth War Graves Commission (CWGC) website has searchable lists of casualties and cemeteries for both world wars, and civilians killed during the Second World War at: www.cwgc.org.

Case Study

A Family's Sacrifice

Two poignant entries in the family Bible, and a faded but long-treasured newspaper cutting tucked inside its pages, record the deaths of two of the author's great-uncles, Herbert and Harry (Henry) Dickman, in 1916 during the First World War. Both men worked at Agecroft Colliery.

A search for their names on the CWGC website quickly elicited their service numbers, rank, dates of death, regiment and the section numbers of the panels where their names are commemorated on the war memorial at Loos.

Harry Dickman (service number 15080) was a private in the 16th Battalion of the Lancashire Fusiliers; his date of death was given as 30 July 1916, age 'unknown'.

His brother Herbert Dickman (service number 15647) served as a private in the 8th Battalion of the Royal Fusiliers, and his date of death is given as 7 March 1916, aged 25. The 'casualty details' for Herbert include the names of his parents, William and Annie Dickman, and their address.

The author next searched the First World War medals index on TNA's Our Online Records. There are six soldiers' records (each with the same initial) on each copy of the medal index cards, so you need to check the service number to ensure you have the correct record.

The brothers' names and service numbers were also checked on the First World War Roll of Honour Death Index (GRO).

The card for Harry Dickman states that he entered France on 23 November 1915. He was awarded the Victory, the British and the Star medals. Puzzlingly, the card states that he was 'K in A [Killed in Action] on 30 July 1918' (WO/372/6). The date when deceased does not match the CWGC website records, but the service number matches, so there may have been an error when the medal card was compiled.

Herbert Dickman's card reveals that he entered Western France on 29 December 1915 and that he 'D of W whilst P of W [died of wounds while a POW] on 2 May 1916'. He was awarded two medals: the Victory and the Star (WO/372/6, Crown copyright TNA).

William and Annie Dickman lost a grandson, too, just a few weeks after Herbert's death. In July 1916 John William Dickman was killed on the Somme. John served in the 8th Battalion of the East Lancashire Regiment; his name is recorded on the Thiepval Memorial.

Brothers Harry and Herbert are commemorated on the Agecroft Colliery war memorial, along with the names of their workmates who died in the 'war to end all wars'.

Undated newspaper cutting of the death of the author's great-uncle Harry Dickman (1916) in the First World War.

The First World War memorial at Agecroft commemorates the sacrifice of the men of the colliery owned by Andrew Knowsley & Sons. (© Sue Wilkes)

The End of an Era

The future looked bright for Lancashire industries as Queen Victoria's immensely long reign ended. The cotton trade had gradually recovered from the cotton famine of the 1860s; at the end of the nineteenth century, cotton goods were still Britain's biggest export. Cotton production peaked at 8,000 million yards of cloth before the First World War. In 1912, 622,000 people were directly employed in the Lancashire cotton industry.

New inventions brought new industries such as aeronautical engineering: the A. V. Roe factory began building aircraft at Great Ancoats Street, Manchester in 1910. The First World War had a positive impact on Lancashire industries such as the ammunitions factories and the Barrow shipyards and chemical-works prospered. Women took over many jobs that were previously the province of men such as munitions work. However, the cotton mills struggled to keep their machinery running during wartime because so many workers left to man the trenches.

106

An early twentieth-century postcard showing a cotton weaving shed and a Lancashire lass in holiday finery.

The Second World War, too, increased employment and wages in the engineering industries, especially factories making aircraft, aero parts and munitions. But the industrial towns were major targets for German bombers and thousands of civilians were killed and injured in Barrow, Liverpool, Manchester and other places. Children were evacuated from the towns to the countryside. Liverpool people suffered terribly: the city was second only to London for the number of bombing raids carried out.

After the end of the First and the Second World Wars, the cotton industry witnessed a brief renaissance, boosted by peacetime and high demand. But during the early 1950s, increasing foreign competition from India and Japan, and failure by British manufacturers to modernize, sounded the death knell for the cotton industry.

By the end of the decade, Britain imported more cotton cloth than it produced. The government paid mill-owners to scrap mule-spinning machinery. Some firms modernized and fitted 'ring-spinning' machines (like those made by Platt Saco Lowell) which had been used in the USA for years. The industry was still undercut by cheap wares from abroad, however, and the number of cotton workers in the county plummeted to 120,000 in the late 1960s.

This was a disaster nationally as well as locally, because the north-west of England was home to 90 per cent of the British textile manufacturing capacity. According to the Lancashire and Merseyside Industrial Development Association's 1967 report on *The Decline of the Cotton and Coal Mining Industries of Lancashire*, the number of mills and finishing works fell to less than 750: less than half those operating in 1951. One by one, the mills closed their gates to workers, and the clatter of machinery was hushed. Cotton's long dominance was over.

The decline of cotton was mirrored in Lancashire's coal industry. A lack of investment by colliery owners, declining demand for coal and problems with geology (Lancashire seams were notoriously narrow and deep) all took their toll. Wages were at rock-bottom levels, working conditions were dangerous and the miners grew increasingly militant. The Great Strike of 1926 was the culmination of years of fighting for higher wages, but the miners were forced back to work. The industry was part-nationalized during the Second World War, then fully nationalized when the National Coal Board (NCB) took over all privately owned mines in 1947.

The number of pits fell from 70 in 1950 to 20 in the late 1960s, although two 'new' collieries – Agecroft Colliery at Pendlebury and Parkside at Newton-le-Willows – began production in the 1960s. (The Agecroft pit had closed in the early 1930s.)

Unemployment increased sharply. However, coal production, while falling, did not drop as markedly as might have been expected owing to the increased efficiency of mine working. There was more bad news for Lancashire miners when Mosley Common Pit, the county's biggest modern colliery employing 2,850 men, was earmarked by the NCB for closure in 1967. Pits continued to shut throughout the twentieth century.

Mining Records

TNA has many collections with relevance to coal mining (there is an online guide) but staff records are more likely to be held at local record offices. Individual mines may be mentioned in estate records, deeds, leases or plans.

LRO's collections of mining records (NC) date from the late fifteenth century to the 1960s. The series includes the NCB and its predecessors, miners' associations such as the Lancashire and Cheshire Miners' Welfare Committee (NCLm), accident and compensation registers, relief societies, cash books, pension records, wage books, etc., and the Salford Museum of Mining collection. Records for local branches of the National Union of Mineworkers can be found at local record offices such as Bolton Archives and Local Studies and Salford City Archives. The main National Union of Mineworkers' archive is held at its Barnsley office.

The loss of the county's traditional industries had a big impact on the districts dependent on them and the populations of towns such as Preston, Blackburn and Bolton fell. After the Second World War, there was social unrest as the county's population mix changed with the arrival of Afro-Caribbean, Asian, Chinese and Indian immigrants.

Many old factory chimneys which littered the Lancashire landscape have been demolished, but new uses were found for some old textile mills. Not all the historic county's industries have disappeared: ships are still built at Barrow-in-Furness, trucks are manufactured near Leyland and currently the aerospace industry remains an important employer.

You can see documentary footage of your ancestors' past lives at the North West Film Archive, which has hours of film of Lancashire people at home and at play. Oral histories are another wonderful way to explore the momentous changes that affected Lancashire society during the twentieth century. The North West Sound Archive at Clitheroe has thousands of recordings of people's memories (explore its collections using the LRO catalogue).

Some oral histories are available in print, e.g., Elizabeth Roberts, *A Woman's Place: An Oral History of Working Class Women, 1890–1940* (Wiley-Blackwell, 1995) which includes interviews with women from Barrow, Lancaster and Preston. Several vivid autobiographical accounts of Lancashire life have been published including Robert Roberts, *The Classic Slum* (Pelican, 1980) and William Woodruff, *The Road to Nab End* (Abacus, 2002).

The Centre for Regional Studies (Lancaster University) has oral history archives. Museums, local studies libraries and record offices may also have collections.

Chapter 7

BEGINNING YOUR SEARCH

Gather as much information as possible at home before you research further afield. Ask family members if they have any names, addresses or dates for previous generations of the family, or if they have any friends who could help with your search. Make a note or make copies of any records that the family have kept such as birth, marriage and death certificates (BMDs), passports, work records, etc., and write down their memories of potentially useful clues such as the names of schools, places of work or previous homes.

Information from family members should be checked whenever possible against original records, because memories may have become confused or inaccurate over time, or family members may have been given incorrect information in the first place.

If you know where your ancestor was living, perhaps from family information but ideally from the address noted on a birth, marriage or death certificate or electoral register, you can search the census records for that address (see Chapter 6).

Use the nineteenth-century censuses to discover your ancestors' families, occupations, birthplaces and children who moved out. Remember that during the nineteenth century, children started work at much earlier ages than today. You may find different branches of the same family living fairly close to each other.

Tip

Families sometimes gave their children the mother's or grandmother's maiden name as a middle name. If one of the children of a marriage has a middle name that looks like a surname, this is a potential clue, worth trying as a 'keyword' when searching online censuses and other records. Alternatively, sometimes parents gave their children their mother's forename as a middle name. Occasionally a child was given the surname of its godparents as a middle name.

The author's grandparents' wedding, 1925. The bride and groom, Frank Dickman and Annie Tudge, are in the centre, with witnesses John Fray Tudge and Hilda Tudge.

Work back in time methodically from the present day. This is important because otherwise you may inadvertently 'skip' a generation. The same forenames often crop up across the generations, and this can cause real confusion when searching through the records.

It is vital to ensure you are researching the correct family tree. Some surnames were extremely common in the county (sometimes within quite a small area) and it is very easy to get muddled when searching the censuses. Check that the names and ages of spouses and children match the family you are hunting for.

BMDs, parish registers, bishop's transcripts, wills, monumental inscriptions (MIs), censuses, rent or rate books, electoral registers, occupational records, pension records, telephone directories, street or trade directories and the many other types of records described in this book can all be pressed into service. Look for lists of householders such as burgess rolls, electoral rolls, lay subsidy rolls, hearth taxes and so on.

Birth, Marriage and Death Certificates and Indexes

In 1837 the civil registration of births, marriages and deaths became compulsory. Birth certificates show the date and location of the person's birth, name, sex, father's name, mother's maiden name and residence, father's occupation, date when the birth was registered and the name and address of the person who registered the birth.

Marriage certificates give the date when the couple married, place where the marriage was solemnized, names and occupations of the bride and groom, their residence at the time of marriage, and names and occupations of the fathers of the bride and groom. The witnesses to the marriage may be relatives of the couple. The bride and groom sometimes gave their planned future address if they needed to fulfil residence requirements.

Death certificates give the person's age and occupation, date of death and residence at time of death, cause of death, date when the death was registered and the name and address of the person who registered the death.

One particular elephant trap to avoid – don't assume that the name of a female ancestor before her marriage is her maiden name – she may have been married before. Re-marriage was very common because life expectancy was lower than in modern times. A marriage certificate should show the bride's previous names.

Copies of BMDs can be ordered from local register offices (see Section C). The BMD registers were indexed by each local register office. The Lancashire BMD website has a searchable database for local register office indexes. Not all the county's birth, marriage and death indexes are online yet, but if you do find an entry for your ancestor on the website, you can order a copy of the certificate from the appropriate register office by post. At the time of writing, it costs about £9 to purchase a birth, marriage or death certificate.

Copies of the registers at local register offices were sent to the GRO every three months. Indexes are available for BMDs. For the birth indexes, the mother's maiden name was not included until 1911. For marriage indexes, the surnames of husband and wife (maiden name) were not listed together until 1912. Death indexes only include the person's age from 1866 onwards.

You can use the index reference and correct quarter of the year to order copies of certificates from the GRO. The registers were formerly kept at St Catherine's House, and you may find these indexes referred to as St Catherine's House indexes on some websites.

Please note that local register indexes are not the same as the GRO indexes, so you cannot use an index reference number from a local register office to order a certificate from the GRO at Southport, or vice versa. The local register office indexes are more accurate than the GRO indexes because errors may have crept in when the details were being transcribed.

Your local record office or reference library may have microfilm copies of the GRO indexes, or access to them via their computers to genealogy subscription websites. Partial coverage of the indexes is available on the Free BMD website.

Locating Parish Registers

If you wish to consult the parish register entries for your ancestors, you must establish the parish and diocese in which they lived or died. Begin by looking for churches near their last known address, but bear in mind that it was quite common for families to change address frequently. Census records include parish of residence. The LRO guides (online and in folders at the archive) give the location of Lancashire parish registers kept at the record office and elsewhere. Parishes are listed in the guides in alphabetical order.

Parish registers for the Manchester, Liverpool, and Wigan areas are usually kept at their diocesan record offices in their original parish (except when still held by their original church): GMCRO, Liverpool Record Office and Wigan Archives respectively. For example, most Bolton parish registers are currently kept at GMCRO as Bolton is in the diocese of Manchester.

The Manchester & Lancashire Family History Society (MLFHS) has published *Registers in Manchester Archives and Local Studies* (2011) which lists dates available and reference numbers for parish registers kept at Manchester.

Not all registers are kept at their diocesan record office. For example, for the diocese of Liverpool, LRO has records for the deaneries of North Meols, Ormskirk and St Helens, and Sefton deanery (Altcar, Formy, Hightown and Sefton). LRO also has parish registers for the diocese of Blackburn.

Original parish records for places in the administrative county of Lancashire before 1974 but now in Cumbria are kept at Cumbria Archives, which has four offices (see Section A). To give another example, registers for St Peter's Church in Finsthwaite parish are held at Kendal, and registers for St George's church, in the parish of Barrow-in-Furness, are kept at Barrow.

Tip

Original archive materials for the Manchester area are currently held at GMCRO on Marshall Street. Microfilm copies of parish registers, and other family history materials, are available at the Manchester Room@City Library, Elliot House, Deansgate. When the new Archives+ facility opens at the Central Library (early 2014), this will be the new home for Manchester archival materials, local studies and family history facilities (see Section A).

Parish registers for places formerly in Lancashire but now in Cheshire, such as Warrington, Culcheth and Winwick, are kept at Cheshire Archives and Local Studies.

In order to protect original parish registers, in general you will only be permitted to view copies of them on microfilm or fiche. This can be very slow and time-consuming. Record offices sometimes have indexed transcripts of the registers, and if these are available you will find it quicker and easier to check the indexes first to see if the record you want is there.

LRO holds some original bishop's transcripts (BTs), e.g., for the dioceses of Blackburn, Liverpool and Manchester. It has microfilm copies of those kept elsewhere in the county, and your local record office or reference library may also have microfilm copies. The original BTs for Furness (diocese of Carlisle) are kept at the Barrow office of Cumbria Archives.

Burial records in parish registers may give the date when the person died, sometimes with the cause of death. Cemetery, crematoria records and memorial (gravestone) inscriptions are all helpful sources. Cemetery and crematorium records are usually kept at the cemetery or crematorium office. LRO has a guide with the addresses and locations of cemetery/crematorium records. Manchester and Lancashire FHS has a list of cemeteries and crematoria for the Manchester area on its website. Your local reference library or record office may have copies of burial or cemetery records on microfilm, especially if the cemetery has closed.

National Burials Index

The National Burials Index, produced by the FFHS, covers England and Wales. The index includes Nonconformist, Roman Catholic and Quaker burials as well as Anglican church burials. The index has been compiled from parish registers, BTs and cemetery records. It does not include MIs. Your local archives, reference library or FHS may have a reference copy. It is also available to buy on CD-ROM from FFHS Services at: www.ffhs.org.uk/projects/nbi/nbi-v3.php.

The dates and locations of Lancashire burials covered by the index are also listed at: www.ffhs.org.uk/projects/nbi/lan3.php.

The Lancashire Parish Register Society (LPRS), family history societies and record societies have transcribed many parish registers, burial records and MIs and published them in book form or on CD-ROM.

Other useful sources of parish register information are Boyd's Marriage Index, Pallot's Baptisms and Marriages Indexes and the International Genealogical Index (IGI, Church of Jesus Christ of Latter-day Saints, available on some subscription websites; your local record office or archive may have copies. Search the IGI index free on FamilySearch at: https://www.familysearch.org.

114

Nonconformists

Original Nonconformist registers are kept at TNA and are available on the BMD Registers website at: www.bmdregisters.co.uk. LRO has transcripts and indexes for some Nonconformist registers.

Nonconformists and Roman Catholics (not Quakers or Jews) had to marry in the Established Church from 1754–1837 and you should search these registers first for weddings.

Roman Catholic Records

LRO is the diocesan record office for the Roman Catholic dioceses of Lancaster, Liverpool and Salford but many registers are still held at their home church. Copies on microfilm, transcripts and indexes are available for some registers. There are special access restrictions for Roman Catholic registers: more details are available in the guide to Roman Catholic records on the LRO website.

The Catholic Record Society has published transcripts of parish registers, returns of papists and other documents relating to convicted recusants in Lancashire during the reign of Charles II.

The Revd Oliver Heywood and Revd T. Dickenson, *Nonconformist Register of Birth, Marriages and Deaths for 1644–1702, 1702–1752 also known as the Northowram or Coley Register*, ed. by J. Horsfall Turner (Brighouse, 1881) includes Puritans and Catholic recusants from Lancashire families. This book is available on the Internet Archive, and an indexed version can be accessed on the GENUKI website at: www.genuki.org.uk/big/eng/YKS/northowram.

The quarter session records (Q), Kenyon of Peel papers (DDKE/7) and other family collections at LRO include lists of recusants and other papers relating to recusancy and the Jacobite plot of 1692–1694.

TNA holds the 'recusant rolls' recording payments of fines and other penalties by recusants (Exchequer records) and a 'Return of Papists' from Lancaster in 1714 (KB 18). The State Paper Office (SP) series has many records relating to Catholics.

Lancashire Online Parish Clerks

No genealogist can afford to miss this ambitious and invaluable project. This free online database includes Lancashire records from a wide variety of sources: parish registers, BTs, censuses, returns of papists, cemetery records, directories and much, much more. The website is regularly updated.

Records range from the early sixteenth century until the beginning of the twentieth century. You can browse the site by parish. A new webpage opens for each parish where you can explore the records available. Churches are listed for each parish, and if their records have been put online, there is a 'link' to a webpage dedicated to that church where you can browse the registers.

Full dates, locations and sources are given for each event so that researchers can check the original sources for themselves and obtain copies if they wish. Or you can use this information to order BMDs from register offices (after 1837).

Surname indexes are available (only for online parish registers). The website has a 'search' page where you can explore the databases by name, date, parents or spouses at: www.lan-opc.org.uk.

Case Study

The author knew from her research that her great-great-grand-father was Henry Tudge, a collier who lived in the Little Hulton area and was born sometime around 1827 (inferred from the censuses). A search on Lancashire OPC for 'Henry Tudge' elicited seven results. The first result was a possible baptism for Henry:

> Baptisms: 1 Mar 1829 at St John the Evangelist, Farnworth with Kearsley, Lancashire
> Henry Tudge: Child of Richard Tudge & Mary
> Abode: Little Hulton
> Occupation: Collier
> Baptised by: G. Marriott
> Register: Baptisms 1826–1840, Page 27, Entry 210
> Source: LDS Film 1538438.

The other six results revealed Henry's first marriage to Mary Ann Matts (1849), his second marriage to widow Mary Partington in 1861, a possible burial for Henry in 1886 and the baptism, marriage and burial of one of his sons, William Henry. A further search for 'Tudge' without a forename elicited over 250 results, dating from the 1770s to the late 1950s: plenty of food for thought.

Tip

New records uploaded to Lancashire OPC are not always immediately available on the searchable database. Visit the 'What's New' page to see which records have recently been added.

116

John Owen Manuscripts

This collection is of vital importance because it contains thousands of transcripts of material such as memorial inscriptions that are no longer extant. Owen, a Bolton man, spent many years compiling genealogy information for north-west England. His research, which filled eighty-nine notebooks, is kept at GMCRO and is available on microfilm at the Manchester Room@City Library. The Manchester and Lancashire FHS has a microfilm copy in its library at Clayton House, and has published an index: *Index to the Owen Manuscripts* (MLFHS, 2003). Some of Owen's transcripts of parish registers for Flixton, Gorton and Newton are available in Find My Past's Manchester Collection.

Where There's a Will

Wills Before 1858
Wills and administration bonds ('admons') were proved in ecclesiastical courts until 1858. The archdeaconry courts were generally used by the 'middling' members of society. Very poor people, who had no property to leave, are unlikely to have left a will.

Unfortunately for genealogists, finding a will proved before 1858 is not always an easy task, especially for Lancashire, because the jurisdiction of ecclesiastical courts did not follow the county boundaries.

When looking for a person's will, one needs to know in which diocese they died or held property or lands in. If you don't know whether they held any land or property, then begin by checking in which diocese the town or village where they died (or were last known to have lived) was situated.

Prior to the Reformation, since south Lancashire was part of the diocese of Lichfield, wills proved in the Lichfield court still extant from before 1540 (if any) will be held by Lichfield Record Office.

Archdeaconry of Richmond
The archdeaconry of Richmond, as previously noted, was responsible for the area of Lancashire north of the River Ribble, and so its court was used for probate purposes. Unfortunately, many early wills for the archdeaconry of Richmond (particularly Amounderness) were lost sometime around 1750. The wills were moved in open carts from Lancaster to Richmond because the commissary court changed location.

Lancashire wills (western deaneries) proved in the archdeaconry of Richmond from 1457–1858 are kept at LRO: W/RW. Copeland deanery (Cumberland) was also in the archdeaconry of Richmond and its probate records form part of this collection.

The University of Lancashire has compiled an index for all surviving probate records for the western deaneries of the archdeaconry of Richmond for 1748–1858. This index is available on the LRO online catalogue.

There is more information about the index, with free alphabetical lists of surnames and townships on the university website at: www.uclan.ac.uk/ ahss/education_social_sciences/history/probate_index.php.

Archdeaconry of Chester

The archdeaconry Court of Chester was responsible for Lancashire south of the Ribble. Lancashire wills proved at Chester from 1487–1858 are kept at LRO (WC); few survive prior to 1541.

In Chester diocese, wills for estates less than £40 in value were known as 'infra' wills, and those for estates of more than £40 in value were known as 'supra' wills. The latter were proved in the bishop's court (sometimes called a consistory or commissary court).

Some early wills proved at Chester were lost or irreparably damaged owing to the poor conditions in which they were kept for many years. However, many missing wills were recorded in the bishop's registers or 'Act books' and abstracts of these wills were published by the Chetham Society. There's an online searchable index which you can use to order copies of wills proved at Chester 1540–1940 (see Section E).

Peculiars

Some 'peculiar' parishes were not controlled by the archdeaconries of Richmond or Chester. The manor of Halton was a 'peculiar' in the deanery of Kendal and its probate records are kept at LRO.

The parishes of Broughton, Kirkby Ireleth and Seathwaite were under the jurisdiction of the Dean and Chapter of York; these parishes' probate records are kept at the Borthwick Institute. For probate purposes, the township of Aighton, Chaigley and Bailey was under the jurisdiction of the Exchequer Court of York and its records, too, are held at the Borthwick Institute. Parishes/townships that were York peculiars are indexed on Origins.net at: www.origins.net/help/aboutNWI-ypec-par.aspx.

Complicated Estates

If a person held property or land in more than one archdeaconry but within the same diocese, then probate was proved in the bishop's court. If an estate was scattered over more than one diocese, or the deceased left goods worth more than £5, then probate was granted by a senior court: the archbishop's prerogative court.

For Lancashire, this was the Prerogative Court of York (PCY), because the county was in the ecclesiastical province of York. The Borthwick Institute,

York holds the original PCY records which are indexed on Origins.net. Copies of wills can be ordered through Origins.net (except 1501–1730 currently) and from the Borthwick Institute.

The most senior church court was the Prerogative Court of Canterbury (PCC). When a person held property in both the ecclesiastical provinces of York and Canterbury, the PCC was used to prove probate, and its records are kept at TNA. Although the majority of the PCC records (PROB 11) relate to people living in the southern counties of England, and Wales, this series includes the wills of thousands of Lancashire people.

The PROB 11 series has been indexed and can be searched on the TNA website, where you can download copies of PCC wills from 1384–1858 from TNA's Our Online Records.

The LCRS has published indexes and lists of wills and administrations proved in the consistory court of Chester, the archdeaconry of Richmond (up to the mid-nineteenth century) and in the PCC. 'Supra', 'infra' and 'diocesan' wills are indexed separately. Your local record office or main library may have copies of the indexes; some wills mentioned in these indexes no longer exist.

The Society of Genealogists has microfilm copies of the will indexes and some abstracts of wills, and has published books of will indexes. Remember that the dates in the will indexes are the date when probate was granted for the will, not the date of the person's death; months or even years may have passed before a will was proved.

If you are having problems tracing a will between 1796 and 1858, try checking the death duty registers. These registers (usually for estates worth more than £20) can be useful because they contain a great deal of family information, such as the deceased's address and last occupation, the date of the will, when and where probate was granted, details (including addresses) of the executors and beneficiaries under the will, and much more.

Death duty registers (IR 26 at TNA) include courts other than the PCC, such as the diocesan court of Chester, known as 'country courts'. These were indexed separately from 1796–1811: IR 27. Series IR 26 and IR 27 can be searched at TNA's Our Online Records; the IR 27 series can also be searched on the Find My Past website.

The following books are helpful: Jeremy Gibson and Else Churchill, *Probate Jurisdictions: Where to Look for Wills* (Federation of Family History Societies, 2002) and Nigel Taylor and Karen Grannum, *Wills and Probate Records: A Guide for Family Historians* (TNA, 2009).

Summary for Wills Before 1858
The National Wills Index (Origins.net) has searchable indexes (fee payable to view records) at: www.nationalwillsindex.com.

LRO holds probate records for north and south of the River Ribble, i.e., the archdeaconries of Chester and Richmond.

- First check which archdeaconry your ancestor might have died in, then consult the LRO will indexes;
- If the will is not at LRO, try the PCY indexes (Borthwick Institute or Origins.net);
- If the will is not in the PCY indexes, try the PCC indexes at TNA.

Wills After 1858

Finding a will proved after 11 January 1858 is a much easier task because the ecclesiastical courts were no longer responsible for probate in England and Wales. Wills were now proved in district probate registries (see Section C).

The district probate registries sent copies of wills to the Principal Probate Registry (now the Principal Registry of the Family Division). The National Probate Calendar is the index to wills after 1858. It can be viewed at the Probate Search Room, First Avenue House, 42–49 High Holborn, London, WC1V 6NP.

LRO, the Manchester Room@City Library, GMCRO and other local archives have indexes of the National Probate Calendar (not all dates are available at each facility). The Society of Genealogists, FamilySearch centres, TNA, local probate registries and some genealogy subscription websites have partial indexes.

The probate calendar gives details of which probate court the will was proved in, and you can use this information to order a copy from Leeds District Probate Registry or your local district probate registry. (You may find York District Probate Registry mentioned on some family history materials, but it no longer deals with probate enquiries.)

Original Lancashire wills after 1858 are not kept at LRO but the archive has some copies of wills proved at Lancaster (1858–1938) and Liverpool (1858–1940). From 1858 registers were kept of estates liable for death duties and indexes and some registers on microfilm are available at TNA.

When is a County not a County?

Lancashire is one of the most complicated counties to research with respect to its administrative records. As a consequence of successive local government reorganizations and diocesan boundary changes, the task of locating records is not as straightforward as one could wish.

Before civil registration began, any reference to the 'county' of Lancashire in a historical record will generally mean the ancient or historic county. As discussed earlier, in 1837 civil registration districts were formed for the purpose of registering births, marriages and deaths. These districts should be used to order certificates (unless you are using the GRO index).

120

As discussed in Chapter 6, these registration districts, which did not necessarily coincide with the historic county boundaries, were used for recording the 1841 census. Then in 1851, the GRO defined 'registration counties' for census purposes and these should be used to consult census records.

In 1888 the Local Government Act defined new administrative units: 'county boroughs' and 'administrative counties' based on the ancient counties and urban and rural sanitary districts. These administrative units did not coincide with the registration districts or the historic county boundaries either. There were now eighteen administrative bodies for 'Lancashire': Lancashire County Council and seventeen county borough councils including Blackburn, Liverpool, Manchester, Salford and Wigan.

The Local Government Act of 1972 added another layer of complexity. In 1974 there were major changes to local government boundaries.

Liverpool and south-west Lancashire, and Manchester and south-east Lancashire, were transformed into the metropolitan counties of Merseyside and Greater Manchester respectively. The northernmost part of Lancashire, comprising the Furness peninsula and Cartmel, became part of Cumbria. The Warrington and Widnes areas were transferred to Cheshire, and some parts of Yorkshire became part of Lancashire.

These reorganizations were changes to administrative county boundaries, not Lancashire's historic boundaries. However, 1974 has been used as a convenient reference point for this book. This is because local authorities have the responsibility for keeping and maintaining archives for their areas, and the locations of many archival collections were influenced by these boundary changes and those that followed.

The metropolitan counties in their turn became defunct in 1986, and unitary authorities such as Manchester City Council were formed. There was yet another local government reorganization in 1998 when unitary authorities such as Blackburn with Darwen were created. With each re-organisation, a new set of records was generated.

Over time, the archival collections for the historic county were split between the record offices of the modern administrative counties of Lancashire, Cheshire and Cumbria, and Greater Manchester and Merseyside. For example, LRO holds the records for Lancashire County Council, which include areas such as Blackburn before they became unitary authorities.

Records for county boroughs and unitary authorities after they split from the Lancashire County Council are highly likely to be found at the record offices in those areas. For example, GMCRO has the records for Manchester City Council. However, some administrative records for the geographical areas covered by these authorities may also be held at LRO, depending on their date.

121

Thomas Baines, FSA (1806–1881), Yorkshire-born Lancashire historian. (Thomas Baines, *Lancashire and Cheshire Past and Present Vol. I* (William Mackenzie, London, c. 1867))

The important thing to bear in mind when searching for a record of a particular event or date, is that you need to check which particular administrative body or area is likely to be associated with it.

If all this sounds daunting and confusing, don't worry, a great deal of help is available such as maps and gazetteers. The archives and record offices have many finding aids, both online and in print.

If you are unsure whether a record is kept at a particular archive, perhaps because you cannot access its online catalogue, contact the archive. Even if the archive does not have the record in its collections they may be able to suggest where else you should look.

You may wish to join one of the family history or local history societies associated with the county (see Section C). The societies have built up a treasure trove of expert knowledge and often have their own library. If you have access to the Internet, there are online forums where you can 'chat' with other family historians.

If you would like to take your family history research a step further, you could consider joining the Guild of One-Name Studies. A 'one-name study' explores facts and history associated with a particular name as well as all the branches of a family tree. Over 8,000 surnames are now registered with the Guild.

Useful Sources in Print

The main archives and reference libraries may have (or the libraries can order), copies of the books listed in this section; you may be able to source second-hand copies. More books are listed where relevant in previous chapters.

The *Victoria History of the County of Lancaster*, mentioned earlier, details the principal landowners and important families for each area under discussion, and its text has plentiful footnotes with the names and dates of important documents relevant to a particular family or place.

Several volumes of the *Victoria County History* have been published on the British History Online website at: www.british-history.ac.uk and on the Internet Archive website at: www.archive.org.

The *Lancashire Bibliography* series, later the *Bibliography of North West England* series (seventeen volumes to date), was published from the 1960s–1990s (various authors and titles) and covers different time periods and historical topics.

Terry Wyke and Nigel Rudyard, *Directory of Local Studies in North West England* (Bibliography of North West England Vol. 14, 1993) is a guide to the area's many archives, libraries, societies, etc. Please note that contact details for the repositories listed may now be out of date.

Before you begin trawling through lots of different records, check first to see if the information you need, or a finding aid such as an index, has already been published. The Chetham Society, the LCRS, the Historic Society of Lancashire and Cheshire, and the Lancashire and Cheshire Antiquarian Society have published medieval records, court leet records, probate indexes, transcriptions of parish registers, MIs and more. The county's family history societies (see Section C) have also published many genealogical treasures.

Stuart A. Raymond, *Lancashire: A Genealogical Bibliography* (3 vols, Federation of Family History Societies, 1996) is a comprehensive list of published resources. Vol. 1 of the bibliography covers Lancashire genealogical sources such as parish histories, directories, censuses and census substitutes, etc., listed alphabetically by area. The 'occupational sources' section describes sources for workers such as clock-makers, soldiers and weavers. Vol. 2 lists published works on parish registers (including non-parochial), MIs and will transcripts and indexes. Vol. 3 covers Lancashire family histories and pedigrees.

Each volume of the *Genealogical Bibliography* contains an author index, place-name index and family name index. Although more publications will have become available for each topic of interest since Raymond's bibliography was published, it is still an extremely helpful starting point for researchers.

Sydney Horrocks, *Registers (parochial, non-parochial), Monumental Inscriptions, Names, Wills*, Vol. 5 (Bibliography of North West England, 1973) is now out of date but still useful.

Oral histories, diaries and journals can help to bring the past to life and some have been published by the historical societies. The North West Sound Archive has a major collection of oral histories by Lancashire people.

Andrew Gritt (ed.), *Family History in Lancashire: Issues and Approaches* (Cambridge Scholars, 2009) is a collection of essays by eminent historians exploring the structure and role of the family in the county through the ages. It contains some fascinating case studies, statistics and other information, such as Alan Crosby's examination of the Shaw family. Elizabeth Roberts reports on how twentieth-century working class families tried to make ends meet, with quotes from oral histories. A chapter by Michael Anderson updates his landmark 1971 study of Victorian Preston using censuses and other data (see also Michael Anderson, *Family Structure in Nineteenth Century Lancashire* (Cambridge University Press, 1971).

Readers who wish to find out more about the history of surnames in the county should consult Richard McKinley, *The Surnames of Lancashire* (Leopard's Head Press, 1981).

Calendars

The dates on old documents, particularly medieval documents, can cause real difficulties for genealogists. Official documents were dated by the number of years the sovereign had reigned, and saint's feast days rather than a particular day of the month. In addition, until 1752 the new year began on 25 March, not 1 January, and this calendar was used by the public, the Church and the courts. In 1752, the beginning of the new year was changed to 1 January, and in addition, the 'old style' Julian calendar was superseded by the 'new style' Gregorian calendar. Several books have been published on the complexities of understanding dates on old documents, including Cliff Webb, *Dates and Calendars for the Genealogist* (Society of Genealogists, 1989) and C. R. Cheney (ed.), *Handbook of Dates for Students of English History* (Cambridge, 1995).

Maps

If you are having difficulty working out which township, parish or census district your ancestor lived in at a given date, a good map or gazetteer is essential.

John Peter Smith, *Genealogist's Atlas of Lancashire* (Henry Young & Sons, 1930) is now out of print; you may be able to source a copy on CD-ROM from genealogy suppliers. The Institute of Heraldic and Genealogical Studies has published a map of Lancashire parishes that shows the dates when each parish's registers began, and probate jurisdictions. The institute has also published maps of registration districts in England and Wales.

The Lancashire Family History and Heraldry Society has published Andrew Todd's 1851 map of Lancashire as a 'hard copy' and on CD-ROM. The map shows registration districts and sub-districts of births, marriages and deaths, parishes, townships and all Anglican churches in existence in 1851 with their dedications and dates of their earliest registers.

LRO has a wonderful map collection, and its website has digital copies of old maps of Lancashire dating from the 1360s onwards, tithe maps, Ordnance Survey (OS) 6in maps (1845 and 1910), OS 25in maps (1890) and more at: www.lancashire.gov.uk/environment/oldmap/index.asp.

Tithe maps and enclosure award maps are often extremely detailed. In 1836, when the Tithe Commutation Act was passed, people were permitted to pay tithes in cash instead of payment in kind. Where the Act was implemented, accurate maps were made of the land in each parish, and the landowners and tenants noted. Three copies were made of each map and tithe apportionment record; one for the parish chest, one for the Tithe Commissioners and one for the diocesan register office.

The Commissioners' copies of tithe maps are held at TNA (IR 29 and 30) and LRO holds the parish and diocesan copies. (Some parishes converted to money payments before the Act, and no commutation records exist for these.) LRO has a Tithes Index on its website.

For a more in-depth discussion, see Eric J. Evans and Alan G. Crosby, *Tithes – Maps, Apportionments and the 1836 Act: a guide for local historians* (3rd edn, British Association for Local History, 1997).

Books and Newspapers Online

Your library service may subscribe to online resources such as the Oxford Dictionary of National Biography and the Times Digital Library.

Times Digital Library

Searchable copies of newspapers 1785–1985. Search by date and/or key words. *The Times* concentrated on London news but included regular updates from the provinces. Major news stories such as strikes were often reported. *The Times* published the names of soldiers killed in action or who died of their wounds during the world wars.

British Library's Newspaper Library

This online library with searchable catalogue has British national and regional newspapers 1800–1900. Articles from the *Penny Illustrated Paper* and the *Graphic* can be viewed free of charge. For other publications, purchase a 'day pass' to view up to 100 articles at: http://newspapers11.bl.uk/blcs.

British Newspapers Archive

This is a new but growing online resource hosting digital images of local newspapers such as the *Burnley Express, Bury Times, Lancaster Gazette, Manchester Mercury*, etc. You can search the archive by personal name, e.g., for your family's birth, marriage and death notices or obituaries. You can also browse the archive by location.

It is free to search, but you must purchase credits to view the page image. The credits are 'time-limited', i.e., you buy a 'credits package' for two days or thirty days, or twelve months of unlimited credits. The older newspapers (published over 107 years ago) are cheaper to view than more recent publications. Currently, you can search the archive from 1700 to 1949, but only a specific date range may be available for a particular title.

When you search the archive, the results give the name of publication, the date and a 'snippet' of the text at: www.britishnewspaperarchive.co.uk.

British History Online

Many Lancashire sources including the *Victoria History of the County of Lancaster*, records of bishops and higher clergy (*Fasti Ecclesiae Anglicanae*), a calendar of *Lancashire Assize Rolls 4 John–13 Edward I, Catalogue of Ancient Deeds* (at TNA), calendars of *Close Rolls* and *Inquisitions Post Mortems* (various reigns), the *Final Concords* ('feet of fines'), topographical dictionaries and much, much more at: www.british-history.ac.uk.

The *Guardian* and *Observer* Digital Archive

Issues of the *Guardian* 1791–2000. Free to search, but if you wish to read or print off an article in full, purchasing a 'day pass' allows you to download an unlimited number of articles for twenty-four hours at: http:/archive.guardian.co.uk.

Members of Manchester Libraries can access the *Guardian* digital archive free (you can join the library online).

London Gazette

This newspaper published legal notices, military promotions and gallantry awards. Search by name or date. If you find a published legal notice concerning one of your ancestors, you can download a free PDF of one page, or purchase a copy of the *Gazette* at: www.london-gazette.co.uk/search.

Internet Archive

Some transcriptions of Lancashire records published in the nineteenth century can be viewed online free, e.g., Preston Court Leet records, early parish registers for Pennington in Furness, Lancaster, Middleton etc., Roman Catholic registers (Catholic Record Society), Chetham Society publications (including heralds' visitations), LCRS publications such as the *Final Concords of the County of Lancaster* ('feet of fines'), and more. Try searches for 'Lancashire records' and 'Lancashire registers' at: www.archive.org.

Google Books
Digital copies of many thousands of books on Lancashire history and people, including some Chetham Society publications at: http://books.google.com.

Online Censuses, Parish Registers and More

Section D lists some free resources online including searchable transcripts of censuses, parish registers and BMD indexes. These databases are compiled by volunteers and only partial coverage of the county may be available, but they are certainly worth browsing if you are on a tight budget. Section E is a brief overview of subscription services offering access to censuses, parish registers and other records.

There are many titles in print that discuss information available online for family historians, such as Peter Christian, *The Genealogist's Internet* (TNA, 2009) and Chris Paton, *Tracing Your Family History on the Internet* (Pen & Sword, 2011).

If you have found your ancestor's address in the censuses or in parish records, and that street still exists, try using the 'Street View' facility on Google Maps to explore the general area at: http://maps.google.co.uk/intl/en/help/maps/streetview.

It could give you a tantalising glimpse of the places where your ancestors spent their childhood, did their shopping or carried on their business. Bear in mind that over the years, streets may have changed name, and buildings may have altered or disappeared altogether.

Lancashire has such a rich, varied and wonderful history that it has only been possible to give the reader a taster of the hundreds of resources available that could shed light on your family's life stories. Your journey into the past may be emotive and exciting, sometimes even frustrating, but there is always something new to discover about your Lancashire ancestors.

Part 2

RESEARCH GUIDE

A

ARCHIVES AND REPOSITORIES

This section is a directory of the most important archives and record offices holding materials relevant to Lancashire family history. Collections held by TNA are listed first. Every effort has been made to ensure that the archival materials and contact details listed below and in the following sections are as up to date as possible.

However, collections may have moved, or websites and contact details for archives may have changed since going to press. Some records may be held off-site and may require ordering several days in advance.

Whenever possible, check the record office catalogue online or contact the archive before travelling to ensure that the records you wish to consult are available. Most archives offer a research service (fee payable) if you are unable to visit the archive in person.

Many local record offices require you to have a CARN (County Archives Research Network) ticket to consult the collections; bring proof of identity on your first visit. Once issued, a CARN ticket can be used at any archive which is a member of the scheme. Please note that Liverpool Record Office is not a member of CARN. It issues its own reader's tickets but accepts a CARN ticket as partial proof of ID. A list of member archives is available on the CARN website at: www.archives.org.uk/general/county-archive-research-network-carn.html.

Cataloguing is an on-going process and many records may not yet be listed on catalogues online. If this is the case, try the Access to Archives (A2A) search engine (www.nationalarchives.gov.uk/a2a), but note it is no longer being updated.

The Accessions to Repositories database on the NRA index is an overview of records recently acquired by archives.

You can explore this database by year and by topic, e.g., 'religion' or 'transport' at: www.nationalarchives.gov.uk/accessions.

The ARCHON directory lists all archives and repositories, with contact details, in Britain and abroad with collections noted in the NRA index at: www.nationalarchives.gov.uk/archon.

The Archives Hub is a finding aid for specialist library and repository resources at: http://archiveshub.ac.uk.

Directory of Archives and Repositories

The National Archives

It is impossible to do justice to TNA's vast collections and only a brief overview is given here. You must have a reader's ticket to view original documents at TNA; identification is required (details on the website). A reader's ticket is not needed to view copies of documents on microfilm or microfiche such as census records.

The website has research guides on canal, railway, merchant shipping sources, labour history and many other subjects. The online catalogue gives a description of each record series at: www.nationalarchives.gov.uk/catalogue/default.asp. The new Discovery catalogue can be accessed at: http://discovery.nationalarchives.gov.uk.

Collections of Lancashire records at TNA are discussed in Walford D. Selby, *Lancashire and Cheshire Records Preserved in the Public Record Office* (Lancashire and Cheshire Record Society, Vols 7 and 8, 1882, 1883). These works are very out of date now but you may still find them a useful introduction.

Exchequer Records (E)

Clerical taxes: E 179, E 331–E 344, E 347. Justices of the Forest (eyres) records include plea rolls: E 32. Recusants' fines: E 372, E 376, E 377. Taxation records 1640–1822 include hearth taxes, lay subsidy rolls, poll taxes, pensions, land tax, estate taxes and much more for Lancashire: E 179. Sheriffs' accounts: E 199. Exchequer pipe rolls: E 372 (copies in E 352).

Series E 179 can be searched by date, location or type of document (surnames of people mentioned in the documents are not in the database) at: www.nationalarchives.gov.uk/e179/default.asp.

Duchy of Lancaster

The Duchy of Lancaster records (DL) contain over fifty series.

Court of Duchy Chamber

Pleadings: DL 1, DL 3–4. Entry books of decrees and orders (for equity pleadings): DL 5. Original affidavits, certificates, reports and petitions: DL 9. Sealed depositions (for equity pleadings): DL 48. Royal charters: DL 10. Duchy of Lancaster civil plea rolls 1351–1360: DL 35 and PL 15. Papers in lawsuits: DL 49. Online indexes with surnames available for some Duchy Chamber series.

Palatinate Records

The Palatinate records (PL) contain over fifty series.

Chancery patent rolls for 1380–1506 include grants, pardons, appointments and leases: PL 1. Chancery close rolls, which include orders to law officers, 1409–1470: PL 2 (see also DL 37). Court of Common Pleas 1400–1848 (many years missing): PL 15. Common pleas heard at Westminster 1361–1377, when the palatine had lapsed: CP 40. Feet of fines (final concords) for Lancashire 1377–1834: PL 17; feet of fines 1351–1377: CP 25.

Inquisitions post-mortem: PL 4, DL 7, WARD 7.

Crown Court of Duchy of Lancaster (mostly assize rolls) from 1422–1843: PL 25. Crown court indictment files and coroners' reports 1660–1867: PL 26. Crown court depositions for 1663–1867: PL 27.

Crown minute books 1686–1877 record the business of each court session, often with names of jurors, names of prisoners tried, their offences, verdicts and sentences: PL 28.

Series JUST 1 (English, French and Latin) contains plea rolls for the Palatinate and JUST 3 includes gaol delivery rolls for 1351–1361 (French and Latin). Records of appointments of sheriff of the county palatine 1684–1876: DL 21.

Assize records for the northern circuit (includes Lancashire after 1876): ASSI 51–52. Copies (estreats) of northern circuit assize records relating to fines and penalties 1843–1890: ASSI 46.

Northern circuit 'order books' detail sentences given by judges against convicts (name, offence and sentence) 1879–1924 (some years missing): ASSI 53. Northern circuit civil minute books 1877–1971 for civil cases referred to the local court by the High Court (nisi prius), give names of plaintiff, defendant and judge, date and location (many decades missing): ASSI 54.

Calendars of prisons and prison registers including Lancashire prisons 1770–1949 at: www.nationalarchives.gov.uk/records/looking-for-person/prisoners.htm.

Nonconformist registers (RG 4) includes Necropolis Burial Ground, Everton, Liverpool (1825–1837). Royalist Composition Papers: SP 23. Treason trials of Lancashire rebels in 1715 (Jacobite rebellion): KB 8/66. Returns of papists in Lancaster 1715–1716: KB 18.

National Land Company (Chartist) shareholders' register: BT 41/474/2659, BT 41/475/2659, BT 41/476/2659.

Our Online Records

Fee payable for most records. Death-duty registers: IR 26. PCC wills: PROB 11. Regimental diaries include wartime diary of Accrington Pals. Many First and Second World War records for servicemen and women available. Office of the Commander in Chief: Monthly Returns to the Adjutant General 1754–

Postcard of Heysham village, 1908.

1866: WO 17 (War Office). Royal Lancashire Volunteers Regiment 1779–1802: WO 17/237.

Copies of Liverpool Vestry Poor Law and workhouse records for 1834–1856 (MH 12) are free at: www.nationalarchives.gov.uk/records/our-online-records.htm.

Digital Microfilm Project (Free)
Fast broadband connection needed. Several series (unindexed) can be downloaded including Convict Transportation Registers HO 11; GRO indexes to foreign returns of BMDs RG 43; Register of Apprentices IR 1; PCC wills PROB 10 at: www.nationalarchives.gov.uk/records/digital-microfilm.htm.

Wills and Probate Records Guide
www.nationalarchives.gov.uk/records/research-guides/wills-and-probate-records.htm.

The National Archives, Kew, Richmond, Surrey, TW9 4DU; www.national archives.gov.uk; email contact form: www.nationalarchives.gov.uk/contact/form; tel: 0208 876 3444.

Ahmed Iqbal Ullah Race Relations Resource Centre, University of Manchester
Race and ethnic history library with an important oral history collection. Steve Cohen collection of memorabilia from anti-deportation and immigration campaigns in Manchester from the 1970s–1990s. Untold Histories resources.

Library catalogue at: www.racearchive.man.ac.uk.

Ahmed Iqbal Ullah Race Relations Resource Centre, The University of Manchester, J14, J Floor, Sackville Street Building, Sackville Street Area, M60 1QD; www.manchester.ac.uk/aboutus/ahmediqbal; email: rrarchive@manchester.ac.uk; tel: 0161 275 2920.

Archives+, Manchester Central Library

The new Archives+ facility is currently scheduled to open in early 2014. It will become the major centre for family history research in Manchester. Archives+ will be a 'one-stop shop' for family history researchers with archival materials, books, maps, online access and exhibitions. The city's records will be located in one building for the first time. The archive will form part of the redeveloped Manchester Central Library. Archives+ will be a partnership between Manchester Archives and Local Studies, GMCRO, MLFHS, Ahmed Iqbal Ullah Race Relations Resource Centre, North West Film Archive and British Film Institute Mediatheque. Check the website for updates to the archive's opening and contact details.

Archives+, St Peter's Square, Manchester, M2 5PD; www.manchester.gov.uk/libraries/arls.

Barclays Group Archives, Manchester

The archive serves the whole of Barclays Group. It cannot carry out blanket searches for names and there are only limited systematic name indexes for customers and employees. Searches can only be conducted if an enquirer can show that an ancestor worked for or banked with one of the constituent banks. Barclays did not have an important Lancashire presence until the mid-1900s but the archive has some records for Martins Bank (Head Office at Liverpool) and the Union Bank of Manchester (acquired by Barclays in 1919). These records include 'signature books': lists of names of account holders (sometimes with addresses and occupations). The directors' minutes of these banks (and smaller constituent banks) also contain names of customers (personal and business). Staff appointments and retirement records; some staff lists.

Letter of introduction or ID required to visit archive; appointments must be made in advance. Management records have a 30-year closure rule; for customer records the closure is 100 years.

Barclays Group Archives, Dallimore Road, Wythenshawe, Manchester, M23 9JA; http://group.barclays.com/about-barclays/about-us/our-history/barclays-group-archives; email: grouparchives@barclays.com; tel: 0161 946 3035.

Bolton Archives and Local Studies Service

Business archives, organizations, personal papers, e.g., Samuel Crompton & Co. records 1812–1823: ZCR. Bradford estate (Bridgeman family) records 1636–1898: ZBR.

Boyd's Marriage Index. Cemetery registers from 1856. Early censuses for Great Bolton 1811–1831. Censuses 1841–1901. Parish registers on microfilm. Trade/local directories from 1798. Burgess rolls 1838–1914, electoral registers from 1868, poll books for Bolton Parliamentary Borough (various dates). GRO index, IGI index, probate indexes. Rate books and valuation lists, school admission registers, workhouse registers (indexed). Bolton Borough quarter sessions records: QBO. Local authority records include Bolton County Borough, Bolton Metropolitan Borough, Farnworth Municipal Borough.

Archives and reserve stock only available some weekdays; check the website or contact Bolton History Centre to check availability before travelling.

Bolton Archives indexes at: www.boltonmuseums.org.uk/bolton-archives/archives-indexes.

Collections and images search at: www.boltonmuseums.org.uk/collections/collection-search.

Summary of Church of England parish registers (copies) at: www.bolton museums.org.uk/bolton-archives/archives-indexes/church-records/church-of-england-registers.

Roman Catholic registers at: www.boltonmuseums.org.uk/bolton-archives/archives-indexes/church-records/romancatholic-registers.

Nonconformist registers (some originals) at: www.boltonmuseums.org.uk/bolton-archives/archives-indexes/church-records/nonconformist-registers.

Bolton Archives and Local Studies Service, Bolton History Centre, Le Mans Crescent, Bolton, Lancashire, BL1 1SE; www.boltonmuseums.org.uk/bolton-archives; email: archives.library@bolton.gov.uk; tel: 0120 433 2185.

Borthwick Institute for Archives

Probate records and wills for the PCY, Dean and Chapter of York, and Exchequer Court of York from 1359–1858. Terriers for the archdeaconry of Richmond (Ter/W) and York peculiars (Ter/V). Library. Copies of probate records can be ordered. The institute can search for up to five individuals free of charge so long as the name of testator/testatrix, abode and date of death/probate/burial is supplied. The volume/folio number of the probate record is helpful but not always required. If the above information is not supplied, then a research service is available at a cost of £15 per half hour. Copying charge is £5 per entry for a registered paper or digital copy. Advanced booking to visit the archive is recommended.

Some probate records at Borthwick are indexed on Origins.net (see Section E).

Cause Papers Database of cases heard 1300–1858 in diocese of York church courts at: www.hrionline.ac.uk/causepapers.

Catalogues at: www.york.ac.uk/library/borthwick/catalogues.

Guide to archival holdings at: www.york.ac.uk/library/borthwick/catalogues/archival-holdings.

Guide to genealogical sources at: www.york.ac.uk/media/library/documents/borthwick/gensources.pdf.

Guide to York probate records at: www.york.ac.uk/media/library/documents/borthwick/3.1.1.20guideprob.pdf.

Guide to probate courts and jurisdictions at: www.york.ac.uk/library/borthwick/research-support/probate-courts.

Borthwick Institute for Archives, University of York, Heslington, York, YO10 5DD; www.york.ac.uk/library/borthwick; email: bihr500@york.ac.uk; tel: 0190 432 1166.

British Library
Large collection of books on Lancashire history. Manuscripts collection includes many deeds and charters relating to the county.

Family history guide at: www.bl.uk/familyhistory.html.

Manuscripts catalogue at: www.bl.uk/reshelp/findhelprestype/manu-scripts/msscatalogues/msscatalogues.html.

The British Library, St Pancras, 96 Euston Road, London, NW1 2DB; www.bl.uk; email: reader-services-enquiries@bl.uk; tel: 020 7412 7676.

Bury Archives Service
Bury Borough Magistrates and Bury Petty Sessions records 1872–1975, Bury Area Health Authority 1864–1973. Local government records. Family estate papers include Hutchinson family: FHU. Nonconformist registers. Trade-union records. School records.

Bury Archives catalogue at: http://archives.bury.gov.uk.

Bury Archives Service, Moss Street, Bury, BL9 0DR; www.bury.gov.uk/archives; email: archives@bury.gov.uk; archives tel: 0161 253 6782.

Cheshire and Chester Archives and Local Studies
The archive has major collections relating to Lancashire families; check the catalogue for Lancashire surnames and places. NB Some records catalogued on A2A, particularly the EDC series (consistory court records), lack correct date references. The archive's own catalogue is the best guide to its records.

Archdeaconry of Chester Records: Consistory Court books 1502–1976: ED. Marriage, wills and tithe cases: EDC 1. Court papers 1525–1860: EDC 5. Marriage Act books 1606–1945: EDC 7. Marriage bonds and allegations 1661–1979 for south Lancashire: EDC 8. Abstracts and indexes available.

The J. P. Earwaker collection has information on Lancashire families: ZCR 63. Shakerley family of Hulme papers from twelfth to twentieth century: DSS. Leicester-Warren papers for de Tabley family's Lancashire estates: DLT.

Lancashire County Asylum at Winwick records contains patient registers from 1897 (no case notes): NHW 3. Several Warrington-centred collections including solicitors' files such as Henry Greenall & Co.: DGR.

Catalogue search at: http://archive.cheshire.gov.uk.

Cheshire Archives and Local Studies Service, Cheshire Record Office, Duke Street, Chester, Cheshire, CH1 1RL; http://archives.cheshire.gov.uk; email: recordoffice@cheshiresharedservices.gov.uk; tel: 0124 497 2574.

Cumbria Record Offices
Cumbria Archives has four record offices: Barrow, Carlisle, Kendal and Whitehaven. Use A2A or the online catalogue CASCAT to search each office's collections at: www.cumbria.gov.uk/archives/default.asp and www.archiveweb.cumbria.gov.uk/CalmView/default.aspx.

Cumbria Archives, Barrow
Petty sessions, council records. Census returns for Furness and Cartmel areas. Records of Vickers Shipbuilding and Engineering Ltd include apprentices' registers and time books. Manor of Broughton-in-Furness records: BDBROUGHTON.

Parish records, leases and wills. Local newspapers, maps and photographs and 1911 'Domesday' valuation survey. Original bishop's transcripts for Furness (diocese of Carlisle).

Cumbria Archives and Local Studies Centre, Barrow, 140 Duke Street, Barrow-in-Furness, LA14 1XW; www.cumbria.gov.uk/archives/recordoffices/barec.asp; email: barrow.archives@cumbria.gov.uk; tel: 0122 940 7377.

Cumbria Archives, Carlisle
Parish, business, family, estate and mining papers relating to Lancashire.

Cumbria Archive Centre, Carlisle, Petteril Bank House, Petteril Bank Road, Carlisle, CA1 3AJ; www.cumbria.gov.uk/archives/recordoffices/carec.asp; email: carlisle.archives@cumbria.gov.uk; tel: 0122 822 7285 or 7284.

Cumbria Archives, Kendal
Parish registers for the Cartmel area (formerly in Lancashire north of the Sands).

Probate records (deaneries of Kendal and Furness), and Carlisle Consistory Court (1536–1860). LPRS Transcripts.

Cumbria Archive Centre Kendal, County Offices, Kendal, LA9 4RQ; www. cumbria.gov.uk/archives/recordoffices/knrec.asp; email: kendal.archives @cumbria.gov.uk; tel: 0153 971 3540 or 3539.

Cumbria Archives, Whitehaven
Estate, family, manorial, mining, property and other records relating to Lancashire.

Cumbria Archive and Local Studies Centre Whitehaven, Scotch Street, Whitehaven, CA28 7NL; www.cumbria.gov.uk/archives/recordoffices/ whrec.asp; email: whitehaven.archives@cumbria.gov.uk; tel: 0194 650 6420.

Duchy of Lancaster Office
NB The Duchy reserves the right to make a time charge with respect to enquiries requiring research into Duchy records. Information about the records and charters can be found at: www.duchyoflancaster.com/about-the-duchy/records-charters.

The Duchy of Lancaster, 1 Lancaster Place, Strand, London, WC2E 7ED; www.duchyoflancaster.com; email: info@duchyoflancaster.co.uk.

Duchy of Lancaster Solicitor's Office
The Duchy Solicitor administers the assets of people who die intestate (without a will) in Lancashire, Greater Manchester, Merseyside and Furness. If you wish to discover if the Duchy is dealing with the estate of a relative who died intestate (only within the county palatine), you must write to the Duchy Solicitor with a simple family tree showing your relationship to the deceased.

Solicitor for the Affairs of the Duchy of Lancaster, Farrer & Co., 66 Lincoln's Inn Fields, London, WC2A 3LH; www.farrer.co.uk; tel: 0207 242 2022.

Guildhall Library
Sun Fire Office insurance records.

Guildhall Library, Aldermanbury, London, EC2V 7HH; www.cityoflondon. gov.uk/Corporation/LGNL_Services/Leisure_and_culture/Libraries/City_ of_London_libraries/guildhall_lib.htm; email: guildhall.library@cityoflondon. gov.uk; tel: 0207 332 1868.

Independent Methodist Archives, Wigan

Church records include minute books, account books, completed baptism, marriage and membership records, old photographs and memorabilia.

Independent Methodist Churches Registered Office and Resource Centre, Fleet Street, Pemberton, Wigan, WN5 0DS; www.imcgb.org.uk; email: resourcecentre@imcgb.org.uk; tel: enquiries for archivist John Dolan 0192 548 6380; to arrange a visit phone Andrew Rigby, Connexional Services Manager 0194 222 3526.

Institution of Civil Engineers Library

Important and extensive collection of archives and books on civil engineering history: engineers' reports and drawings, diaries, letters, etc. An appointment is needed to visit the archive.

Guide to the archives at: www.ice.org.uk/Information-resources/Document-Library/Archives-guide.

Library at: www.ice.org.uk/Library.

Virtual Library at: www.icevirtuallibrary.com.

Archivist Mrs Carol Morgan, Archives, Institution of Civil Engineers, 1 Great George Street, Westminster, SW1P 3AA; www.ice.org.uk/topics/historical engineering/Archives; email: archive@ice.org.uk or carol.morgan@ice.org. uk; tel: 0207 665 2043.

Labour History Archive and Local Study Centre, People's History Museum

The museum has exhibitions on the history of Britain's workers. Major collection of historic trade-union and political banners.

Important repository for the archives of working class organizations from the Chartists to New Labour, including the Labour Party and Communist Party of Great Britain. Personal papers of politicians, writers, activists and more. Visits to the archive by appointment.

The website has guides to the collections on the British Union of Fascists, early industrial Manchester, the 1984–1985 miners' strike, general elections, Spanish Civil War, Chartism and women's suffrage at: www.phm.org.uk/archive-study-centre/subjects-covered.

Labour History Archive and Local Study Centre, People's History Museum, Left Bank, Spinningfields, Manchester, M3 3ER; archive www.phm.org.uk/archive-study-centre; museum www.phm.org.uk; archive email: archive @phm.org.uk; museum email: info@phm.org.uk; archive tel: 0161 838 9190; museum tel: 0161 838 9190.

Lancashire Record Office

Only a brief overview of the archive's vast collections can be given here. Reginald Sharpe France, *Guide to the Lancashire Record Office* (Lancashire County Library, 1985) and *Guide to the Lancashire Record Office Supplement 1977–1989*, ed. Janet D. Martin (Lancashire County Library, 1992) are helpful resources. The leaflets *Family History For All* (a beginner's guide on the website) and *Finding folk: a handlist of basic sources for family history in the Lancashire Record Office* (LRO, 2000) may also be useful.

Local government records: Lancashire County Council and district and parish councils, and their predecessors. Electoral registers: EL. Borough of Preston records include Guild Merchant rolls: CNP. Preston County Borough Council records include electoral registers: CBP.

Quarter Sessions 1583–1999: Q. Petty sessions 1583–1972: QS. Calendars of prisoners tried at quarter sessions and assizes 1801–1967: QJC. Coroners' records. Freeholders' lists (those qualified to serve on juries) give name, address and occupation for 1696–1832: QDF. Land-tax assessments: QDL.

Censuses up to 1901. Poor Law Unions and turnpike trusts. Probate registry records for 1858–1940: W/L. School records, including log books and admissions registers.

Maps and plans include tithe, enclosure and estate plans.

Palatinate records 1664–twentieth century: PPLC. Assize rolls (Duchy of Lancaster) for 1664, 1667–1669 and 1672–1673: PPLC 2/1–6. Chancery records: PPLC/3. Palatine assize rolls: DDCM/1.

Family Collections

Manors of Blackburn, and Halton: DDCM. Wills proved in manor of Halton: DDCM/8/1. Hesketh of Rufford c. 1200–1930: DDHE. The manors in the Honour of Clitheroe have been indexed: DDHCL. Hawkshead-Talbot of Chorley 1274–1966: DDHK. Stanley of Knowsley (Earls of Derby) estate papers: DDK.

Kenyon of Peel family papers 1319–1960 include quarter session, sheriff and assize records, and hearth-tax returns: DDKE. Kay-Shuttleworth estate papers: DDKS. Molyneux family (Earls of Sefton) estate papers include manorial records: DDM. Manor of Accrington: DDTO.

De Trafford of Trafford papers, dating from the twelfth–twentieth centuries, include the manors of Barton, Mawdesley and Stretford: DDTR.

Church Records

Records of Anglican parish registers: baptisms, marriages and burials, BTs and MIs. No Bolton-area parish registers except St Katherine's Church, Blackrod. Wills and probate records for the archdeaconries of Chester and Richmond before 1858: W and W/RW. Marriage bonds and allegations for western deaneries of archdeaconry of Richmond for 1615, 1633–1634, 1636,

141

1642, 1648–1854 and 1861: ARR/11. Nonconformist registers: indexed transcripts of some registers, microfilm copies and registers for post-1974 county. Roman Catholic registers for Lancaster, Liverpool and Salford dioceses except where kept at original parish; transcripts and indexes.

Industry records include NCB records: NC. Lancashire and Cheshire miners' welfare committee, colliery doctors' certificates, etc. W. and J. Foster Limited, knitting-machine manufacturers, Preston 1862–1961: DDX 438. Lancashire Football Association 1878–1965: DDX 2708.

The website has research guides on 'Black and Asian History', 'Diaries and Journals', 'Cinemas', 'Militia and Volunteers' (1757 onwards), 'Preston Guild Merchant', 'Theatre and Performance' and 'World War Two' records. 'Cemeteries and Crematoria' Guide details location of records (most are kept at cemetery/crematoria offices) and copies kept at the record office. In-depth community history guides to its holdings on Blackburn with Darwen, Blackpool, Burnley and Pendle.

Online Guide to Lancashire Local Studies and Family History Collections at: www.lancashire.gov.uk/libraries/services/local/guideie.asp.

Online catalogue LANCAT at: http://archivecat.lancashire.gov.uk/calm view.

For the Local Studies library at LRO, use the Lancashire Libraries catalogue at: http://lclcat.lancashire.gov.uk/TalisPrism.

Police Officers Surname Search (Lancashire Constabulary) 1840–1925 at: www.lancashire.gov.uk/education/record_office/records/policesearch.asp.

Lancashire Record Office, Bow Lane, Preston, Lancashire, PR1 2RE; www.lancashire.gov.uk; email: record.office@lancashire.gov.uk; tel: 0177 253 3039.

Lichfield Record Office
Diocese of Lichfield records include south Lancashire before 1540.

Lichfield Record Office, The Friary, Lichfield, WS13 6QG; www.staffordshire.gov.uk/leisure/archives/contact/LichfieldRecordOffice/home.aspx; email: lichfield.record.office@staffordshire.gov.uk; tel: 0154 351 0720.

Liverpool Cathedral Archives
Collection relates to the building and history of the cathedral. Personal access to the collection is not always possible, but the archivist welcomes queries by email and telephone, especially if family members had historic links to the cathedral.

Canon Val Jackson, Liverpool Cathedral Archive Enquiries, St James' House, 20 St James Road, Liverpool, L1 7BY; www.liverpoolcathedral.org.

uk/about/cathedral/cathedral-archives.aspx; email: valjackson@liverpool
cathedral.org.uk; tel: 0151 702 7227.

Liverpool Record Office
Durning and Holt family papers: 920 DUR. Edmund Kirby & Sons,
architects and surveyors: 720 KIR. Molyneux of Sefton family papers
including diaries 1815–1953: 920 SEF. Nicholson papers: 920 NIC. Plumbe
Tempest deeds and papers: 920 PLU. Salisbury manuscripts include manors
of Childwall, Little Woolton, Much Woolton, West Derby, Everton and
Wavertree: 920 SAL. Speke estate records: 920 SPE. Papers of the Stanley
family, Earls of Derby: 920 DER. Quarter sessions court records (1724–1956)
including calendars of prisoners (1882 onwards): 347 QUA.

Council corporation archives including minute books from 1550, school
records, cemetery registers. Roman Catholic registers include city of Liverpool.
Nonconformist archives, Church of England parish registers (some only
available on microfilm). Jewish synagogue registers. Business records include
Imperial Tobacco Company, Ogden branch. Community archives, including
the Merseyside Jewish community. Photographic collections.

Liverpool Central Library is closed until spring 2013; a temporary archive
service is available at Wellington Employment Park (former Merseyside
Record Office). Some family history materials are available at the World
Museum. Online archive catalogue (follow the link from the 'Libraries and
Archives' page on the website). Check the website for updates to services
and location of holdings.

Liverpool in Print, an online catalogue of local studies collection held by
Liverpool Record Office, available at: www.liverpoolinprint.org.uk.

Temporary archives service at former Merseyside Record Office: Unit 33,
Wellington Employment Park South, Dunes Way, L5 9RJ; http://liverpool.
gov.uk/libraries-and-archives/archive-satellite-service.aspx; email: archives
@liverpool.gov.uk; tel: 0151 233 5817.

Temporary service: Horseshoe Gallery, World Museum, William Brown
Street, L3 8EN.

Permanent address: Liverpool Record Office, Central Library, William
Brown Street, Liverpool, L3 8EW; www.liverpool.gov.uk/libraries-and-
archives/archives-local-and-family-history.

London Metropolitan Archives
Trades Union Congress archive. Lloyd's Captains' Registers 1869–1947.

London Metropolitan Archives, 40 Northampton Road, Clerkenwell, London,
EC1R 0HB; www.cityoflondon.gov.uk/lma; email: ask.lma@cityoflondon.
gov.uk; tel: 0207 332 3820.

Manchester Archives and Local Studies, Central Library

Closed for refurbishment until early 2014 when the new Archives+ facility opens. Archive materials currently available at Greater Manchester Record Office by appointment only (see below).

Family history materials on microfilm and reference books available at the Manchester Room@City Library (see Section B). Check website for current contact details, updates to services and location of holdings.

Manchester Central Library, St Peter's Square, Manchester, M2 5PD; www.manchester.gov.uk/libraries/arls; email: libraries@manchester.gov.uk Manchester.

Greater Manchester County Record Office (with Manchester Archives)

Family and estate papers including Asshetons of Middleton (some manorial papers): E7. Egertons of Heaton Hall: E4. Leghs of Lyme Hall: E17. Entwistles of Foxholes: E.FOX.

Business records. Manchester Ship Canal collection includes minute books, financial records, accident registers, cash books, etc.: B10. Calico Printer's Association. Coroners' records (1851–1852, limited collection). Quarter sessions for City of Manchester. Parish registers not available on microfilm, including Methodist records.

Societies' records include Manchester Chamber of Commerce. Jewish records including Manchester Jewish Refugees Committee. Manchester City Council records. Political records include women's suffrage, Manchester Communist Party. Trade-union records. Hospital records. Poor Law and workhouse collection includes industrial schools and Withington Hospital. National Probate index from 1930–1959 as hard copy. Manchester rate books 1902–1956/7. School records include Manchester Grammar: M516. Borough/City of Manchester Quarter Sessions Court: M116. Calendars of Prisoners tried at Lancashire Quarter Sessions (Hundred of Salford) 1821–1840: L27. 1910 Land Tax Valuation Registers: A11. Photographic archive.

GMCRO with Manchester Archives will move to Archives+, Manchester Central Library in early 2014. An appointment is needed to consult archive collections. Some materials are held off-site and at least two weeks' notice may be required.

Greater Manchester Past Finder

The Past Finder project comprises the Bolton, Bury, Manchester, Oldham, Rochdale, Salford, Stockport, Tameside, Trafford, Wigan councils and GMCRO. This searchable database has details of over 4,000 archive collections held by these bodies and can be accessed at: www.dswebhosting. info/Manchester.

Greater Manchester County Record Office, 56 Marshall Street, New Cross, Manchester M4 5FU; www.manchester.gov.uk/libraries/arls; email: archives localstudies@manchester.gov.uk; tel: 0161 832 5284.

Manchester Cathedral Archives

Parochial records include the parish registers from 1573 onwards. (NB The cathedral parish registers are available on microfilm at the Manchester Room@City Library). Banns books. Churchwardens' accounts. Sextons' registers 1732–1848: the registers from 1753 onwards often give age of deceased and cause of death.

The 'Capitular Records' relate to the Dean and Canons and their predecessors: the Warden and Fellows of the Collegiate Church. These papers, dated 1361 to the twenty-first century, include financial records, title deeds, estate records, tithe leases and maps, estate maps and plans, surveys from 1649 and more. Records of the manor court of Newton 1530–1919.

Commonwealth Survey of 1649: Mancath/2/A/3/1.

Use A2A to explore the cathedral's collections.

At least one week's notice is required to access items from the collections, which are produced for viewing at Chetham's Library; contact Michael Powell, the cathedral's Honorary Archivist, at Chetham's Library (see Section B).

Copy certificates of parish registers can be ordered from the cathedral. You must provide a date and name for the register entry you wish to order; send a sae and cheque to the cathedral (payment details are on its website).

Family history and parish register enquiries (no other collections enquiries) should be addressed to: Archives Assistant, Manchester Cathedral, Victoria Street, Manchester, M3 1SX; www.manchestercathedral.org/history/archives; archives@manchestercathedral.org.

Merseyside Maritime Museum Archive and Library, Liverpool

The museum has displays on emigration, smuggling, ships and shipping companies, great ocean liners, including the *Titanic*, the Battle of the Atlantic and more.

Collections relating to the area's maritime history. Records of the Mersey Docks & Harbour Co., many shipping companies, merchants, slave traders, shipping and trade associations, ship-building, seamen's charities, etc.

Family papers include collections on the Earles (slave traders): D/EARLE, the Croppers (abolitionists): D/CR. Danson family. William Davenport (slaver) letter books, wage books, correspondence and miscellaneous papers 1747–1834: D:DAV. The Crosbie-Oates archive is another important genealogical collection relating to the West African palm oil trade. Liverpool shipping registers formerly kept at Customs House (indexes available): C/EX. Non-maritime business and industry collections. Copies of King's (Liverpool) Regiment Battalion Diaries for the First World War.

An appointment may be needed to view collections; some collections are held off-site.

The museum's website has many online guides.

Major collections: www.liverpoolmuseums.org.uk/maritime/archive/majorcollections.aspx.

Maritime Archives & Library, Merseyside Maritime Museum, Albert Dock, Liverpool, L3 4AQ; www.liverpoolmuseums.org.uk/maritime/archive; email form: www.liverpoolmuseums.org.uk/about/contact/maritimearchives enquiry.aspx; tel: 0151 478 4499.

Museum of Science and Industry, Manchester

Working mill engines, textile machinery demonstrations, transport history.

The museum's Collections Centre has a study area and reference library. Archive holdings include materials for the Calico Printers Association, Electricity Council. Mather & Platt business records, Paterson Zochonis, Beyer, Peacock & Co., Ferranti, Metropolitan-Vickers, Linotype & Machinery Co. Ltd, factory records, company minute books, photographs, trade directories, textile samples and designs. Lancashire and Cheshire Miners Federation, Alexandra colliery branch subscription book 1931–1936: U221. Oral histories online collection has mill workers' stories at: www.mosi.org. uk/collections/explore-the-collections/oral-histories-online.

Collections Department, Museum of Science & Industry, Liverpool Road, Castlefield, Manchester, M3 4FP; www.mosi.org.uk/collections/using-the-collections/using-the-archives.aspx; email: collections@mosi.org.uk; Collections Centre tel: 0161 606 0127; Museum tel: 0161 832 2244.

National Co-operative Archive, Manchester

Original records of national co-operative organizations and societies which now form part of the Northern Region of the Co-operative Retail Services, and more. Records of some smaller co-operative societies, and Co-operative Women's Guild (Lancashire Region). Periodicals, books, pamphlets, photographs, films. Society histories include Failsworth Industrial Society. Personal papers of eminent people involved in the movement such as Robert Owen and Edward Owen Greening. National Co-operative Film Archive. Visitors by appointment only.

The archive's catalogues can be explored on the Archives Hub at: http://archiveshub.ac.uk.

Female weaver 'kissing the shuttle' at the factory of Messrs Barlow and Jones, Bolton and Manchester. The weaver sucked the end of a cotton thread through the side of the wooden shuttle so it could be placed into the loom to continue weaving. Oil on the shuttle transferred to the mouth often caused mouth and lip cancers. (Film still NWFA 37 © North West Film Archive, Manchester Metropolitan University)

Some clips from the Film Archive can be viewed online at: www.co-op. ac.uk/our-heritage/national-co-operative-archive/collections/national-co-operative-film-archive.

National Co-operative Archive, Holyoake House, Hanover Street, Manchester, M60 0AS; www.co-op.ac.uk/our-heritage/national-co-operative-archive; email: archive@co-op.ac.uk; tel: 0161 246 2945 or 2937.

National Union of Mineworkers
Appointment needed to consult records.

National Union of Mineworkers Office, 2 Huddersfield Road, Barnsley, South Yorkshire, S70 2LS; www.num.org.uk; tel: 0122 628 4006.

North West Film Archive
The archive holds over 35,000 items of film and video. The collection includes cinema newsreels, documentaries, advertising and promotional

material, educational and travel films, and home movies. Themes covered include work and local industry, leisure, sport and entertainment, local traditions and community activities, transport, housing and wartime experiences. It is not yet possible to view the main collection online, although a very small collection of 'taster' clips can be seen at: www.media.mmu.ac.uk/nwfa25.

You can explore and view the collection of films made by Burnley filmmaker Sam Hanna, and the BBC North West Collection 1966–1986, from the archive's home page (try a different Internet browser if you cannot run the clips).

Researchers are welcome to visit the archive and view the collections by appointment to ensure availability of material.

The archive will relocate to Manchester's new Archives+ facility at the Central Library in early 2014.

North West Film Archive, Manchester Metropolitan University, Minshull House, 47–49 Chorlton Street, Manchester, M1 3EU; www.nwfa.mmu.ac.uk; email: n.w.filmarchive@mmu.ac.uk; tel: 0161 247 3097.

North West Sound Archive

Memories of mill workers, coal miners and other workers. BBC Radio Lancashire and BBC Radio Manchester collections. Interviews with prisoners at Manchester's Strangeways Prison. Bolton Oral History Survey, Manchester Jewish Oral History and many more oral records of north-west England.

An appointment is necessary to visit the archive and listen to recordings. Many items from the collection may be borrowed.

North West Sound Archive, Old Steward's Office, Clitheroe Castle, Clitheroe, Lancashire, BB7 1AZ; www.lancashire.gov.uk; email: nwsa@ed.lancscc.gov.uk; tel: 0120 042 7897.

Salford Diocesan Archives (Roman Catholic)

Private archive. Diocesan records from 1850 onwards (no parish registers) includes minute books, property deed index. Some educational records (very few admission registers). Photographic collection. Contact the archivist Fr David Lannon if you wish to consult the collection or library.

Guide to the archive's collection at: www.churches-online.org.uk/salford archives/Resources/SDADescription.pdf.

St Augustine's Presbytery, Grosvenor Square, All Saints, Manchester, M15 6BW; www.churches-online.org.uk/salfordarchives; email: davelannon@aol.com; tel: 0161 236 6762.

Salford City Archives

Extensive Bridgewater Estates Collection (BW) from the fifteenth to the nineteenth centuries. James Nasmyth collection (U312). Salford City collection. Poor relief records.

Readers wishing to access the collection are advised to check its catalogue via A2A portal first and specify a catalogue number and the item they wish to view before contacting archivist Roseanne McLaughlin to make an appointment.

Salford Local History Library, which has family history material including census returns, is also housed within the same building (no appointment needed).

Salford City Archives, Salford Museum and Art Gallery, Peel Park, The Crescent, Salford, M5 4WU; www.salford.gov.uk/lhlibrary.htm; genealogical sources www.salford.gov.uk/genealogy.htm; archive email: roseanne. mclaughlin@salford.gov.uk; library email: local.history@salford.gov.uk archives; tel: 0161 778 0810; library tel: 0161 778 0810.

Sedbergh School Archive and Heritage Centre

History of Sedbergh School; collection includes documents from 1527 to modern times. Photographs, diaries, registers, etc. An appointment is needed.

The Archivist, Sedbergh School Archive and Heritage Centre, Back Lane, Sedbergh, Cumbria, LA10 5BX; www.sedberghschool.org/the-archive-a-heritage-centre.html; email: ki@sedberghschool.org; tel: 0153 962 2275.

Santander Group Archives, Bootle

Records of Girobank PLC 1965–1979. (NB Records of Alliance & Leicester PLC, its predecessors and subsidiaries from 1853–1997 are not currently open for inspection.)

Santander Group Archives, Room SL2, Santander Bootle HQ, Bridle Road, Bootle, L30 4GB; email archivist Roy Steers: Roy.Steers@Santander.co.uk; tel: 0151 966 2699.

Staffordshire Record Office

www.staffordshire.gov.uk/leisure/archives/contact/sro/home.aspx.

Stonyhurst College Archives

Records of the school's history and former pupils. The libraries have important collections on recusants and biographies of recusant families. Researchers wishing to consult the collections should contact the archivist or library curator.

Stonyhurst College, Stonyhurst, Clitheroe, Lancashire, BB7 9PZ; www.
stonyhurst.ac.uk; archivist David Knight email: d.knight@stonyhurst.ac.uk;
library curator Mrs Jan Graffius: j.graffius@stonyhurst.ac.uk; tel: 0125 482
6345.

Tameside Local Studies and Archives

Records for boroughs of Ashton-under-Lyne and Mossley, and Audenshaw,
Denton and Droylsden Urban District Councils (UDCs), and predecessor
authorities. Business records, school records, trade-union records, etc.
Parish registers on microfilm. Manchester Regiment Archive.

Guide to family history materials at: www.tameside.gov.uk/family
history/archives/material.

Guide to Absent Voters' Lists at: www.tameside.gov.uk/archives/absent
voters.

Search Tameside burial records at: http://public.tameside.gov.uk/candc/
regenq.asp.

Tameside Local Studies and Archives Centre, Central Library, Old Street,
Ashton-under-Lyne, OL6 7SG; www.tameside.gov.uk/archives; tel: 0161
342 4242.

Waterways Archive, Ellesmere Port

Formerly the David Owen Waterways Archive. Company records, waterways staff records, library, photographic collection and more. Booking is
required to visit the archive.

The Waterways Archive (Ellesmere Port), South Pier Road, Ellesmere Port,
Cheshire, CH65 4FW; http://nwm.org.uk/TheWaterwaysArchive.html;
email: Linda.Barley@thewaterwaystrust.org.uk; tel: 0151 373 4378.

West Yorkshire Archives Service

The main archives are at Wakefield, with four sister sites at Bradford,
Calderdale (Halifax), Kirklees (Huddersfield) and Leeds. Medieval records
for Lancashire include manorial court rolls (Leeds office). Wakefield office
has the British Waterways Northern Region collection (C.299) including
the Lancaster Canal, Leeds and Liverpool Canal Co., and more. Wakefield
office has archdeaconry of Richmond probate records indexes on microfilm;
Leeds office has a card index and manuscript index. Bishop's transcripts on
microfilm at Calderdale include Todmorden.

West Yorkshire Archive Service, Registry of Deeds, Newstead Road,
Wakefield, WF1 2DE; www.archives.wyjs.org.uk; email: wakefield@wyjs.
org.uk; tel: 0192 430 5980.

Wigan Archives Service

Standish family papers include eighteenth-century correspondence: DD/St. Also papers relating to the Jacobite Plot or Standish Plot, of the 1690s. Andertons of Ince collection includes Civil War papers: DD/An. Crawford collection has records of the Haigh Estate in the nineteenth and early twentieth centuries: DD/Hai. Census of Wigan township 1765: TR/Ath/F/5. Lancashire and Cheshire Miners' Federation records 1912–1949. Transcripts of 1811 census for Wigan.

The archive is the diocesan record office for the thirty-seven parishes (deaneries of Wigan and Winwick) in the diocese of Liverpool. Parish registers available to view on microfilm.

Borough of Wigan records include burgess lists and court leet. Quarter sessions records include session rolls, calendars of prisoners, case papers and recorder's notebooks 1733–1972: QS.

The archives are located in Leigh Town Hall, but parish registers on microfilm can be viewed at Leigh Library (0194 240 4559) or the Museum of Wigan Life, formerly Wigan History Shop (0194 282 8020).

Family historians should first contact the Museum of Wigan Life or Leigh Library by telephone or via the email address below. An appointment is needed to view records at the archives.

Pennington township tax assessment 1791 at: www.wlct.org/heritage-services/archive-collections.htm.

Wigan Canal Boats Registers at: http://bit.ly/xFjJf0.

Wigan Poor Law Union Vaccination Register 1899–1909 at: www.wlct.org/heritage-services/gwi155.pdf.

Wigan Archive Collections guide at: www.wlct.org/heritage-services/archive-collections.htm.

The catalogue can be explored using the Greater Manchester Past Finder database.

Archivist: Alex Miller, Wigan Archive Service, Town Hall, Leigh, Lancashire, WN7 1DY; www.wlct.org/heritage-services/wigan-archives-service.htm; email: heritage@wlct.org; Wigan Archives tel: 0194 240 4430.

Working Class Movement Library

Library reading room open by appointment only.

Working Class Movement Library, 51 The Crescent, Salford, M5 4WX; www.wcml.org.uk; tel: 0161 736 3601.

York Minster Library

Records of the Dean and Chapter of York include probate registers 1321–1558 and probate Act books 1559–1636 and 1665–1673.

An appointment, and a reader's ticket, are necessary to access the records and manuscripts. Further information about the records may be found at: www.yorkminster.org/learning/the-historic-collections.

The Old Palace, Dean's Park, York, YO1 7JQ; www.yorkminster.org/learning/the-historic-collections; email: petery@yorkminster.org; tel: 0844 939 0021 (ext. 2520).

Yorkshire Archaeological Society (YAS)
Genealogical notes and pedigrees relating to Lancashire families. Grantley collection (Norton family) includes Lancashire deeds: DD53. Deeds relating to Saddleworth for eighteenth and nineteenth centuries: DD75. Medieval documents relating to Salford Hundred: see YAS Vol. 56 MD 102. Bradfer-Lawrence collection includes Lancashire deeds: MD335. Middelton of Stockeld papers for twelfth to nineteenth centuries (MD59) and Anne of Burghwallis (MD218) collection for thirteenth to nineteenth centuries include Lancashire estates.

Copies of LPRS publications. Online catalogues.

Yorkshire Archaeological Society Library and Archives, Claremont, 23 Clarendon Road, Leeds, Yorkshire, LS2 9NZ; www.yas.org.uk/content/archives.html; email: yas.archive@googlemail.com; library tel: 0113 245 7910.

University Libraries

Centre for North West Regional Studies
Elizabeth Roberts Archive: oral histories of Barrow, Lancaster and Preston, and on everyday life. Lune Valley Architectural Survey (photographic collection). Penny Summerfield Childhood and Schooling Archive (Lancashire oral histories 1910–1950). Muriel Humphries Inghamite Archive. Slaidburn Oral History Archive. 'Now the War is Over' – transcripts and tapes of BBC programme. Aldcliffe History Archive. Some subject indexes for the archives are available on the website. An appointment is needed to consult the archives.

Centre for North West Regional Studies, Lancaster University, Fylde College, Lancaster, LA1 4YF; www.lancs.ac.uk/depts/cnwrs; email Centre Administrator Christine Wilkinson: christine.wilkinson@lancs.ac.uk; tel: 0152 459 3770.

John Rylands Library
Library's Special Collections include records of companies, business associations, trade unions, charities, religious institutions, etc. Local family papers

include the Byrom family, Jevons family and more. Estate records, charts and deeds. *Manchester Guardian* archive.

The library is also home to the Methodist Archives and Research Centre, the largest collection of Methodist Connexional records in Britain, including personal papers and other records of ministers.

Members of the public are permitted to visit the library three times, after which they must apply for external membership, for which there is a fee.

A to Z list of the library's special collections at: www.library.manchester. ac.uk/searchresources/guidetospecialcollections/atoz.

The John Rylands Library, 150 Deansgate, Manchester, M3 3EH; www. library.manchester.ac.uk; contact the library: www.library.manchester. ac.uk/aboutus/contact; Special Collections email: jrul.special-collections @manchester.ac.uk; tel: 0161 275 3764; Methodist archive enquiries email: peter.nockles@manchester.ac.uk; tel: 0161 275 3755.

Keele University Library
Raymond Richards Collection has several important collections: the Hatton Wood Collection includes medieval deeds relating to Lancashire, and the William Davenport & Co. Collection (Liverpool slave-trading firm).

Special collections and archives at: www.keele.ac.uk/library/specarc.

Helen Burton (Miss), Special Collections and Archives Administrator, The Library, Keele University, Staffordshire, ST5 5BG; www.keele.ac.uk/library; email: h.burton@lib.keele.ac.uk; tel: 0178 273 3237.

Lancaster University
Special Collections include Lancashire Textiles Project (oral histories of cotton-spinning mills). Austin Langshaw Archive (Austin and Langshaw family papers). An appointment is needed to visit the archive.

The Library, Lancaster University, Lancaster, LA1 4YH; http://lancaster. libguides.com/specialcollections; email: librba@lancaster.ac.uk; tel: 0152 459 2544.

University of Liverpool
Collection on the Norris family of Speke Hall, Lancashire, c. 1220–1637.

Widnes Halmote rolls: 1 copy of court roll, 1748, and 76 rolls recording surrenders, admittances and enfranchisements, 1799–1863. Family and business records of the Rathbone family of Liverpool. David Owen (politician) papers. Gypsy Lore Society collection.

Norris Collection online catalogue at: http://bit.ly/xiaM44.

Special Collections & Archives, Sydney Jones Library, The University of Liverpool, PO Box 123, L69 3DA; http://sca.lib.liv.ac.uk/collections; email: mwatry@liv.ac.uk; tel: 0151 794 2696.

Manchester Metropolitan University

The university's special collections include book illustration and textile design, the Manchester Society of Architects' Library and the North West Film Archive (see above). Free admission to the reading room; contact the archivist in advance.

Special Collections, Sir Kenneth Green Library, All Saints, Manchester, M15 6BH; www.specialcollections.mmu.ac.uk/collections.php; email: lib-spec-coll @mmu.ac.uk; tel: 0161 247 6107.

Oxford University, Bodleian Library

Cartulary of Sir John le Byron of Clayton in Droylsden, Lancashire (Black Book of Clayton): Catalogue No.: 11808, Shelfmark: MS. Rawl. B. 460.
   A reader's ticket is needed to consult library collections.

Main Enquiry Desk, Bodleian Library, Broad Street, Oxford OX1 3BG; www.bodleian.ox.ac.uk; email: reader.services@bodleian.ox.ac.uk; tel: 0186 527 7162.

University of Salford Library

Playwright Arthur Hopcraft papers: AHP. Bartington Hall papers: BAR. Bridgewater Estates Archive: BEA. Richard Badnall papers. Duke of Bridge-water Archive: DBA. Bridgewater collection includes manorial records Worsley 1581–1888; Hulton 1599–1888; Bedford 1802–1888; Cadishead 1859–1888: BW/M. Salford Grammar School records including admission registers: SGS. Salford Royal Technical Institute and Royal Technical College records: RTI.

   Some collections, including the photographic collection, have been digitized and put online, Salford Archives Repository Collection at: http:// usir.salford.ac.uk/archives/.

   Visits by appointment only. To arrange a visit, or for archive queries, email Ian Johnston.

Clifford Whitworth Library, The Library, The University of Salford, The University of Salford, The Crescent, Salford, M5 4WT; www.library.salford. ac.uk/resources/special; archive email: I.Johnston@salford.ac.uk: library email: library@salford.ac.uk; archive tel: 0161 295 6650; library tel: 0161 295 2444.

University of Warwick Library

Employers' associations, trade associations, trade-union records for different industries. Union records do not necessarily include membership registers. Trades Union Congress archive.

Transport and General Workers Union archive (includes National Transport Federation records): MSS 126. Friendly Society of Iron Founders of England, Ireland and Wales: FSIF. Readers should contact the Centre before visiting to check availability.

Business history sources at: www2.warwick.ac.uk/services/library/mrc/explorefurther/subject_guides/business.

Family history guide at: www2.warwick.ac.uk/services/library/mrc/explorefurther/subject_guides/family_history.

Occupational guide to trade unions at: www2.warwick.ac.uk/services/library/mrc/explorefurther/subject_guides/family_history/occupational guide.pdf.

TGWU catalogue at: www2.warwick.ac.uk/services/library/mrc/images/tgwu.

Modern Records Centre, University Library, University of Warwick Coventry, CV4 7AL; www2.warwick.ac.uk/services/library/mrc/holdings/main_archives; email: archives@warwick.ac.uk; tel: 0247 652 4219.

Miscellaneous

Cornucopia at: www.cornucopia.org.uk/html.

North West Regional Archives Council at: www.northwestarchives. org.uk.

B

LOCAL ARCHIVES AND LOCAL STUDIES LIBRARIES

The following is a selection of specialist archives and local history libraries with study materials relating to the historic county. Local studies libraries may only have resources such as census returns, parish registers, rate books and electoral registers for their immediate area. Trade directories were not published every year, and libraries may only have a selection of those published.

Guide to Lancashire Studies and Family History Collections at: www. lancashire.gov.uk/libraries/services/local/guide.asp.

Accrington Community History Library
Library is housed in the old Mechanics' Institute; access through the reference library.

Census returns on microfilm 1841–1901. Parish registers; trade directories from 1818. Burgess rolls and registers of electors from 1878. Poll books. Rate books for Church 1901–1958; Clayton-le-Moors 1935–1967; Oswaldtwistle 1913–1962. Records of Accrington and Hyndburn Borough Councils, Church, Clayton-le-Moors, Great Harwood and Oswaldtwistle UDCs. Local clubs and societies collections. Photographic collection, maps and plans.

Important First World War collection includes cemetery registers, rolls of honour, the seventy-five-volume *Official History of the Great War*, personal memoirs and William Turner's Accrington Pals collection. Microfilm copies of local newspapers from the 1850s.

Accrington Community History Library, St James Street, Accrington, BB5 1NQ; www.lancashire.gov.uk/libraries/services/local/accrington.asp; email: accrington.library@lancashire.gov.uk; tel: 0125 487 2385.

Armitt Library and Museum, Ambleside
Collections of books include medieval Cartmel and Furness at: www.armitt. com/medieval_cumbria.htm.

The Armitt Library & Museum, Rydal Road, Ambleside, Cumbria, LA22 9BL; www.armitt.com; email: almc@armitt.com; tel: 0153 943 1212.

Bacup Library

Electoral registers. No rate books. Census returns 1841–1891. Local directories from 1824 onwards. Bacup Mechanics' Institute minutes and papers 1839–1900. Bacup Relief Fund (1862–1863).

Bacup Library, St James Square, Bacup, Lancashire, OL13 9AH; www. lancashire.gov.uk/libraries/services/local/bacup.asp; email: Bacup.library @lancashire.gov.uk; tel: 0170 687 3324.

Barnoldswick Library

Local directories from 1822 onwards. Rate books (twentieth century), some poll books. Some parish records. Barnoldswick UDC and Earby UDC minute books. Censuses 1841–1891 on microfiche. Maps, plans, photographs, newspapers and more.

Barnoldswick Library, Fern Lea Avenue, Barnoldswick, Colne, Lancashire, BB18 5DW; www.lancashire.gov.uk/libraries/services/local/barnoldswick. asp#1; email: Barnoldswick.library@lancashire.gov.uk; tel: 0128 281 2147.

Blackburn Central Library

Woodfold Estate records: DDX 1936. Records for over twenty business organizations including Blackburn Chamber of Trade. Personal papers include Elizabeth I's letter book and novelist Charles Dickens' correspondence. Censuses 1841–1901, electoral registers, cemetery records, etc. First World War rolls of honour for Blackburn and Darwen. Boyd's marriage index, IGI, Anglican parish registers for Blackburn, GRO index. Trade directories from 1818. An appointment is needed to consult archive collections.

Blackburn Central Library, Town Hall Street, Blackburn, Lancashire, BB2 1AG; www.blackburn.gov.uk; archives email: community.history@blackburn. gov.uk; library email: 0125 466 1221; archives tel: 0125 458 7919; library tel: 0125 466 1221.

Blackpool Family and Local History Centre

Blackpool Family and Local History Centre, Central Library, Queen Street, Blackpool, FY1 1PX; www.blackpool.gov.uk/services/a-f/blackpool libraries/familyandlocalhistory.htm; email: localhistory.centre@blackpool. gov.uk; tel: 0125 347 8090.

Chetham's Library

Founded in 1653, this is the oldest public library in the English-speaking world. Free admission. Many collections relating to local history, particularly for the Manchester area: archives, books, manuscripts, prints and photographs. Visitors should book an appointment before visiting; give at least one day's notice.

Hand-list of Manuscripts at: www.chethams.org.uk/handlist.html.

Library Catalogue at: www.chethams.org.uk/catalogue.html.

Medieval manuscripts at: www.chethams.org.uk/collections_medieval. html.

Chetham's Library, Long Millgate, M3 1SB; www.chethams.org.uk; email: librarian@chethams.org.uk; tel: 0161 834 7961.

Greater Manchester Police Museum & Archives

Displays on the history of policing in Manchester. Aliens Registers for Salford (1914–1969, some gaps), Oldham and Rochdale (late 1940s–1960s). (NB Manchester Aliens Register is no longer extant). Copies of *Police Gazette* on microfilm 1839–1900 (some gaps). Calendars of Prisoners for the Assize Court of Manchester 1882–1964 (some years missing).

For museum opening times, check the website; archive visits by appointment only.

Greater Manchester Police Museum & Archives, 57a Newton Street, Manchester M1 1ET; www.gmp.police.uk; email: Police.Museum@gmp. police.uk; tel: 0161 856 3287.

Harris Library, Preston

Papers of Edward Baines and Edwin Butterworth. Francis Thompson (poet) manuscripts.

Preston Harris Library, Market Square, Preston, PR1 2PP; www.lancashire. gov.uk/libraries; email: harris.library@lancashire.gov.uk; community history tel: 0177 253 2668; library tel: 0177 253 2676.

Leigh Library

Turnpike Centre, Civic Square, Market Street, Leigh, WN7 1EB; www. wlct.org/library-services/library-locations/leigh-library.htm; email: Leigh. Library@wlct.org; tel: 0194 240 4197.

Liverpool Central Library

Currently closed until spring 2013; temporary service at the World Museum (see Liverpool Record Office listing).

Liverpool Central Library and Archive, William Brown Street, Liverpool, Merseyside, L3 8EW; www.liverpool.gov.uk/libraries-and-archives.

158

Manchester Central Library

Currently closed for refurbishment until late 2013 when a new, extended library will open. Main collection is in off-site storage. Some special collections can be accessed at Chetham's Library and other sites but an appointment is needed. Further information is available at: www.manchester.gov.uk/info/447/rare_books_and_special_collections.

Manchester Central Library, St Peter's Square, Manchester, M2 5PD; www.manchester.gov.uk/info/500138/central_library.

Manchester City Library

Local studies and family history resources on microfilm/fiche and computer are available at the Manchester Room@City Library while Manchester Central Library is being redeveloped.

Parish registers on microfilm. National Probate Index 1858–1943 on microfiche. GRO indexes. Will indexes for archdeaconry of Chester. City of Manchester electoral registers on microfilm 1832–2002 (not 1917, 1940–1944): no surname index. Manchester rate books 1706–1901 on microfilm. Trade directories on microfilm. Pre-1925 school admission registers on microfilm. Copies of Court Leet records of the Manor of Manchester 1552–1846. Belle Vue prison records on microfilm. Reference library. Newspapers and periodicals. Some MIs and burial registers on microfilm.

Guide to cemetery records and MIs at: www.manchester.gov.uk/info/448/archives_and_local_studies/462/family_history_in_manchester/5.

List of parish registers for Manchester area available at GMCRO and Manchester Room@City Library at: www.manchester.gov.uk/info/448/archives_and_local_studies/4670/archive_and_local_collections/6.

Online guides to court and prison records at: www.manchester.gov.uk/info/448/archives_and_local_studies/3808/court_and_prison_records/4.

City Library, Elliot House, 151 Deansgate, Manchester, M3 2HN; www.manchester.gov.uk/info/448/archives_and_local_studies; email: archiveslocalstudies@manchester.gov.uk; tel: 0161 234 1979.

Manchester Grammar School Archive

Ian Bailey Archive Library. Some materials held at GMCRO.

Rachel Kneale, The Archivist, The Manchester Grammar School, Old Hall Lane, Manchester, M13 0XT; www.mgs.org/1515-2015/development-office/the-archive-office; email: r.a.kneale@mgs.org; tel: 0161 224 7201.

Manchester High School for Girls Archive

Archive catalogue at: www.mhsgarchive.org/catalogue.php.

Dr Christine A. Joy, School Archivist, Manchester High School for Girls, Grangethorpe Road, Rusholme, Manchester, M14 6HS; www.mhsgarchive. org; email: cjoy@mhsg.manchester.sch.uk; tel: 0161 249 2267.

Manchester Jewish Museum

The museum, housed in the oldest surviving synagogue building in Manchester, tells the story of the Jewish population in the area. Oral histories. Researchers can access the museum's library and collections of documents, tapes and objects by prior appointment. The Jewish Genealogical Society of Great Britain holds meetings at the museum.

Manchester Jewish Museum, 190 Cheetham Hill Road, Manchester, M8 8LW; www.manchesterjewishmuseum.com; curator email: curator@manchester jewishmuseum.com; learning officer email: learning@manchesterjewish museum.com; curator tel: 0161 830 1436; learning officer tel: 0161 830 1432.

Oldham Local Studies and Archives

Butterworth papers (James and Edwin) 1787–1859: D-BU. Highams Ltd records include financial accounts and pensions 1896–1989: D-HI. Family history information on migrant communities (including Asians) in the Oldham area, with photos and oral histories.

Family papers, council records, religious records, business records including textiles, co-operative societies and more.

Parish registers, cemetery and burial records, MIs, censuses, electoral registers, burgess rolls, parish registers, probate indexes, military sources, etc.

List of archive collections at: www.oldham.gov.uk/info/200539/archive_ collections.

Oldham Local Studies and Archives, 84 Union Street, Oldham, OL1 1DN; www.oldham.gov.uk/info/200276/local_studies_and_archives; email: archives @oldham.gov.uk; tel: 0161 770 4654.

Portico Library

Subscription library. Membership fee; restricted number of members. Gallery open to general public. Researchers are welcome to consult the library's collection (membership not required), but only members are permitted to borrow books.

57 Moseley Street, Manchester, M2 3HY; www.theportico.org.uk./Home. html; email: emma.marigliano@theportico.org.uk; tel: 0161 236 6785.

Rochdale Local Studies Library
Collections for the Rochdale area and Castleton, Littleborough, Milnrow, Norden and Wardle. Rochdale County Borough Council records 1725–1968. Online index to parish register holdings.

Local Studies Library, Touchstones Rochdale, The Esplanade, Rochdale, Lancashire, OL16 1AQ; www.link4life.org/index.cfm; tel: 0170 692 4915.

St Helens Local History and Archives Library
St Helens Local History and Archives Library, Central Library, Gamble Institute, Victoria Square, St Helens, WA10 1DY; www.sthelens.gov.uk; email: localhistory&archivesservices@sthelens.gov.uk; tel: 0174 445 6952.

Talbot Library
John Henry Newman collection. Irish studies. Roman Catholic history collections.

Librarian: Revd Deacon Michael Dolan, MA, FCLIP, The Talbot Library, Weston Street, Preston, PR2 2QE; www.talbotlibrary.co.uk; email: talbot library@btconnect.com; tel: 0177 276 0186.

Trafford Local Studies Library
Family history materials and records for Trafford Metropolitan Borough. Searchable database of Trafford images and history at: www.trafford.gov.uk/content/tca/.

Trafford Local Studies Centre, Sale Waterside, Sale, M33 7ZF; www.trafford.gov.uk/leisureandculture/libraries/localandfamilyhistory; email: trafflocals@trafford.gov.uk; tel: 0161 912 3013.

Warrington Library, Museums and Archives Service
South Lancashire Regiment records include register of prisoners of the South Lancashire Regiment Sep–Nov 1916; register of change of addresses 1916–1918 and four volumes of registers arranged alphabetically with names of soldiers, regimental number: WMS 1010, 1090–1092.

Warrington borough records, manorial and court records. Estate and family deeds and papers. Rentals, maps and surveys; militia records. Electoral registers, voters' lists. Records of many local businesses, societies, clubs and institutions and schools. Census returns, parish registers, newspapers on microfilm. Photographic collection.

Warrington Library, Museum Street, Cultural Quarter, Warrington, WA1 1JB; www.warrington.gov.uk/libraries; email: library@warrington.gov.uk; tel: 0192 544 2890.

C

USEFUL ADDRESSES

Barrow Register Office
Barrow Register Office, The Nan Tait Centre, Abbey Road, Barrow-in-Furness, Cumbria, LA14 1LG; www.barrowbc.gov.uk; tel: 0122 940 7510 and 7511.

Blackburn with Darwen Copy Certificate Service
Register Office, King George's Hall, Northgate, Blackburn, BB2 1AA; www.blackburn.gov.uk; registrars@blackburn.gov.uk; tel: 0125 458 8660.

Blackpool Copy Certificate Service
The Register Office, South King Street, Blackpool, FY1 4AX; www.blackpool.gov.uk/Services/A-F/CopyCertificates; tel: 0125 347 7177.

General Register Office (England and Wales)
BMDs for England and Wales from 1 July 1837 onwards. Adopted Children Register from 1927.

General Register Office Certificate Services Section, General Register Office, PO Box 2, Southport, PR8 2JD; www.gro.gov.uk/gro/content/certificates/default.asp; email: certificate.services@ips.gsi.gov.uk; tel: 0300 123 1837.

Lancashire Certificate Service
Copy certificates for births, marriages and deaths in Accrington, Burnley, Chorley, Clitheroe, Fleetwood, Lancaster, Lytham, Ormskirk, Pendle, Preston and Rawtenstall.

Lancashire Certificate Service, Quayside Court, Chain Caul Way, Preston, PR2 2ZP; https://lccsecure.lancashire.gov.uk/online//services/certificate; email: certificateservices@lancashire.gov.uk; tel: 0845 053 0021.

Lancashire Register Offices
There are register offices at Accrington, Burnley, Chorley, Fleetwood, Lancaster, Lytham, Ormskirk and Preston.

www.lancashire.gov.uk/acs/sites/registration/offices.

Land Registry, Lancashire

Land Registry Fylde Office, Wrea Brook Court, Lytham Road, Warton, Preston, Lancashire, PR4 1TE; www.landregistry.gov.uk; email: customer support@landregistry.gsi.gov.uk; tel: 0177 283 6700.

Land Registry

www.landregistry.gov.uk; email: customersupport@landregistry.gsi.gov.uk; tel: 0844 892 1111.

Leeds District Probate Registry

The Postal Searches and Copies Department, Leeds District Probate Registry, York House, York Place, Leeds, LS1 2BA; www.justice.gov.uk/guidance/courts-and-tribunals/courts/probate/probate-registries.htm; email: Leeds DPRenquiries@hmcts.gsi.gov.uk; tel: 0113 389 6133.

Liverpool Copy Certificate Service

Liverpool Register Office, St George's Hall, Heritage Entrance, St George's Place, Liverpool, L1 1JJ; http://liverpool.gov.uk/births-marriage-deaths/copies-of-certificates; tel: 0151 233 3004.

Liverpool District Probate Registry

Liverpool District Probate Registry, Queen Elizabeth II Law Courts, Derby Square, Liverpool, L2 1XA; email: liverpool.dpr@hmcts.gsi.gov.uk; tel: 0151 236 8264.

Manchester Copy Certificate Service

The Register Office, Heron House, 47 Lloyd Street, Manchester, M2 5LE; www.manchester.gov.uk/info/323/birth-historical_searches/1144/registration-copy_certificates/1; email: registeroffice@manchester.gov.uk; tel: 0161 234 5005.

Manchester District Probate Registry

Manchester District Probate Registry, Manchester Civil Justice Centre, Ground Floor, 1 Bridge Street West, PO Box 4240, Manchester, M60 1WJ; email: ManchesterDPRenquiries@hmcts.gsi.gov.uk; tel: 0161 240 5701.

Salford Register Office

Register Office, Town Hall, Chorley Road, Swinton, Salford, M27 5DA; www.salford.gov.uk/bmd.htm; email: birthsanddeaths1@salford.gov.uk; tel: 0161 909 6501.

Wigan and Leigh Register Office
Wigan and Leigh Register Office, Town Hall, Library Street, Wigan, WN1 1YN; www.wigan.gov.uk/Services/CommunityLiving/BirthsDeaths Marriages; email: WiganRegisterOffice@wigan.gov.uk; tel: 0194 270 5000.

Principal Registry of the Family Division (Probate Service)
Where to find a probate registry: www.justice.gov.uk/guidance/courts-and-tribunals/courts/probate/probate-registries.htm.

Guide to probate records in England and Wales: www.justice.gov.uk/guidance/courts-and-tribunals/courts/probate/family-history.htm and www.justice.gov.uk/guidance/courts-and-tribunals/courts/probate/index.htm.

Family History Societies

Federation of Family History Societies
The Federation of Family History Societies, PO Box 8857, Lutterworth, LE17 9BJ; www.ffhs.org.uk; email: info@ffhs.co.uk; tel: 0145 520 3133.

Guild of One-Name Studies
The Guild of One-Name Studies, Box G, 14 Charterhouse Buildings, Goswell Road, London, EC1M 7BA; www.one-name.org; email: guild@one-name.org; tel: 0800 011 2182.

The Institute of Heraldic and Genealogical Studies
IHGS Library holdings for Lancashire at: www.ihgs.ac.uk/library/pdf/lancashire.pdf.

The Institute of Heraldic and Genealogical Studies, 79–82 Northgate, Canterbury, Kent, CT1 1BA; www.ihgs.ac.uk/index.html; tel: 0122 776 8664.

Society of Genealogists
National Library and Education Centre for Family History at: www.sog.org.uk/library/intro.shtml.

Lancashire resources available at the Society's Library at: www.sog.org.uk/prc/lancashire.shtml.

Society of Genealogists, 14 Charterhouse Buildings, Goswell Road, London, EC1M 7BA; www.societyofgenealogists.com; email: membership@sog.org.uk; tel: 0207 251 8799.

Local Family History Societies

North West Group of Family History Societies
www.nwgfhs.org.uk.

Bolton and District FHS
www.familyhistorybolton.tk; enquiries@famhistbolton.freeiz.com.

FHS of Cheshire
FHSC Sources and Location of MIs in Cheshire at: http://bit.ly/zNqpT2.

Membership enrolment secretary: Mrs Sue McNulty, 59 Cedarway, Bollington, Macclesfield, Cheshire, SK10 5NR; www.fhsc.org.uk.

Cumbria FHS
Membership: Janet Arnison, Membership Secretary, Cumbria FHS, Jack Dike, Cliburn, Penrith, Cumbria, CA10 3AL; http://cumbriafhs.com/cgi-bin/site/main.pl; email: membership@cumbriafhs.com.

Institute of Local and Family History
The institute holds regular conferences and study days which are open to members and non-members. Members of the Institute receive discounts on events, and a free copy of the *Bulletin of Local and Family History*. Members' Area of the website has full access to the probate index for the western deaneries of the archdeaconry of Richmond (1748–1858).

Institute of Local and Family History, University of Central Lancashire, Preston, Lancashire, PR1 2HE; www.uclan.ac.uk/schools/education_social_sciences/history/local_family_history.php; email: lfhistory@uclan.ac.uk; tel: 0177 289 3053.

Lancashire Family History and Heraldry Society
Lancashire Family History and Heraldry Society, 2 Straits, Oswaldtwistle, Lancashire, BB5 3LU; www.lfhhs.org.uk; email: secretary@lfhhs.org.uk; membership@lfhhs.org.uk; tel: 0125 423 9919.

Furness FHS
Membership enquiries: J. Grisedale, 5 Mowings Lane, Ulverston, LA12 7DB; www.furnessfhs.co.uk; general secretary email: julia.fairbairn@furnessfhs.co.uk; membership secretary email: jacquie.grisdale@furnessfhs.co.uk.

Lancashire Parish Register Society
Alphabetical list of parish registers published by the Society at: www.genuki.org.uk/big/eng/LAN/lprs/parishes.shtml.

LPRS Publication Sales, Mr Neil Hudson, Lancashire Parish Register Society, Raising House, Leece, Nr Ulverston, Cumbria, LA12 0QP; www.lprs.org.uk.

Lancaster FH Group
Membership Secretary: 46 Westham Street, Lancaster, LA1 3AU; www. lfhg.org; membership email: membership@lfhg.org; general secretary email: secretary@lfhg.org.

Liverpool & S.W. Lancs FHS
General secretary: Miss P. McEvoy, 6 Kirkmore Road, Liverpool L18 4QN. Membership secretary: Diane Banahan, 39 Belmont Street, Southport, Merseyside PR8 1LY; www.liverpool-genealogy.org.uk; general secretary email: secretary@liverpool-genealogy.org.uk; membership secretary email: membership@liverpool-genealogy.org.uk.

Manchester & Lancashire Family History Society
The Society plans to move to the Archives+ facility in the renovated Manchester Central Library in 2014 (see Section A).

The MLFHS has four branches: Bolton & District, Oldham & District, Irish Ancestry and Anglo-Scottish Ancestry FHS.

Several free searchable databases online including Manchester 'strays', Manchester war memorial inscriptions, Manchester Crematorium obituaries, memorial inscriptions, Roman Catholic register index, Paradise Mill (Oldham) wages book 1852–1858 and more. Complete data for some databases restricted to members only. Access at: http://mlfhs.org.uk/data/ online data.php.

MLFHS, Clayton House, 59 Piccadilly, Manchester Ml 2AQ; www.mlfhs. org.uk; email enquiry form: www.mlfhs.org.uk/contact/mailme.php; tel: 0161 236 9750.

North Meols (Southport) FHS
General Secretary Jane Scarisbrick, 6 Millars Place, Marshside, Southport, Lancashire, PR9 9FU; www.nmfhssouthport.co.uk; general secretary email: secretary@nmfhssouthport.co.uk; membership secretary: membership @nmfhssouthport.co.uk.

Ormskirk & District FHS
The Society has created a canal-boat families website with an online index of family names from the late eighteenth century onwards. A database is available on CD-ROM of boatmen and families in Burscough and the surrounding area.

www.boatfamilies.org.uk; email: boatfamilies@odfhs.org.uk; ODFHS, PO Box 213 Aughton, Ormskirk, Lancs, L39 5WT; www.odfhs.org.uk; email: secretary@odfhs.org.uk.

Pendle & Burnley
Member of Lancashire Family History and Heraldry Society.

Membership: David Burgess, 10 St Andrews Drive, Alwoodley, Leeds, LS17 7TR; www.lfhhs-pendleandburnley.org.uk; email: enquiry@lfhhs-pendleand burnley.org.uk.

Rossendale
Member of Lancashire Family History and Heraldry Society.

www.rossendale-fhhs.org.uk; secretary Rita Hirst email: rossendale@lfhhs. org.uk.

St Helens Townships FHS
Secretary Mrs Pauline Hurst, St Helens Townships FHS, 6 Gainford Close, Widnes, WA8 4UN; www.sthelenstownshipsfhs.org.uk; email: contactus @sthelenstownshipsfhs.org.uk.

Ulverston: Heritage First!
The Membership Secretary, Heritage First!, c/o Tower House, 57 Lightburn Avenue, Ulverston, Cumbria, LA12 0DL; www.rootsweb.ancestry.com/ ~ukuhc; email: ulverstonheritage@hotmail.co.uk.

Wigan Family & Local History Society
Mr Tony Haslam, 15 Welbeck Road, Ashton-in-Makerfield, Wigan, WN4 8AR; www.wiganworld.co.uk/familyhistory; email: wigan.fhs@gmail.com.

FamilySearch Centres (Church of Jesus Christ of Latter-day Saints)

A large collection of Lancashire records are available on microfilm at FamilySearch Centres including parish registers, probate records and census returns on microfilm (except 1911). FamilySearch census microfilms are catalogued by the historic counties and parishes, not census registration districts. You can order microfilms to view in advance (a fee may be payable). The 1911 census can be accessed free online at Centres with an Internet connection. Opening hours are on the FamilySearch website; you may need to make an appointment to visit. NB These centres cannot answer postal enquiries, so access at: www.familysearch.org/Eng/Library/FHC/frameset_fhc.asp.

Ashton-under-Lyne
Patterdale Road, Crowhill Estate, Ashton-under-Lyne, Tameside; tel: 0161 330 3453.

Barrow-in-Furness
Abbey Road, Barrow-in-Furness, Cumbria; tel: 0122 982 0050.

Blackpool
Warren Drive, Cleveleys, Blackpool, Lancashire; tel: 0125 386 3868.

Chorley
Temple Way, Hartwood Green, Chorley; tel: 0125 722 6145.

Manchester
Altrincham Road, Wythenshawe, Manchester; tel: 0161 902 9279.

Historical and Heritage Societies

Lancashire Local History Federation (LLHF)
Lancashire is blessed with a large number of historical and heritage societies. There is a list of members on the LLHF website at: www.lancashirehistory.org and www.lancashirehistory.org/membersoci.htm.

Barrow-in-Furness Civic and Local History Society
www.barrowhistorysociety.org.uk.

Catholic Record Society
The society is devoted to the history of Roman Catholicism and cannot help with family history research.

www.catholic-history.org.uk/index.php.

Chetham Society
List of Chetham Society publications at: www.chethams.org.uk/chetham_society_pubs.pdf.

Chris Hunwick, Alnwick Castle, Alnwick Northumberland, NE66 1NQ; membership email: memsec.chethamsoc@googlemail.com; general enquiry email: hunwickc@alnwickcastle.com.

168

Historic Society of Lancashire and Cheshire

The society has a comprehensive library of works on the history of the two counties. The earlier volumes of the Society's journals (up to 1999) have been digitized and put on their website.

Index of journals published at: http://bit.ly/zNXazK.

Membership: Mr Simon Hill, Department of History, Liverpool John Moores University, 68 Hope Street, Liverpool, L1 9BZ; www.hslc.org.uk; online membership form: www.hslc.org.uk/forms/membershipform.pdf.

Lancashire and Cheshire Antiquarian Society

Mr Roy Westall, Honorary Membership Secretary, Lancashire and Cheshire Antiquarian Society, 349 Andrew Street, Compstall, Stockport, Cheshire, SK6 5HW; www.landcas.org.uk; email: roy@landcas.org.uk.

Lancashire and Cheshire Record Society

Publications at: www.royalhistoricalsociety.org/lanc&cheshirerecsoc.pdf.

Liverpool History Society

Hon. Membership Secretary, Liverpool History Society, 55 Greenloons Drive, Formby, Merseyside, L37 2LX; www.liverpoolhistorysociety.org.uk; email: membershipsecretary@liverpoolhistorysociety.org.uk.

North West Catholic History Society

Membership: Brian Farrimond, The Treasurer, 11 Tower Hill, Ormskirk, Lancashire, L39 2EE; www.catholic-history.org.uk/nwchs/index.htm.

Ranulf Higden Society

The Society transcribes and translates medieval Latin documents associated with Lancashire, Cheshire, Staffordshire and Derbyshire.

The Secretary, Ranulf Higden Society, Southerton, Hazler Road, Church Stretton, Salop, SY6 7AQ; www.ranulfhigden.org.uk.

D

FREE ONLINE RESOURCES

Lots of free resources are available online including datasets compiled by volunteers. These websites have been included as useful starting points for your research, but the author cannot guarantee the accuracy of online transcriptions and databases, which may be subject to human error. Ideally, you should always locate and consult the original document whenever possible.

Key points to remember about online databases:

- Not all records have been transcribed;
- They may not be 100 per cent accurate;
- They do not constitute real 'proof' of an ancestor's details.

FamilySearch (The Church of Jesus Christ of Latter-day Saints)
Church records for about two-thirds of Lancashire parishes: baptism, marriage and burial records including BTs. Many indexed church records. Historical record collections include over 330,000 images of parish registers from the diocese of Manchester free to view online ('click' on your ancestor's name to view image if available). Oldham Cemetery Registers 1797–2004.

Cheshire marriage bonds and allegations (including Lancashire marriages in the diocese of Chester). Summaries of census returns, including the 1911 census. The website has a free index (which includes place of birth) to the 1911 census with links to the census return images at the Find My Past website.

See Section C for the location of FamilySearch Centres. The website has links to subscription sites if no image is available of a record.

An interactive map (1851) shows the county's jurisdictions by parish, diocese, deanery, Poor Law Union, civil registration district and more at: http://maps.familysearch.org.

Familysearch Wiki for Lancashire has over 900 articles at: https://wiki.familysearch.org/en/Lancashire.

www.FamilySearch.org.

Apprentices

Ancestry offers a free index to the Register of Duties Paid on Apprentices' Indentures (IR 1 at TNA) 1710–1811.

http://search.ancestry.co.uk/search/db.aspx?dbid=1851.

British Jewry North West

Tips for researching Jews living in north-west England.

www.british-jewry.org.uk/northwest.html.

Cemetery Records Online: Lancashire

An incomplete list of burials.

www.interment.net/uk/eng/lancashire.htm.

CemSearch

Searchable MIs.

www.cemsearch.co.uk.

Chadwick Family (Wigan)

Gwynne Chadwick's family history research into the Chadwick/Chadock family tree includes many other Wigan surnames including the Sharrock family.

www.rafbridgnorth.org.uk/familyhistory/chfamily/chindex.html.

Chartist Ancestors

Mark Crail's wonderfully informative website includes lists of Chartists.

www.chartists.net.

Convict Transportation Registers Database

The registers, dating from 1787–1867, have details for over 123,000 of the estimated 160,000 convicts transported to Australia in the eighteenth and nineteenth centuries: names, term of years, transport ships and more.

www.slq.qld.gov.au/info/fh/convicts.

Cumbrian Manorial Records

www.lancs.ac.uk/fass/projects/manorialrecords/index.htm and www.lancs.ac.uk/fass/projects/manorialrecords/cumbria/lancashirelist.htm.

Cyndi's List for Lancashire
Over 400 useful links.

www.cyndislist.com/uk/eng/counties/lan.

Earlam Family History
http://earlamfamilyhistory.com/index.htm.

Entwistle Family History
www.entwistlefamily.org.uk/index.htm.

Free 1881 Census
Free to search and view on Ancestry.

www.ancestry.co.uk.

Free Reg
Parish registers including Nonconformist.

www.freereg.org.uk.

Free UK BMDs
Free GRO indexes for England and Wales (not deaths overseas). Images of original GRO index pages available. Check the transcription of the GRO reference against the index before ordering the certificate from the GRO at Southport.

www.freebmd.org.uk.

Free UK Census 1841–1891
Currently, FreeCen has only partial coverage for Lancashire returns for 1861 and 1891; none for other census years. However, you can search the databases by birth county, so you can find Lancashire-born ancestors living outside the county (full coverage not yet available).

www.freecen.org.uk.

GENUKI Lancashire
www.genuki.org.uk/big/eng/LAN.

Great Harwood Register of Recusants 1682 and Returns of Papists 1767
www.great-harwood.org.uk/about/History/Documents/recusants.htm.

Grimshaw Origins and History
www.grimshaworigin.org.

Hearth Tax Online
This tax was levied from 1662–1689 on every householder according to the number of hearths in their house. Currently, Lancashire transcripts are not yet online, but should be in the near future.

www.hearthtax.org.uk/index.html.

Hibernia
Irish family history in the Liverpool area.

http://freepages.genealogy.rootsweb.ancestry.com/~hibernia.

Kirkby Ireleth (Irelyth) Wills
www.history-of-kirkby.org/Archives.htm.

Lancashire Life and Times E-Resource Network
Searchable image archive. Indexes for armed forces, obituaries and censuses (mostly for Burnley). Newspaper index (chiefly Preston, Chorley and East Lancashire). Transactions index (historical societies' publications).

http://lantern.lancashire.gov.uk.

Lancashire Family History: Dr Craig Thornber
Dr Thornber has constructed some family trees for the Crabtree, Cragg, Eastham, Lancaster, Stanworth, Thornber and other families. Photographs and genealogy information, including details of transcriptions of some Lancashire parish registers, particularly for East Lancashire and the Clitheroe area. (NB Dr Thornber cannot absolutely guarantee the accuracy of any family relationships mentioned.)

www.thornber.net, www.thornber.net/famhist/htmlfiles/holden.html and www.thornber.net/famhist/htmlfiles/churches.html.

Lancashire Look-Up Exchange
Volunteer 'look-ups' and searchable online resources. Requests for information should be as specific and detailed as possible, not 'blanket' searches for a particular family or location.

www.rootsweb.ancestry.com/~uklancs.

Lancashire Newspapers

Richard Heaton's family history site has transcripts of some Lancashire newspapers.

Surname index.

http://freepages.genealogy.rootsweb.ancestry.com/~dutillieul/ZOtherPapers/Index/Dates.htm.

Lancashire Online Parish Clerks

This invaluable resource contains a wealth of information to help you start constructing your family tree (see Chapter 7).

www.lan-opc.org.uk.

Lancashire Wills Search (Before 1858)

www.xmission.com/~nelsonb/lws.htm.

Lancashire Wills Transcriptions Online

Only a limited number of transcriptions at present.

www.willtranscriptions.co.uk/counties/lancashire.htm.

Lancaster Castle Convict Database

Searchable database of people tried and sentenced at Lancaster Assizes.

www.lancastercastle.com/html/convict/default.php.

Lichfield Wills

List of wills proved in the diocese of Lichfield before 1541.

www.historicalresources.myzen.co.uk/WILLS/lichweb.pdf.

Liverpool History Projects

Project includes Liverpool graveyards, Roman Catholic baptisms, marriages and burials.

www.liverpoolhistoryprojects.co.uk.

Manchester Archives Images

www.flickr.com/photos/manchesterarchiveplus/sets.

Manchester Chinese Archive

The story of Manchester's Chinese community. The website discusses the problems facing people researching their Chinese ancestors in the Greater

Manchester area. Useful pages on census entries, Chinese genealogy and archives, and businesses. Currently the archive is kept at GMCRO.

www.manchesterchinesearchive.org.uk.

Manchester Family History Research
Gerald Lodge's website has many extremely informative pages, especially one about Manchester court records.

www.manchester-family-history-research.co.uk and www.manchester-family-history-research.co.uk/new_page_3.htm.

Manchester General Cemetery Transcriptions Project
http://mgctp.moonfruit.com.

Manchester Historical Maps (beta)
http://manchester.publicprofiler.org/beta.

Manchester Local Images Collection
http://images.manchester.gov.uk/index.php.

Medieval Genealogy
Lots of helpful information on medieval records, with Lancashire resources, a guide to probate records, and links to free e-books.

www.medievalgenealogy.org.uk, www.medievalgenealogy.org.uk/och/lancashire.shtml and www.medievalgenealogy.org.uk/sources/probate.shtml.

Moving Here
Tips on tracing family history of immigrants to Britain.

www.movinghere.org.uk.

North-West England: Family and Business Database 1760–1820
Small family businesses such as retailers, manufacturers and service providers. Database can be searched by family name, business or documents such as family correspondence, diaries, court proceedings or wills. Images of some documents.

www.northwestfamilybusiness.arts.manchester.ac.uk.

Old Mersey Times

Transcriptions from old newspapers on life in Liverpool and Merseyside. Includes trades and occupations such as mining, births, marriages and deaths, MIs and much more.

www.old-merseytimes.co.uk/index.html.

Prestwich & Whitefield Heritage

www.prestwichheritage.co.uk/local-resources-for-family-history.

Recusant Historian's Handbook

www.catholic-history.org.uk/nwchs/recushandbook.htm.

Rootsweb

Lancashire at: www.rootsweb.ancestry.com/~englan. Lancashire Genealogy mailing list at: http://lists.rootsweb.ancestry.com/index/intl/ENG/LANCSGEN.html. Lancashire Life mailing list at: http://lists.rootsweb.ancestry.com/index/intl/ENG/LANCSLIFE.html.

Salford Hundred Medieval Documentation

Blog on medieval sources for Salford Hundred; other Lancashire sources also mentioned, with links to free e-books.

http://salfordhundred.wordpress.com.

Tameside Family History

Many useful links. Includes transcripts for the parish of Ashton-under-Lyne in 1811 census: Ashton town, Heyrod, Mossley and Lees.

http://tamesidefamilyhistory.co.uk/index.htm.

Tatham History Society

Includes articles and transcripts of census data for Tatham, tithes, hearth taxes, MIs and more. Searchable parish registers (pre-1837).

www.tathamhistory.org.uk/index.php.

Together Trust

Formerly the Manchester and Salford Boys and Girls Refuges and Homes. The trust has an archive relating to children who were in its care. The website has a list of children's homes run by the charity. Access at: www.togethertrust.org.uk/about/history. Archive blog at: www.togethertrustarchive.blogspot.com. Contact the archivist for family history enquiries at: www.togethertrust.org.uk/contact/new.

Toxteth Park Cemetery Burials Index
Searchable database for surnames. Database includes deceased's name, age and address, date of burial, grave number and folio number of the original record. Maps of the cemetery.

www.toxtethparkcemetery.co.uk.

Toxteth Park Cemetery Database
http://freepages.genealogy.rootsweb.ancestry.com/~toxtethparkcemetery.

Trade Union Ancestors
Tips for finding union ancestors. Short trade-union histories. Mark Crail's site lists every trade union known to have existed.

www.unionancestors.co.uk.

Tudge Family History
Dave Lane's website has plenty of detailed information on Tudges, particularly in the Bolton area.

www.d.lane.btinternet.co.uk/tudge.htm.

UK BMD
Brett Langston's index of civil parishes (England and Wales) 1837–1974 shows each place's county and civil registration district at: www.ukbmd. org.uk/genuki/places/regindex2-1.pdf. Langston's list of civil registration districts in England and Wales for 1837–1974.

www.ukbmd.org.uk/genuki/reg   and   ww.ukbmd.org.uk/genuki/reg/ districts/index.html.

UK Genealogy Archives
Links to online databases. Images of some published parish registers for Lancashire.

www.uk-genealogy.org.uk/Registers/parish_registers.html.

Wigan Genealogy
Forum. Incomplete transcript of 1811 census.

www.wiganworld.co.uk/communicate/genealogy.php   and   www.wigan world.co.uk/communicate/mb.php?opt=f3.

177

Wills and Inventories for Archdeaconry of Richmond
Surtees Society publication, 1853. Some wills in Latin, some in English.

www.uiowa.edu/~c030149a/northern/richmondtext.pdf.

E

SUBSCRIPTION AND 'PAY PER VIEW' WEBSITES

Family History Resources

The family history subscription websites constantly update their databases and more record collections will have been added since going to press. Local record offices and the county libraries usually give their members free access via their library computers to one of these services. It is not possible to recommend any particular subscription service because so much depends on which particular databases are most relevant to your family tree, and also your preferred method of working. Each service presents its searchable datasets in a different format. Subscription services often offer 'free trials' for a limited period, which are helpful if you are on a tight budget.

Ancestry

UK Census Collection 1841–1911 includes reconstructions of the 'unfilmed' Manchester 1851 census returns damaged by water. Free BMD indexes for England and Wales for 1837–1915. National Probate Calendar. Extracted probate records.

British Army WWI Service Records and Pension Records 1914–1920.

UK Soldiers Died in the Great War 1914–1919 includes Lancashire regiments.

England & Wales, Criminal Registers. UK Railway Employment Records. British Postal Service Appointment Books.

Chorley parish registers. Croston parish registers. Rochdale parish registers. Trade directories.

Liverpool Collection includes Quaker registers, Church of England registers and Roman Catholic registers.

www.ancestry.co.uk.

British Origins

British & Irish Passenger Lists (to USA and Canada) 1890, 1891. Militia Attestations Index (WO 96) 1860–1915 includes Lancashire regiments (attestations are forms with recruits' personal details). National Wills Index includes York Medieval Probate Index 1267–1500. Probate index for Prerogative & Exchequer Courts of York 1688–1858. Probate indexes include York peculiars (Broughton, Kirkby Ireleth and Seathwaite) 1383–1883. Indexes to York marriage bonds available at: www.nationalwillsindex.com and www.origins.net/NWIWelcome.aspx.

www.origins.net/Welcome.aspx.

Family Relatives
BMD indexes. Medical registers. Parish registers. School records. First and Second World War death indexes and many other military records.

www.familyrelatives.com.

Find My Past
Free to search, but to view original record or transcript you must buy a subscription or 'Pay As You Go' credits. BMD indexes for Lancashire from 1837–2006. Censuses from 1841–1911 include 'unfilmed' Manchester 1851 returns. Militia service records. Not all years available; more details on the website of coverage. Parish registers Chadderton St Matthew, Failsworth St John, Friarmere St Thomas, Hey St John, Heaton Norris St Thomas, Heyside Friends, Hollinwood St Margaret, Moorside St Thomas, Oldham St Mary, Oldham St Peter, Pleasington Priory St Mary and St John the Baptist, Prestwich St Mary, Richmond St Anne's, Royton St Paul, Saddleworth St Chad, Shaw Holy Trinity, Waterhead Holy Trinity and Wrightington Hall.

Manchester Collection includes apprentice records 1700–1849 (mostly, but not all, parish apprentices); Ardwick cemetery and MIs, Cheetham Hill Wesleyan Cemetery burial registers, Chorlton-upon-Medlock Rusholme Road burial registers. Giles Shaw transcripts of baptism, marriage and burial registers from Oldham St Mary. John Owen transcripts for Gorton, Newton and Flixton 1571–1785. School admission registers; industrial school registers; prison registers; workhouse registers.

Cheshire Collection has Diocese of Chester bishop's transcripts of parish registers; Anglican parish registers; Chester wills and probate; marriage licence bonds and allegations.

www.findmypast.com.

The Genealogist
Official site for Nonconformist records for England and Wales, dating back to 1538 with baptisms, marriages and burials. BMD indexes and transcripts. Censuses from 1841–1911. Keyword search available. Roman Catholic Registers: Robert Hall and Hornby, Co. Lancaster, Culcheth, registers of Fr Thomas Worthington, Southworth Hall. Trade directories. Military

records include Roll of Officers of the York and Lancaster Regiment records and 'Soldiers Died in the Great War'. Heralds' visitations.
   Royalist Composition Papers. Wills.

www.thegenealogist.co.uk.

Genes Reunited
BMD indexes. British Newspaper Archive. Censuses. Parish registers. Passenger lists. First and Second World War death indexes.

www.thegenesreunited.co.uk.

BMDs, Censuses and More

1911 Census
www.1911census.co.uk.

Ancestors On Board
TNA's Outward Passenger Lists (BT 27) for long-distance voyages leaving Britain 1890–1960.

www.ancestorsonboard.com.

Cheshire BMDs
www.cheshirebmd.org.uk.

Cheshire Wills
Search the online database, then order a copy of the will.

http://archives.cheshire.gov.uk/family_history/wills_and_probate_records. aspx and http://archivedatabases.cheshire.gov.uk/RecordOfficeWillEPay-ments/search.aspx.

Lancashire BMDs
Indexes not currently complete, but site is constantly updated. Online ordering of certificates available.

www.lancashirebmd.org.uk.

Lancashire Census (S & N Genealogy)
www.lancashirecensus.co.uk.

Manchester Online Burial Records Search
www.burialrecords.manchester.gov.uk/GenSearch.aspx.

Mocavo
www.mocavo.co.uk.

Official Non-Conformist and Non-Parochial BMD Service
www.bmdregisters.co.uk.

UK BMDs
www.ukbmd.org.uk.

UK Census Online
Censuses 1841–1901.

www.ukcensusonline.com.

Gazetteer of British Place Names (Association of British Counties)
www.gazetteer.co.uk.

F

USEFUL WEBSITES

Coal

Coal Mining History Resource Centre
Ian Winstanley's comprehensive website is a mine of information. Searchable database of mining deaths and injuries. Photographic gallery and mining literature. Download the 1842 Children's Employment Commission (CEC) Report at: www.cmhrc.co.uk/site/literature/royalcommissionreports/index.html.

North Lancashire CEC report at: www.cmhrc.co.uk/cms/document/1842_N_Lancs.pdf.

www.cmhrc.co.uk/site/home/index.html.

Jack Nadin's Lancashire Coal Mining History
www.jnadin1.50megs.com.

National Mining Memorabilia Association
www.mining-memorabilia.co.uk.

Cotton

Cotton Threads
This project from Bury Museum and Archive Service investigates links between cotton and slavery through the Hutchinson family's story.

www.cotton-threads.org.uk.

Cotton Times
Doug Peacock's exploration of the industry, its history and people.

www.cottontimes.co.uk.

Cotton Town – Blackburn with Darwen
This website has many illustrations and information about the cotton industry, as well as the area's other industries such as textile bleaching,

printing and dyeing, chemical industries, coal mining, wallpaper manufacture, etc. There are also rolls of honour and war memories.

www.cottontown.org.

Spinning the Web
All aspects of the cotton industry – history, workers' lives and archive
images.

www.spinningtheweb.org.uk.

General

Ancestor Search
www.ancestor-search.info.

British GENES blog (news and events)
http://britishgenes.blogspot.com.

British & Irish Genealogy Blog
www.bi-gen.blogspot.com.

Calendars – Convert Old Style Dates to New Style
http://people.albion.edu/imacinnes/calendar//Old_&_New_Style_Da-
tes.html.

Currency Converter
Converts old currency into decimal currency, and gives examples of 'buying
power'.

www.nationalarchives.gov.uk/currency.

Fleetwood Online Archive of Trawlers
Photographic collection.

http://float-trawlers.lancashire.gov.uk.

Friends of Lancashire Archives
http://bit.ly/yEjAWM.

Friends of Real Lancashire
Campaign to promote the historic county boundaries.

www.forl.co.uk.

Guide to Record Societies and their Publications (Texts and Calendars)
www.royalhistoricalsociety.org/textandcalendars.php.

Hospital Records Database (TNA)
Includes Grangethorpe Hospital, Manchester.

www.nationalarchives.gov.uk/hospitalrecords/search.asp.

Lancashire Online Reference Library
Some resources on this website can only be accessed by members of Lancashire libraries, but others are freely available.

www.lancashire.gov.uk/onrl/index.asp.

The Lancashire Society
Devoted to preserving the county's literary and spoken heritage. Online aural, visual and literature archives.

www.thelancashiresociety.org.uk.

Manchester Association for Masonic Research (MAMR)
The Association covers freemasonry for East and West Lancashire, and Cheshire.

www.pglel.co.uk/MAMR/MAMR.asp.

Manchester's Radical History
Blog with articles exploring Manchester's Radical past.

http://radicalmanchester.wordpress.com.

Mersey Gateway
This 'Gateway to Learning' includes an introduction to local archive sources and topics such as the slave trade, the history of the port and its people.

www.mersey-gateway.org.

Old Liverpool
www.old-liverpool.co.uk.

185

Online Historical Population Reports Website
Examples of blank census schedules and essays on the censuses and population statistics.

www.histpop.org/ohpr/servlet/Show?page=Home.

Palaeography (Old Handwriting) Online Tutorial
www.nationalarchives.gov.uk/palaeography.

Railway Ancestors Family History Society
www.railwayancestors.org.uk.

Revealing Histories: Remembering Slavery
www.revealinghistories.org.uk/home.html.

Stuart Raymond (Genealogical Bookman)
www.stuartraymond.co.uk.

Transatlantic Slave Trade Database
Voyages database, images and searchable African names database.

www.slavevoyages.org/tast/index.faces.

Victoria County History of Lancashire
www.victoriacountyhistory.ac.uk/counties/lancashire, www.british-history.ac.uk and www.british-history.ac.uk/place.aspx?gid=20&region=6.

Victorian Times Project
Download some parliamentary papers and publications on many occupations including cotton.

http://victoria.cdlr.strath.ac.uk/index.php.

Virtual Waterways Archive Catalogue
Online catalogue gives location of British Waterways and early canal company records in fifteen partner repositories. (NB Some hyperlinks on this website are out of date.)

www.virtualwaterways.co.uk/home.html and www.virtualwaterways.co.uk/Family_History_introduction.html.

Vision of Britain

Historical statistics for Lancashire, resized for the modern county boundaries. It has a useful overview of administrative districts and boundary changes for places in the county with source references.

www.visionofbritain.org.uk.

Wigan Images Online

Archive of photographs from the late nineteenth century to modern times.

http://wiganimages.wlct.org.

G

MILITARY RESOURCES

Regimental Archives and Museums

King's Own Royal Border Regiment Museum, Carlisle
http://kingsownbordermuseum.btck.co.uk.

King's Own Royal Regiment Museum, Lancaster
Archives include eighteenth-century 'order books', First World War battalion archives and much more. An appointment is needed to view collections in store. Rolls of honour on the website.

Archives collection: www.kingsownmuseum.plus.com/mus03arch.htm; Peter Donnelly, Curator, King's Own Royal Regiment Museum, Market Square, Lancaster, LA1 1HT; www.kingsownmuseum.plus.com; email: kingsownmuseum@iname.com; curator tel: 0152 455 5619; museum tel: 0152 464 637.

Lancashire Fusiliers
Collections relating to the XX Lancashire Fusiliers and the Royal Regiment of Fusiliers. Archive includes medal rolls 1799–1902, casualty lists, records of honours and awards, regimental diaries and more. Fee for searches.

The Fusilier Museum, Moss Street, Bury, BL9 0DF; www.fusiliermuseum. com; email: enquiries@fusiliermuseum.com; tel: 0161 763 8950.

Liverpool Scottish Regimental Archive, Museum
The former museum is currently closed, but part of the collection will be displayed at the new Museum of Liverpool. Visits to the regimental archive at Artists Club, 5 Eberle Street, Liverpool, L2 2AG by appointment only (no correspondence to this address). The website has the Second World War Roll of Honour for the regiment.

Liverpool Scottish Regimental Museum, c/o 51a Common Lane, Culcheth, Warrington WA3 4EY; www.liverpoolscottish.org.uk; email Major I. L. Riley: ilriley@liverpoolscottish.org.uk; tel: 0192 576 6157.

Manchester Regiment Archive, Tameside

The Regiment's archive is deposited with Tameside Local Studies and Archives (see Section A) at: www.tameside.gov.uk/archives/manchester regiment. Search the Manchester Regiment Image Archive at: www.manchester-regiment.org.uk.

Museum of the Manchester Regiment

This museum does not have regimental records.

Museum of the Manchester Regiment, Ashton Town Hall, Market Place, Ashton-under-Lyne, OL6 6DL; www.tameside.gov.uk/museumsgalleries/mom; tel: 0161 342 2254.

Lancashire Infantry Museum

Story of the Queen's Lancashire and its preceding regiments; The Loyal North Lancashire Rgt, East Lancashire Rgt, Lancashire Rgt (Prince of Wales's Volunteers), South Lancashire Rgt and former Regiments of Foot: 30th, 40th, 47th, 59th, 81st and 82nd.

Regimental Archive at the museum open to visitors by appointment only. Research service (fee payable). Please allow ten weeks for completion of requests.

The Curator, The Lancashire Infantry Museum, Fulwood Barracks, Preston, PR2 8AA; www.lancashireinfantrymuseum.org.uk/; email: qlrmuseum@btconnect.com; tel: 0177 226 0362.

Websites

Accrington Absent Voters' List 1918

www.pals.org.uk/avl/index.htm.

Accrington Pals

Website dedicated to the famous Accrington, Sheffield and Barnsley Pals. Lots of helpful general information for readers trying to trace ancestors who served in the First World War.

www.pals.org.uk/research.htm.

Ashton Pals

Searchable website dedicated to the Ashton Territorials, 9th Battalion of the Manchester Regiment.

http://ashtonpals.webs.com.

Blackburn and Darwen Rolls of Honour
www.cottontown.org.

British War Graves
Free photographs of war graves. Access at: www.britishwargraves.co.uk.

Burnley in the Great War
Excellent website with a roll of honour for Burnley men who died in the First World War with photographs of men and memorials.

http://burnleyinthegreatwar.info.

Commonwealth War Graves Commission
Search the 'Debt of Honour Register' database for a casualty who died in First or Second World Wars. Searchable database of cemeteries, and database of Commonwealth citizens killed in the Second World War. Casualty details sometimes include name and address of next of kin.

www.cwgc.org.

King's Regiment (Liverpool)
Tips on researching soldiers in the regiment. The King's Regiment First World War searchable database is at: www.liverpoolmuseums.org.uk/mol/kingsreg.

www.liverpoolmuseums.org.uk/mol/history/citysoldiers/research.

Lancashire and Yorkshire Railway Society
The society's website has a Roll of Honour for Lancashire and Yorkshire Railwaymen who died in the First World War at: www.lyrs.org.uk/genealogy/rollofhonour.html.

www.lyrs.org.uk.

The Long, Long Trail
Comprehensive website with help for family historians. Assistance with finding soldiers' records at: www.1914-1918.net/records.html and Lancashire Fusiliers at: www.1914-1918.net/lancsfus.htm.

www.1914-1918.net/index.html.

Manchester Regiment Group
www.themanchesters.org.

Manchester Regiments Group Forum
www.themanchesters.org/forum/index.php.

Regimental War Diaries
TNA's Our Online Records service includes some Lancashire regiments. TNA Guide to records for war dead for the First and Second World Wars is at: www.nationalarchives.gov.uk/documents/research-guides/war-dead-first-second-world-wars.pdf.

https://www.nationalarchives.gov.uk/war-diaries-ww1.htm.

Roll of Honour
Searchable databases online for those who served in both the First and Second World Wars and more recent conflicts at: www.roll-of-honour.com/Databases/index.html. Includes photographs of war memorials.

www.roll-of-honour.com.

Royal Lancashire Volunteer Regiment
Online index of the regiment's register of recruits (Wilton Militia) 1779–1782. Each man's name, occupation, place of origin, height and weight is listed.

www.manchester.gov.uk/downloads/download/4205/royal_lancashire_regiment.

Spinning the Web
Rolls of honour for 1914–1918 for Manchester and Salford.

www.spinningtheweb.org.uk.

War Graves Photographic Project
War grave photographs available for a fee.

http://twgpp.org.

H

PLACES TO VISIT

A selection of the dozens of heritage sites related to historic Lancashire.

Astley Green Colliery Museum
The only surviving pit head gear and colliery engine house in Lancashire.

The Secretary, Astley Green Colliery Museum, Higher Green Lane, Astley Green, Tyldesley, Manchester, M29 7JB; www.agcm.org.uk; email: info @agcm.org.uk.

Blackburn Museum and Art Gallery
Social history galleries tell the story of life in the town and its industries.

Blackburn Museum and Art Gallery, Museum Street, Blackburn, BB1 7AJ; www.blackburn.gov.uk; email: museum@blackburn.gov.uk; tel: 0125 466 7130.

British Commercial Vehicle Museum
Online image database. The museum's archive includes records for British Leyland Motor Corporation Ltd.

The British Commercial Vehicle Museum, King Steet, Leyland, Lancashire, PR25 2LE; www.bcvmt.co.uk; tel: 0177 245 1011.

The Dock Museum, Barrow-in-Furness
Ship-building and social history exhibitions. Vickers photographic archive.

The Dock Museum, North Road, Barrow-in-Furness, Cumbria, LA14 2PW; www.dockmuseum.org.uk; email: dockmuseum@barrowbc.gov.uk; tel: 0122 987 6400.

Helmshore Mills Textile Museums, Rossendale Valley
Helmshore Mills Textile Museum, Holcombe Road, Helmshore, Rossendale, BB4 4NP; www.lancashire.gov.uk/acs/sites/museums/venues/helmshore; email: helmshoremuseum@lancashire.gov.uk; tel: 0170 622 6459.

Imperial War Museum North
The Quays, Trafford Wharf Road, Manchester, M17 1T; www.iwm.org.uk/ visits/iwm-north; email: iwmnorth@iwm.org.uk; tel: 0161 836 4000.

International Slavery Museum
International Slavery Museum, Albert Dock, Liverpool, L3 4AQ; www. liverpoolmuseums.org.uk/ism; tel: 0151 478 4499.

Lancaster Maritime Museum
Lancaster Maritime Museum, Custom House, St George's Quay, Lancaster, LA1 1RB; www.lancashire.gov.uk/acs/sites/museums/venues/lanc-maritime/index.asp; email: lancastermaritimemuseum@lancashire.gov.uk; tel: 0152 438 2264.

Museum of Liverpool
City Soldiers gallery tells the story of the King's Regiment.

Museum of Liverpool, Pier Head, Liverpool, L3 1DG; www.liverpool museums.org.uk/mol; tel: 0151 478 4545.

Museum of Lancashire
Museum of Lancashire, Stanley Street, Preston, PR1 4YP; www.lancashire. gov.uk/acs/sites/museums/venues/mol/index.asp; email: museumof lancashire@lancashire.gov.uk; tel: 0177 253 4075.

Queen Street Mill Textile Museum, Burnley
The museum has a library with over 7,000 books, journals and other items on the Lancashire textile industry; members of the public can consult the collection by appointment.

Queen Street Mill Textile Museum, Harle Syke, Burnley, BB10 2HX; www. lancashire.gov.uk/acs/sites/museums/venues/qsm; email: queenstreetmill @lancashire.gov.uk; tel: 0128 2412 555.

Rochdale Pioneers Museum
31 Toad Lane, Rochdale, Lancashire, OL12 0NU; www.co-op.ac.uk/our-heritage/rochdale-pioneers-museum; email: museum@co-op.ac.uk.

Stott Park Bobbin Mill
Stott Park Bobbin Mill, Colton, Ulverston, Cumbria, LA12 8AX; www. english-heritage.org.uk/daysout/properties/stott-park-bobbin-mill; email: customers@english-heritage.org.uk; tel: 0870 333 1181.

Trencherfield Mill Steam Engine

Machinery hall and engine house. World's largest working horizontal triple expansion steam engine in its original location.

Wigan Pier Quarter, Heritage Way, Wigan WN3 4EF; www.wlct.org/ heritage-services/trencherfield-mill-engine.htm; email: heritage@wlct.org; tel: 0194 282 8128 or 0194 277 7566 (Sundays).

Museum of Wigan Life

Museum of Wigan Life, Library Street, Wigan, WN1 1NU; www.wlct.org/ heritage-services/museum-of-wigan-life.htm; email: heritage@wlct.org; tel: 0194 282 8128.

World of Glass

Explore underground passageways below the Victorian furnace building. Glass-making demonstrations.

The World of Glass, Chalon Way East, St Helens, Merseyside, WA10 1BX; www.worldofglass.com; tel: 0174 422 766.

SELECT BIBLIOGRAPHY

Contemporary Works

Annual Register 1867, Annual Register, Vol. 109, London, 1868

Children's Employment Commission: Report on Mines, XV, 1842

Fifth Report of the Children's Employment Commission (1862): Printing and Miscellaneous Trades [13273], XXIV, 1866

Report from the Select Committee on Handloom Weavers' Petitions, with Minutes of Evidence [341], XIII, 1835

Report from the Select Committee on the State of Children Employed in Manufactories, 1816

Report from the Select Committee on the State and Condition of Children Employed in Manufactories, 1819

Reports of the Inspectors of Factories for the half year ending 30 April 1876, 1876

Third Report of the Children's Employment Commission: Metal Manufactures (3414-1), XXII, 1864

Anon., *History of Preston in Lancashire, together with the Guild Merchant*, London, 1822

Anon., *Parliamentary Gazetteer of England and Wales*, A. Fullarton & Co., 1840

Abram, W. A., *History of Blackburn*, Blackburn, 1877

Abram, W. Alexander, *The Rolls of Burgesses of the Guilds Merchant of the Borough of Preston 1397–1682*, Lancashire and Cheshire Record Society, Vol. IX, 1884

Austin, S., Harwood, J. and Pyne, G. and. C., *Lancashire Illustrated*, London, 1831

Axon, William E. A., *The Annals of Manchester*, London, 1886

Baines, Edward, *History of the Cotton Manufacture*, London, 1835

Baines, Edward, *History, Directory and Gazetteer of the County Palatinate of Lancaster Vol. 1*, Longman, Hurst & Co., 1824

Baines, Thomas, *History of the Commerce and Town of Liverpool*, Longman & Co., 1852

Baines, Thomas, *Lancashire and Cheshire Past and Present Vol. I*, William Mackenzie, c. 1867

Beeton, Samuel O., *Dictionary of National Biography*, Ward, Lock & Tyler, c. 1870

Britton, John, *The Beauties of England and Wales Vol. IX*, London, 1807

Crossley, James (ed.), *Pott's Discovery of Witches in the County of Lancaster* (1613), Chetham Society Old Series, 1845

Croston, James, *County Families of Lancashire and Cheshire*, London, 1887

Earwaker, J. P. (ed.), *The Court Leet Records of Manchester Vol. III*, Manchester, 1886

Earwaker, J. P. (ed.), *An Index to the Wills and Inventories now preserved at the Court of Probate at Chester 1545–1620*, Lancashire and Cheshire Record Society Vol. II, 1879

Earwaker, J. P. (ed.), *An Index to the Wills and Inventories now preserved at the Court of Probate at Chester 1621–1650*, Lancashire and Cheshire Record Society, Vol. IV, 1881

Ecroyd, Thomas Backhouse, *The Registers of the Parish Church of Whalley in the County of Lancaster 1538–1601*, Lancashire Parish Register Society, 1900

Espinasse, Francis, *Lancashire Worthies: Second Series*, London, 1877

Farrer, William (ed.), *Final Concords of the County of Lancaster ... or feet of fines, preserved in the Public Record Office, London*, Lancashire and Cheshire Record Society Vol. XXXIX, 1899

Fishwick, Henry, (ed.), *Lancashire and Cheshire Church Surveys 1649–1655 Vol. 1*, Lancashire and Cheshire Record Society, 1879

Gibson, Revd T. Ellison, *Crosby Records: A Cavalier's Notebook*, Longmans, Green & Co., 1880

Graham, George, *The Census of Great Britain in 1851*, Longman, Brown, Green & Longmans, 1854

Halley, Robert, *Lancashire: Its Puritanism and Nonconformity*, 2nd edn, Manchester, 1872

Harland, John (ed.), *Mamecestre, Being Chapters from the Early Recorded History of the Barony Vol. I*, Chetham Society, 1861

Harland, John (ed.), *The pole booke for Manchester, May ye 22d 1690, Chetham Miscellanies Vol. 3*, Chetham Society Old Series 57, 1862

Hibbert, Samuel, *Illustration of the Customs of a Manor in the North of England during the Fifteenth Century*, Edinburgh, 1822

Holt, John, *General View of the Agriculture of Lancashire*, London, 1794

Humber, William (ed.), *A Record of the Progress of Modern Engineering ... 1866*, London, 1868

Jopling, Charles M., *Sketch of Furness and Cartmel, comprising Lonsdale North of the Sands*, London, 1843

Langton, William (ed.), *The Visitation of Lancashire and a Part of Cheshire ... AD 1533, Part II*, Vol. CX, Chetham Society, 1882

Lewis, Samuel, *A Topographical Dictionary of England Vol. III*, S. Lewis & Co., 1831

Lyon, Revd P. A., *Two 'Compoti' of the Lancashire and Cheshire Manors of Henry de Lacey, Earl of Lincoln, XXIV and XXXIII Edward I*, Chetham Society, 1884

Maxwell-Lyte, H. C. (ed.), *Calendar of the Patent Rolls preserved in the Public Record Office, Edward I, 1301–1307*, HMSO, 1898

Oats, Henry Carne, 'On the Social Statistics of certain Boroughs and Townships in Lancashire and Cheshire during the last Twenty Years', *Transactions of the Manchester Statistical Society*, Session 1866–1867, Manchester, 1867

Ormerod, George (ed.), *Tracts relating to Military Proceedings in Lancashire during the Great Civil War*, Chetham Society Vol. II, Manchester, 1844

Raines, James, *Wills and Inventories from the Registry of the Archdeaconry of Richmond: Surtees Society Publications XXVI*, Surtees Society, 1853

Redding, Cyrus, Beard, J. R. and Taylor, W. C., *Pictorial History of the County of Lancaster*, George Routledge, 1844

Roby, J., *Traditions of Lancashire Vol. I*, Longman, Rees, Orme, Brown & Green, 1829

Roscoe, E., 'The Industries of the English Lake District', *English Illustrated Magazine 1883–1884*, Macmillan & Co., 1884

Smiles, Samuel, *Brindley and the Early Engineers*, John Murray, 1874

Smiles, Samuel, *Industrial Biography: Iron Workers and Tool Makers*, John Murray, 1863

Smith, Jeremiah Finch (ed.), *The Admission Register of the Manchester School*, Vol. 2 (1776–1807), Chetham Society Old Series 73, 1868

Smithers, Henry, *Liverpool: Its Commerce, Statistics and Institutions*, Liverpool, 1825

Timperley, Charles Henry, *Manchester Historical Recorder*, Manchester, c. 1875

Waugh, Evelyn, *Home Life of the Lancashire Factory Folk During the Cotton Famine*, Simpkin, Marshall & Co., 1867

West, Thomas and Close, William (ed.), *The Antiquities of Furness*, Ulverston, 1805

Willis, William (ed.), *History of the House of Stanley*, Manchester, 1840

Modern Works

The Decline of the Cotton and Coal Mining Industries of Lancashire, Lancashire and Merseyside Industrial Development Association, Manchester, 1967

Aldcroft, Derek and Freeman, Michael, *Transport in the Industrial Revolution*, Manchester University Press, 1983

Ashmore, Owen, *The Industrial Archaeology of North-West England*, Chetham Society Third Series, No. 29, Manchester University Press, 1982

Ashworth, Elizabeth, *Champion Lancastrians*, Sigma Press, 2010

Aspin, Chris, *The Cotton Industry*, Shire Publications Ltd, 1995

Aspin, Chris, *Lancashire: The First Industrial Society*, Carnegie, 1995

Aylmer, G. E., *The Crown's Servants: Government and Civil Service under Charles II, 1660–1685*, Oxford University Press, 2002

Bagley, J. J., *A History of Lancashire*, Phillimore, 1976

Barker, T. C. and Harris, J. R., *A Merseyside Town in the Industrial Revolution: St. Helens 1750–1900*, Liverpool University Press, 1954

Benson, John, *British Coalminers in the Nineteenth Century*, Gill & Macmillan, 1980

Blackwood, B. G., *Lancashire Gentry and the Great Rebellion 1640–60*, Chetham Society Third Series, Vol. 25, Manchester, 1975

Brand, Jack, *Local Government Reform in England 1888–1974*, Croom Helm, 1974

Browning, Charles H., *Magna Charta Barons and their Descendants*, Genealogical Publishing Company, 2002

Broxap, E., *The Great Civil War in Lancashire 1642–51*, Manchester University Press, 1973

Burton, Anthony, *The Miners*, Futura Publications, 1977

Chadwick, Edwin and Flinn, M. W. (ed.), *The Sanitary Population of the Labouring Population of Britain 1842*, Edinburgh University Press, 1965

Challinor, Raymond, *The Lancashire and Cheshire Miners*, Frank Graham, 1972

Chaloner, W. H., *Industry and Innovation: Selected Essays*, Frank Cass & Co., 1990

Chapman, Sydney J., *The Lancashire Cotton Industry*, Manchester University Press, 1904

Christian, Peter and Annal, David, *Census: The Expert Guide*, TNA, 2008

Clayton, Gerald (ed.), *Registers of the Parish Church of Walton-le-Dale in the County of Lancaster*, LPRS, Vol. 37, 1910

Clemesha, H. W., *A History of Preston in Amounderness*, Manchester University Press, 1912

Crofton, H. T., *A History of the Ancient Chapel of Stretford in the Parish of Manchester Vol. 3*, Chetham Society New Series 51, 1903

Cunningham, H. Stuart, 'Married at the Collegiate and Parish Church of Manchester', *The Manchester Genealogist Vol. 34*, Issue 4, MLFHS, 1999

Daniels, George W., *The Early English Cotton Industry*, Manchester University Press, 1920

Emmison, F. G., *Archives and Local History*, Methuen, 1966

Farrer, William (ed.), *The Chartulary of Cockersand Abbey, Vol. II, Pt. 2*, Chetham Society New Series, Vol. 43, Manchester, 1900

Farrer, W. (ed.), *The Lancashire Pipe Rolls of 31 Henry I., A.D. 1130, and of the reigns of Henry II., A.D. 1155–1189; Richard I., A.D. 1189–1199; and King John, A.D. 1199–1216*, Liverpool, 1902

Farrer, W. (ed.), *Some Court Rolls of the Lordships, Wapentakes, and Demesne Manors of Thomas, Earl of Lancaster, for the 17th and 18th years of the Reign of Edward II, AD 1323–4*, Vol. XLI, Lancashire and Cheshire Record Society, 1901

Farrer, W., *Victoria County History of the County of Lancaster Vol. 1*, Constable & Co., 1906

Farrer, W. and Brownbill, J., *Victoria County History of the County of Lancaster Vol. 3*, Constable & Co., 1907

Farrer, W. and Brownbill, J., *Victoria County History of the County of Lancaster Vol. 4*, Constable & Co., 1911

Farrer, W. and Brownbill, J., *Victoria County History of the County of Lancaster Vol. 8*, Constable & Co., 1914

Finer, Samuel Edward, *The Life and Times of Sir Edwin Chadwick*, Methuen & Co., 1980

Fishwick, Henry, *The History of the Parish of Preston in Amounderness in the County of Lancaster*, London, 1900

Fowler, Simon, *A Guide to Military History on the Internet*, Pen & Sword, 2007

George, David, *Lancashire, Records of Early English Drama*, University of Toronto, 1991

Gibson, Jeremy, *Electoral Registers 1832–1948 and Burgess Rolls*, 3rd edn, Family History Partnership, 2008

Gregg, Pauline, *A Social and Economic History of Britain 1760–1970*, 6th edn, G. Harrap & Co. Ltd, 1971

Gritt, Andrew (ed.), *Family History in Lancashire: Issues and Approaches*, Cambridge Scholars, 2009

Hadfield, Charles and Biddle, Gordon, *Canals of North-West England*, 2 vols, David & Charles, 1970

Haigh, Christopher, *Last Days of the Lancashire Monasteries and the Pilgrimage of Grace*, Manchester University Press, 1969

Haigh, C. A., 'Slander and the church courts in the sixteenth century', *Transactions of the Lancashire and Cheshire Antiquarian Society, Vol. 78*, Manchester, 1975

Henderson, William Otto, *The Lancashire Cotton Famine 1861–1865*, 2nd edn, Manchester University Press, 1969

Holman, Tom, *A Lancashire Miscellany*, Frances Lincoln, 2010

Holmes, Richard, *Tommy: The British Soldier on the Western Front 1914–1918*, Harper Perennial, 2005

Hovell, Mark, *The Chartist Movement*, ed. T. Tout, Longmans, Green & Co., 1918

Kenyon, Denise, *The Origins of Lancashire*, Manchester University Press, 1991

Knowles, David, *The Religious Orders in England Vol. III: The Tudor Age*, Cambridge University Press, 1959

Lacey, Margaret de, *Prison Reform in Lancashire 1700–1850*, Manchester University Press, 1985

Lawson, Richard (ed.), *The Census and Social Structure*, Frank Cass, 1978

Lowe, Norman, *The Lancashire Textile Industry during the Sixteenth Century*, Chetham Society, 1972

Marshall, J. D., *Furness and the Industrial Revolution*, Michael Moon, 1981

Marshall, J. D., *Lancashire*, David & Charles, 1974

Marshall, J. D. (ed.), *The autobiography of William Stout of Lancaster, 1665–1752*, Chetham Society Third Series, No. 14, 1967

Martinez, A. J., 'Palatinate administration and local society in the palatinate of Lancashire under the Lancastrian kings, 1399–1461', *Transactions of the Historic Society of Lancashire and Cheshire, Vol. 156*, 2008, 1–25

Midwinter, E. C., *Law and Order in Early Victorian Lancashire*, Borthwick Papers No. 34, York, 1968

Midwinter, E. C., *Social Administration in Lancashire 1830–1860*, Manchester University Press, 1969

Morgan, Nicholas J., 'Lancashire Quakers and the Tithe 1660–1730', *Bulletin of the John Rylands University Library of Manchester 70, no. 3*, Autumn 1988, 61–75

Mumford, Alfred A., *Manchester Grammar School 1515–1915*, Longmans, Green & Co., 1919

Nicholson, Albert, *The Chetham Hospital and Library*, Sherratt & Hughes, 1910

Outhwaite, R. B., *Clandestine Marriage in England 1500–1850*, Hambledon Press, 1995

Owen, David E., *The Manchester Ship Canal*, Manchester University Press, 1983

Parker, Colonel John, *A Calendar of the Lancashire Assize Rolls Preserved in the Public Record Office Part 1*, Lancashire and Cheshire Record Society, 1904

Phillips, C. B. and Smith, J. H., *Lancashire and Cheshire from AD 1540*, Regional History of England, Longman, 1994

Pinchbeck, Ivy, *Women Workers and the Industrial Revolution 1750–1850*, Virago, 1981

Pounds, N. J. G., *A History of the English Parish*, Cambridge University Press, 2004

Pratt, David H., *Researching British Probate Records 1354–1858: Northern England*, The Church of Jesus Christ of Latter-day Saints, 1992

Raymond, Stuart A., *Lancashire: A Genealogical Bibliography*, 3 vols, Federation of Family History Societies, Birmingham, 1996

Redford, Arthur, *Labour Migration in England 1800–1850*, 3rd edn, Manchester University Press, 1976

Richardson, David, Schwarz, Suzanne and Tibbles, Anthony, *Liverpool and Transatlantic Slavery*, Liverpool University Press, 2007

Richardson, R. C., *Puritanism in North-West England: A Regional Study of the Diocese of Chester to 1642*, Manchester University Press, 1972

Rogers, Colin Darlington, *The Family Tree Detective*, 2nd edn, Manchester University Press, 1985

Schaefer, Christina K., *Instant Information on the Internet! A Genealogists' Handbook*, Genealogical Publishing Co., 2000

Scola, Roger, *Feeding the Victorian City: The Food Supply of Manchester 1780–1870*, Manchester University Press 1992

Sheridan, Richard B., *Sugar and Slavery: The Economic History of the British West Indies 1623–1775*, University of West Indies, 2000

Silbey, David, *The British Working Class and Enthusiasm for War 1914–1916*, Frank Cass, 2005

Smith, J. P. (ed.), *Lancashire Registers IV: Brindle and Samlesbury*, Catholic Record Society, 1922

Smith, Lucy Toulmin (ed.), *Leland's Itinerary in England and Wales in … 1535–1543 Parts VII and VIII*, George Bell & Sons, 1909

Starkey, H. F., *Schooner Port: Two Centuries of Upper Mersey Sail*, G. W. & A. Hesketh, 1983

Stephens, W. B., *Sources for English Local History*, Cambridge University Press, 1994

Sterling, Jane, *The Civil War in Lancashire*, Dalesman Publishing Co., 1971

Sterling, Jane, *Elizabethan and Jacobean Lancashire*, Dalesman Publishing Co., 1973

Sumner, Jeremy and Churchill, Else, *Probate Jurisdictions: Where to Look for Wills*, 5th edn, Federation of Family History Societies, 2002

Tait, James, *Mediaeval Manchester and the Beginnings of Lancashire*, Manchester University Press, 1904

Tate, W. E., *The Parish Chest*, 3rd edn, Cambridge University Press, 1979

Thirsk, Joan, *The Agrarian History of England and Wales Vol. IV: 1500–1640*, Cambridge University Press, 2011

Timmins, Geoffrey, *The Last Shift: the Decline of Handloom Weaving in Nineteenth Century Lancashire*, Manchester University Press, 1993

Timmins, Geoffrey, *Made in Lancashire: A History of Regional Industrialization*, Manchester University Press, 1998

Turnbull, G., *History of the Calico-Printing Industry of Great Britain*, John Sherratt & Sons, 1951

Uglow, Jenny, *Elizabeth Gaskell*, Faber and Faber, 1994

Wadsworth, Alfred P. and Mann, Julia de Lacy, *The Cotton Trade and Industrial Lancashire 1600–1780*, Manchester University Press, 1931

Walton, John K., *Lancashire: A Social History 1558–1939*, Manchester University Press, 1987

Webb, Sidney and Beatrice, *English Local Government: English Poor Law History*, 2 vols, Longmans, 1927

Webb, Sidney and Beatrice, *English Local Government: Statutory Bodies for Special Purposes*, Longmans, Green & Co., 1922

Whiteley, J. M., 'The Turnpike Roads and Traffic up to 1830', *Diversion*, 1984

Wilkes, Sue, *The Children History Forgot*, Robert Hale Ltd, 2011

Wilkes, Sue, *Narrow Windows, Narrow Lives: The Industrial Revolution in Lancashire*, History Press, 2008

Wilkes, Sue, *Regency Cheshire*, Robert Hale, 2009

Wilkes, Sue, *Tracing Your Canal Ancestors*, Pen & Sword, 2011

Williams, Bill, *The Making of Manchester Jewry*, Manchester University Press, 1985

Wood, J. F., *The Story of Manchester*, T. Werner Laurie, c. 1912

Online Sources

British History Online

'Assizes at Lancaster: 4 John – 26 Henry III', *Lancashire Assize Rolls: 4 John – 13 Edward I*, 1903, pp. 1–4; www.british-history.ac.uk/report.aspx?compid= 69815; date accessed: 10 November 2011

'Lonsdale hundred: Introduction and map', *A History of the County of Lancaster: Volume 8*, 1914, pp. 1–3; www.british-history.ac.uk/report.aspx? compid=53255&strquery=deaneries; date accessed: 4 November 2011

'The parish of Lancaster (in Lonsdale hundred): General history and castle', *A History of the County of Lancaster: Volume 8*, 1914, pp. 4–22; http://www. british-history.ac.uk/report.aspx?compid=53256&strquery=assizes; date accessed: 8 February 2012

'MANCHESTER: Introduction', *Fasti Ecclesiae Anglicanae 1541–1857*, Vol. 11: Carlisle, Chester, Durham, Manchester, Ripon, and Sodor and Man dioceses, 2004, pp. 117–118; www.british-history.ac.uk/report.aspx? compid=35870; date accessed: 6 December 2011

'Manchester: The parish and advowson', *A History of the County of Lancaster: Volume 4*, 1911, pp. 192–204; www.british-history.ac.uk/report.aspx? compid=41406&strquery=deaneries; date accessed: 4 November 2011

'The parish of Preston', *A History of the County of Lancaster: Volume 7*, 1912, pp. 72–91; www.british-history.ac.uk/report.aspx?compid=53190&strquery =plague; date accessed: 22 November 2011

Oxford Dictionary of National Biography

Hawkins, Angus, 'Stanley, Edward George Geoffrey Smith, fourteenth earl of Derby (1799–1869)', *Oxford Dictionary of National Biography*, Oxford University Press, 2004; online edn, May 2009; http://www.oxforddnb. com/view/article/26265; date accessed: 10 February 2012

Purvis, June, 'Pankhurst, Emmeline (1858–1928)', *Oxford Dictionary of National Biography*, Oxford University Press, 2004; online edn, Jan 2011; http:// www.oxforddnb.com/view/article/35376; date accessed: 15 November 2011

Manchester Centre for Regional History

Rogers, Colin D., 'Parish Registers in the Salford Hundred of Lancashire', *Manchester Region History Review*, Vol. 1 No. 1, Spring 1987; www. mcrh.mmu.ac.uk/pubs/pdf/mrhr_01i_rogers.pdf

Stanley, Jo, 'Mangoes to Moss Side: Caribbean Migration to Manchester in the 1950s and 1960s', *Manchester Region History Review*, Vol. 16, 2002–3; www.mcrh.mmu.ac.uk/pubs/pdf/mrhr_16_stanley.pdf

Medieval Genealogy
www.medievalgenealogy.org.uk/guide/sta.shtml

Medieval Documentation for Salford Hundred
http://salfordhundred.wordpress.com

INDEX